Japanese Intelligence in World War II

OSPREY
PUBLISHING

JAPANESE INTELLIGENCE IN WORLD WAR II

KEN KOTANI

Translated by Chiharu Kotani

First published in English in Great Britain in 2009 by Osprey Publishing,
Midland House, West Way, Botley, Oxford OX2 0PH, United Kingdom.
443 Park Avenue South, New York, NY 10016, USA.
Email: info@ospreypublishing.com

A CIP catalog record for this book is available from the British Library.

ISBN-13: 978 1 84603 425 1

Page layout by Myriam Bell Design, France
Index by Mike Parkin
Typeset in Perpetua MT, Bell Gothic, Quay Sans ITC
Originated by PPS Grasmere Ltd
Printed in China through Worldprint

09 10 11 12 13   10 9 8 7 6 5 4 3 2 1

FOR A CATALOGUE OF ALL BOOKS PUBLISHED BY OSPREY MILITARY
AND AVIATION PLEASE CONTACT:

Osprey Direct, c/o Random House Distribution Center,
400 Hahn Road, Westminster, MD 21157
Email: uscustomerservice@ospreypublishing.com

Osprey Direct, The Book Service Ltd, Distribution Centre,
Colchester Road, Frating Green, Colchester, Essex, CO7 7DW
E-mail: customerservice@ospreypublishing.com

www.ospreypublishing.com

CONTENTS

FOREWORD

Since the early 1970s with the outing of Ultra, historians have had a field day with the complex story of intelligence in World War II and its impact on every level from the sharp end of combat operations all the way to the formulation of grand strategy. At least in terms of the European theater of operations, what has emerged is a general picture of the enormous superiority the Allies enjoyed over the Italians and the Germans in the field on intelligence. The contribution of intelligence to military operations and deception operations on both the Eastern and Western Front represented a major enabler to Allied victory over Nazi Germany. Moreover, historians have also had access to the other side of the hill in Europe. Thus, we have been able to untangle the strengths and weaknesses of the Axis powers in the field of intelligence and gain a thorough understanding of the cultural, bureaucratic, and ideological factors that contributed to the many and egregious failures in intelligence, strategic analysis, and cryptanalysis that characterized not only Hitler's but the German military's conduct of the war..

While the advantages that the Allies enjoyed in the field of intelligence in the Pacific was clear far earlier than was the case in the Europe with the impact of code breaking, for example, on battles such as Midway revealed almost in the immediate aftermath of the Second World War, the tangled history of Japanese intelligence has remained largely obscure due to the language barrier. Ken Kotani of the National Institute of Defense Studies has now rectified that gap in our knowledge of Japanese intelligence in this splendid study. He has provided the English speaking public with a detailed examination of the bureaucratic, organizational, and cultural aspects of Japanese intelligence. In the larger sense, the story has been known in its bare outline. But this study reveals a Japanese military that was in most respects dysfunctional in the field of intelligence.

It was not so much a failure of the intelligence organizations themselves as a massive failure of the culture and bureaucratic organization of the Japanese military from top to bottom. And in some cases the details take one's breath away at the sheer, unadulterated inability of the system to function in the interest of Japan's national security. Thus, when the Japanese Army's code breakers not only managed to decipher American machines at times, but discovered that the Americans were reading Japanese naval codes, the army failed to provide the navy with either the means to break these codes or the warning that its own codes had been compromised.

Thus, in every respect this study represents a major contribution to our understanding of the war in the Pacific. It is in every way a sad story of incompetence and cultural bias. And yet perhaps that very incompetence not only contributed to the Allied victory, but lessened the suffering the Japanese people would suffer in the catastrophic war of their own making.

Williamson Murray
Professor Emeritus
 Ohio State University

PREFACE AND ACKNOWLEDGEMENTS

I began work on the subject of Japanese intelligence in World War II in 2004. Before that time I had studied as a graduate student at King's College London and Kyoto University, working on British intelligence operations in the Far East. After writing my PhD thesis on this topic, I was naturally curious about the state of current Japanese intelligence reform, which is still under discussion in the Japanese government. There are lots of arguments on the issue, but I noted that there has been little academic study on the history of this fascinating area of Japanese military and security operations.

Fortunately, I am now working at the National Institute for Defense Studies (NIDS), part of the Ministry of Defense, which possesses one of the largest military archives in Japan. Although the Imperial Japanese Army (IJA) and Navy (IJN) systematically destroyed documents on intelligence, there nevertheless remain enough files and papers to explore the topic. I dug up and struggled with the fragmented primary sources and published the findings as *Nihon Gun no Intelligence* (Intelligence of the IJA and IJN) in 2007; this book is its translation.

While writing the book, I discovered that present-day Japanese intelligence has inherited many of the negative aspects of wartime IJA and IJN intelligence, namely: 1) the poor status of the intelligence section of government; 2) a lack of central intelligence organization; and 3) inefficiencies in the intelligence 'cycle' (the processing of data). In addition, modern Japanese intelligence collection is much more vulnerable in comparison with that of World War II because of a lack of counter-intelligence capability and a very limited intelligence budget. Japan also does not have national secrecy or anti-spy laws – legally there is almost no penalty if a Japanese intelligence officer intentionally leaks national secrets to a foreigner, a crime that can result in the death penalty or decades of imprisonment in many other countries.

I would like to express my appreciation to my colleagues: Hajime Kitaoka of the Ministry of Foreign Affairs, Kotaro Ochiai of the Tokyo University of Technology, and Masafumi Kaneko of the PHP Research Institute, who guided me through the world of modern intelligence affairs. There are also many specialists in military history at NIDS who have given me valuable advice: former Major General Tadashi Kagatani, director of the Military History Department, Takahiko Tsukamoto, Junichiro Shoji, Kiyoshi Aizawa, Tomoyuki Ishizu, Kyoichi Tachikawa, Hiroyuki Shindo, Shingo Nakajima, Nobu Iwatani, and Hiroshi Yamazoe. I am also indebted to Tsuyoshi Hara, Atsusi Moriyama, and Hiroyasu Miyasugi for reading my draft paper and providing many useful comments and observations.

I have spent several years in the UK as a graduate student and visiting fellow of the Royal United Services Institute (RUSI), and had the good fortune to talk with British and US scholars, who gave me further assistance in the process of writing intelligence history. These include Christopher Andrew (University of Cambridge), Michael Herman (University of Nottingham), David Kahn, Williamson Murray (Institute for Defense Analyses), Brian Bond, Michael Dockrill, Michael Goodman, and Alessio Patalano (King's College London), Ian Nish and Antony Best (London School of Economics), James Harris (University of Leeds), Paul Maddrell (Aberystwyth University), Philip Davies (Brunel University), Douglas Ford (University of Salford), and Andrew Oros (Washington College). Moreover, I have been fortunate to collaborate on this book with Ruth Sheppard, Jaqueline Mitchell, and Philip Smith at Osprey Publishing.

I also express my gratitude to Terumasa Nakanishi, my supervisor at Kyoto University, who was a graduate student of Sir Harry Hinsley at Cambridge in the 1970s. Finally, my deepest thanks go out to my better half Chiharu, who took on the tough job of translating my book, and to our little baby Kei, a hope for the future.

(When referring to Japanese names, I have adopted the western style of personal names preceding family names)

INTRODUCTION

In Japan, intelligence studies have been ignored until recent times. This omission is largely because the IJA and IJN destroyed most intelligence documents at the end of the war. In addition, intelligence officers of the IJA and IJN were unwilling to talk about their roles, as they were afraid of being punished by the victorious Allies. These conditions made it difficult to examine Japanese intelligence activities during World War II. There remain, however, fragmented collections of documents at the military archives of the National Institute for Defense Studies (NIDS), as well as equally fragmented memoirs of ex-officers, which can be cross-checked against diplomatic and historical sources.

A fundamental problem with researching this topic is that intelligence studies have not been treated with academic respect in Japan. Even studies of diplomatic or military history have not carefully examined intelligence factors, and as a result, intelligence studies have often been consigned to the realms of conspiracy theories or political plots. Conspiracy theories relating to the attack on Pearl Harbor, for example, have not been fully examined by academics (revisionist claims that President Roosevelt knew about the impending Japanese attack on Hawaii through intelligence sources, but deliberately witheld warnings to the US Pacific fleet and used the attack as an excuse to wage a war against Axis countries).

Given this situation, it is useful to provide a review of the existing literature on Japanese intelligence. At long last, ex-Colonel Tsutao Ariga published *Nihon Riku Kai Gun no Jyoho Kiko to Sono Katsudo* (The Organization and Activities of the IJA and IJN) in 1994, which paved the way for further studies of Japanese intelligence history.[1] There are also several key memoirs from former officers that provide illumination on Japanese wartime intelligence activities. Former Major General Takeo Imai wrote *Showa no Boryaku* (Conspiracies in the Showa Era) in 1967 and ex-Lieutenant Colonel Saburo Hayashi wrote *Kanto-Gun to*

1

Kyokuto Soren-Gun (The Kwantung Army and the Soviet Far Eastern Army) in 1974, which revealed espionage and conspiracy activities by the IJA's *Tokumu Kikan* (Special Duty Agency; SDA) in China and Manchuria. Ex-Colonel Yukio Nishihara also wrote about the SDA in Harbin, and explained Japanese special duties against the Soviets in the 1930s and 1940s, and ex-Lieutenant Colonel Iwaichi Fujiwara, who led the *F Kikan* (F Agency: Fujiwara Agency) in India, wrote a book based on his experiences.[2]

The largest work on Japanese intelligence history was *Rikugun Nakano Gakko* (Army Nakano School), edited by graduates of the school and published in 1978.[3] The book provides a comprehensive survey of the IJA's espionage training and activities during the Sino-Japanese and Pacific Wars, and also delivers a brief history of Japanese intelligence. The Nakano School was the exclusive intelligence training school of Japan, and turned out competent intelligence officers for service in Manchuria, China, Southeast Asia, and islands in the West Pacific. One of the graduates, ex-Second Lieutenant Hiroo Onoda, had engaged in espionage missions on Lubang Island, Philippines, until 1974, 29 years after the end of the war. There are other books about the Nakano School published in Japan, but the *Rikugun Nakano Gakko* is the landmark work.

In 1987, ex-Colonel Ichiji Sugita published *Joho Naki Senso Shido* (War Command Without Intelligence) in 1987, which reflected the demerits of the IJA's intelligence management during the war. He was an intelligence specialist in the IJA General Staff, becoming the intelligence section chief in the last stage of the war. Sugita's junior staff officer Eizo Hori also wrote a famous book, *Nichibei Joho Senki* (Record of the US–Japanese Intelligence War), in 1989.[4]

Regarding counter-intelligence, *Nihon Bocho shi* (History of Japanese Counter-Intelligence) is a classic book on Japanese counter-intelligence history, written by the prosecutor Ishiki Yamamoto in 1942. The book covered a long history, from the 8th to the 20th century. Japanese counter-intelligence was undertaken by the *Kenpei-tai* (Military Police) in World War II, and the Military Police HQ edited an official history called *Nihon Kenpei Showa Shi* (History of the Japanese Military Police in the Showa Era) in 1939. After the

Pacific War, the ex-Military Police officers' association produced *Nihon Kenpei Seishi* (Orthodox History of the Japanese Military Police) in 1975 and *Nihon Kenpei Gaishi* (Another History of the Military Police) in 1983. There are plenty of extant memoirs of ex-Military Police officers: the significant books are ex-Colonel Keijiro Otani's *Showa Kenpei shi* (History of the Military Police in the Showa Era) and ex-Lieutenant Yutaka Kudo's *Cho-ho Kenpei* (Espionage and the Military Police). Otani was a senior Military Police officer during the war, and Kudo engaged in covert actions against the Soviets in Manchuria.[5]

As far as the IJN is concerned, ex-Vice Admiral Toshiyuki Yokoi wrote *Nihon no Kimitsushitsu* (Japanese Black Chamber) in 1951, which revealed the IJN's codebreaking activities from the 1920s to the end of the Pacific War, and ex-Captain Yuzuru Sanematsu wrote a famous book, *Joho Senso* (Intelligence War), in 1972. Sanematsu engaged in US-directed intelligence as a senior staff member of the Navy intelligence section and the Navy General Staff during the war, and the IJN's intelligence activities are explored in this book. Ex-Lieutenant Kenichi Nakamuta recollected his codebreaking missions in the Pacific War in *Joho Shikan no Kaiso* (Memoir of an Intelligence Officer) published in 1974. Ex-Captain Motonao Samejima left vast amounts of private papers, and parts of his writings were published in 1981 as *Moto Gunreibu Tsushin Kacho no Kaiso* (Memoir of an Ex-Chief of Communications, Navy General Staff), which explored the IJN's radio communications and codebreaking in the Pacific War.[6] There have been several studies on Japanese intelligence in China, such as Hisashi Takahashi's "Nihon Rikugun to Taichu Joho" (The IJA and its Intelligence in China),[7] and Ryouichi Tobe's *Nihon Rikugun to Chugoku: 'Shina-tsu' ni Miru Yume to Satetsu* (The Japanese Imperial Army and China: Dream and Failure of China-hands).[8]

There are various books on Japanese intelligence published in English. On the Chinese side of operations there are works such as David Barrett and Larry Shyu's *Chinese Collaboration with Japan 1932–1945* and Timothy Brook's *Collaboration*.[9] Furthermore, in 1968 David Kahn examined Japanese codebreaking in his book *The Codebreakers*, written with the help of Naotsune Watanabe, a professor of archeology at the University of Tokyo who had spent the war working as a Japanese naval cryptanalyst of American codes.[10] Gordon Prange's *At Dawn We Slept* (1981) is a classic book for understanding Japanese information gathering during the run-up to the Pearl Harbor attack, and it is useful for examining revisionist views on that particular action. Famous conspiracy theory titles are Charles Beard, *President Roosevelt and the Coming of the War 1941* (1948), George Morgenstern's *Pearl Harbor* (1947), Charles Tansill's *Back Door to War* (1952), Robert Theobald's *The Final Secret of Pearl Harbor* (1954), John Toland's *Infamy* (1982), James Rusbridger's *Betrayal at Pearl Harbor* (1991), and Robert Stinnett's *Day of Deceit* (2000). A recent reappraisal of the Pearl Harbor attack is Timothy Wilford's *Pearl Harbor Redefined* (2001).

Historians are also able to study Japanese intelligence in World War II through Allied intelligence efforts. Arthur Marder wrote on historical relations between the Royal Navy (RN) and the IJN and he also mentioned the IJN's intelligence.[11] Richard Aldrich's *Intelligence and the War against Japan* (2000) and Antony Best's *British Intelligence and the Japanese Challenge in Asia, 1914–41* (2002) further revealed the struggle between UK and Japanese intelligence before and during the war.

The intricate affairs of Richard Sorge provide insight into Japanese counter-intelligence. He was a Soviet spy and was used to send Japanese military and political secrets back to Moscow from 1933. Sorge was investigated by the *Tokko* (Special Political Police) and the Military Police and was finally arrested in October 1941. The books by F. W. Deakin and G. R. Storry and Gordon Prange are classic studies of Sorge affairs.[12] The Fujiwara Agency, which supported the Indian independence movement during World War II, has attracted limited UK and US scholarship,[13] although the studies that have been produced and those on the Sorge affairs are more developed than similar Japanese-language works.

In 1982 Richard Deacon wrote *A History of the Japanese Secret Service*, a comprehensive study of Japanese intelligence since the 19th century, but in places his writing is based on outdated ideas. Also in the 1980s, Louis Allen, Ian Nish, J. W. M. Chapman, and Michael Barnhart sought to examine Japanese intelligence management, and their arguments remain persuasive.[14]

4

More recently, Tony Matthews' *Shadow Dancing* and Stephen Mercado's *The Shadow Warriors of Nakano* added further insights into Japanese covert actions during the war.[15]

Studies focusing specifically on Japanese signals intelligence during World War II have, however, been rare, compared to the plethora of material on the Allied equivalent. The imbalance between these two histories sometimes leads to too much emphasis on Allied signals intelligence and its influence on the course of the war. It is now commonly believed, therefore, that Japanese signals intelligence was almost negligible. It is true that the Japanese diplomatic, naval, and military ciphers were decrypted by Allied codebreakers.[16] After the war, the US Military Intelligence Section (MIS) delivered a report entitled "The Japanese Intelligence System" on September 4, 1945. The report stated that "Signals intelligence is a prime source of information for the field units of the Japanese Army and Navy. Although Japanese signals intelligence has apparently not succeeded in reading any high-grade American or British cryptographic systems, it has had considerable success with Chinese systems of all types and has been able to read several low grade British and American systems, principally weather and aircraft codes."[17]

By contrast, British intelligence documents, which were recently opened at the UK National Archives, show that Japanese signals intelligence achieved steady results in codebreaking.[18] As mentioned above, most documents related to intelligence were burnt at the end of the war and officers have largely kept silent on the matter, but there are some memoirs of Japanese ex-intelligence officers published after the 1970s. There have appeared some recent academic works on Japanese signals intelligence and other studies have shone a light on the performance of Japanese wartime signals intelligence using fragmented documents and officers' memoirs.[19] The studies demonstrate that the IJA and IJN did in fact break the US, UK, Soviet, Chinese, and French diplomatic ciphers in addition to several Allied military ciphers before the Pacific War.[20] Nevertheless, there is no overall account of Japanese signals and human intelligence in World War II, a deficit this book seeks to address.

1
JAPANESE INTELLIGENCE: A BRIEF HISTORY

EARLY JAPANESE INTELLIGENCE

The root of Japanese intelligence lies in Sun Tzu's *The Art of War*, written during the 6th century BC. Japanese military thinkers such as Soko Yamaga (1622–85), Shozan Sakuma (1811–64), and Shoin Yoshida (1830–59) studied and interpreted Sun's words, including the maxim "If you know the enemy and know yourself, you need not fear the result of a hundred battles."[21] Yamaga, especially, developed this idea and wrote that military planning and information gathering should be a coherent process.[22] Here was a primitive stage in the idea of the "intelligence cycle," and it became a tradition that was inherited by modern war planners in the late 19th century and applied to war against China and Russia.

From the establishment of the IJA and IJN in 1868, both branches of service had regulated their own intelligence apparatus.[23] The IJA's intelligence activities abroad began in 1878 when the Army General Staff placed military attachés in China. However, there was no espionage network at that time and the IJA asked Ginko Kishida, a private trader in China, to collect information. In 1890, Captain Sei Arai established the *Nisshin Boueki Kenkyu-jyo* (Institute for Sino-Japanese Trade) and the institution became a base of Japanese intelligence activities in China.[24]

In 1894, Japan began a war against China. It had been estimated that the Chinese Army was far greater than the IJA in numbers, but the IJA realized that the Chinese had military and political weaknesses through the reports of General Yasumasa Fukushima, military attaché to China, and Lieutenant General Souroku Kawakami, Vice Chief of Staff, who traveled to see China just before the war.[25] (Fukushima served in both the First Sino-Japanese War (1894–95) and Russo-Japanese War (1904–5) as an outstanding intelligence officer, one who adhered rigidly to the principles of Sun Tzu.) The IJN also obtained information through a British citizen, J. M. James, who was personally hired by Admiral Tsugumichi Saigo, Navy Minister. He collected information in Tientsin city and Saigo rewarded him with 7,000 yen (10 million yen today) for his information gathering.[26] Based on the intelligence, Japan was confident about entering the war with China.

After the defeat of China, Russia became the serious menace for Japan. The IJA and IJN did ad hoc information gathering before the Sino-Japanese War, but the same system seemed to cause difficulties in the case of a war with Russia. In 1903 the IJN established the 3rd Department, whose duty was collecting foreign intelligence, while the IJA did not alter its ways at all – General Soroku Kawakami, IJA Chief of Staff, was afraid of causing trouble by making a drastic system change just before the war. Instead of setting up a new intelligence department, the IJA established the *Kaigai Joho Hensan Iinkai* (Committee of Foreign Intelligence Compilation; CFIC) headed by Fukushima, which was the central body for gathering Russian intelligence in the IJA.[27] The committee dealt with vast amounts of information from military attachés abroad and foreign agents in China and Russia, and submitted intelligence assessments to operations staff of the Army General Staff.

In July 1903, Fukushima reported his estimations to the Army General Staff: "As far as land operations are concerned, earlier war is better because the Russians are now constructing the trans-Siberian railway. After completion of the railway, it would be quite difficult for the IJA to beat the Russian Army. On the other hand, we can be more optimistic about sea operations. The ratio between the Japanese Navy and Russian Far Eastern Navy is 4 to 3. If we can damage the Baltic Fleet dispatched from the west, we have a chance of winning."[28]

During the subsequent Russo-Japanese War, a famous intelligence officer, Colonel Motojiro Akashi, military attaché to St. Petersburg, supported political movements in Finland and Poland. He met Lenin in Geneva and persuaded him to return to Russia for his revolution. His espionage activities were published as *Rakka Ryusui* and the book would be used as a textbook at the Nakano School, the IJA's espionage training school.[29] Also, Major Nobuzumi Aoki engaged in intelligence activities in China and Makiyo Ishimitsu collected Russian information in Manchuria.

In 1907, Japan laid down a *Teikoku Kokubo Hoshin* (Imperial National Defense Plan). Japan had learned lessons from the Russo-Japanese War and restructured her military organization, which was out of date compared with those of the Western nations. Before the Russo-Japanese War, the IJA's foreign intelligence was regionally divided between 1st and 2nd Departments, but the system was not based on systematic management, but on ad hoc arrangements for the war. In 1908, the IJA set up the 2nd Department within the Army General Staff, which would focus on information collection and analysis.

Fundamentally, Japanese intelligence had a tactical focus because it was heavily influenced by the Prussian style of limited war used at the end of the 19th century. In fact, Japanese tactical intelligence led to victories in the First Sino-Japanese and the Russo-Japanese Wars, and the IJA and IJN thought that tactical intelligence could compensate for their deficiencies on the battlefield. In addition, the Japanese forces did not really take part in World War I, and they failed to understand the concept of total war as a whole. Michael Herman wrote: "The First World War had indeed shown that total war needed total intelligence; foreign military power had come to depend on factors of industrial capacity, demography and morale which fell outside the analysis of normal military and naval intelligence."[30] However, Japanese intelligence failed to adopt the "total intelligence" approach after World War I.

Japanese intelligence responsibilities had been mainly assumed by the IJA and IJN from the 1920s onwards. The 2nd Department of the Army General Staff and the 3rd Department of the Navy General Staff were the central bodies of intelligence, which aggregated information from military attachés abroad, plus from the *Toku-Jo Han* (Special Intelligence Section; SIS) and the special duty agencies (SDA). The SIS engaged in eavesdropping and codebreaking duties and the SDAs engaged in espionage and conspiracy duties. The War Ministry operated the Military Police, which performed counter-intelligence activities.

SOURCES OF INTELLIGENCE IN WORLD WAR II

According to the *Joho Kinmu no Sanko* (Textbook for the Intelligence Service) used in the North China Area Army, the sources of Japanese intelligence in World War II were as follows: 1) attachés, expeditionary troops abroad, and special agencies providing human intelligence (HUMINT) and open source intelligence (OSINT); 2) signals intelligence (SIGINT); 3) scout groups; 4) captured documents; and 5) intelligence agents.[31]

The HQ of the Expeditionary Army to China published monthly the *Nai Gai Josei no Gaiyo Hyo* (Summary of Domestic and Foreign Affairs), which summarized the international affairs of Japan, the United States, the United Kingdom, China, Germany, the Soviet Union, Italy, the Middle East, South America, and Southeast Asia and the course of the Pacific War and the war in Europe. The summary showed information sources, which were newspapers, signals intelligence, attaché reports, and SDA reports in China.[32] The Navy General Staff has also left the *Jokyo Handan Shiryo* (Situation Estimate Document), which was the daily intelligence report from the Intelligence Department to the Operations Department at the last stage of the Pacific War.[33] Based on this report, the information sources of the IJN were as follows:

Source	Number of reports collected October 1, 1944–July 10, 1945
Signals intelligence	393
Attaché reports	102
POW information	27
Captured documents	2
Foreign agents	7
IJA	11
Foreign Ministry	2
Open source (radio etc.)	110
Open source (newspapers etc.)	769
Others	23
Unclear	38
Total	1,484

From this data, it is apparent that the IJN depended on SIGINT for its best information. The SIS had engaged in codebreaking activities since the 1920s and they had broken the US, UK, and Chinese diplomatic ciphers and a part of their military ciphers. Colonel Yuzuru Sanematsu, senior staff of the Navy Intelligence Department (NID), wrote that "Signals intelligence was a great help for operations staff, although it was sometimes evaluated too much."[34]

Japanese naval attachés were sent to the United States, the United Kingdom, Germany, France, the Soviet Union, Italy, China, Spain, Holland, Argentina, Turkey, Mexico, Canada, Thailand, Palau, Romania, Brazil, and Chile before the Pacific War, and after the outbreak of war the IJN collected information through naval attachés in Sweden and Thailand. POWs were also an important source of information during the war. Commander Nobuhiko Imai, an IJN intelligence officer, interrogated Allied POWs at the Ofuna camp, Kanagawa. He was good at posing leading questions and through these collected small fragments of information, patching these together in a larger picture. He wrote: "I chatted with the POWs and collected bits of information. They [the POWs] were not so serious in daily conversations. We doggedly repeated the conversations and finally could draw up schedules and positions of the US submarines in the Pacific area."[35] Captured documents were naturally appreciated as intelligence sources. Sanematsu and Imai wrote that the documents entitled "US Planning of Amphibious Operations in Okinawa" and "US Navy Task Binder" were very useful for estimating US naval strength before the battle of Okinawa.[36]

Facts about foreign agents hired by the Japanese are still unclear, but the German Bernard Kühn and Britisher F. J. Rutland were famous spies for the IJN. Although both of them were arrested before the Pacific War, there seems to have been some continuing reports from foreign agents during the conflict. Imai wrote: "We succeeded in infiltrating the US government, but after the outbreak of the war the agents were obliged to move to Mexico, Argentina, and Chile. On the other hand, we hired native Chinese and Australians in New Guinea, but they eventually double-crossed."[37]

As far as OSINT was concerned, the Domei press agency collected world news and translated it for the Japanese government.[38] According to the IJN's document, OSINT depended on Reuters, Associated Press, United Press, *Life*, *Time*, *News Chronicle*, *The New York Times*, *The New York Herald Tribune*, and military magazines overseas. During the war the material was obtained in neutral countries, such as Sweden and Argentina. Masao Tsuda, the Domei press agency, and Colonel Makoto Onodera, military attaché to Sweden, gathered press sources and sent them to Tokyo.[39] The Navy war planners sometimes happened upon genuinely useful information by chance in an open source. For example, the British battleship *King George V* arrived in the United States carrying the new ambassador, Lord Halifax, and the photos were published in *Life* magazine on February 3, 1941. When this issue reached Japan a month later, the IJN learned about the new British anti-aircraft guns.[40]

The IJN exchanged information with Germany. On May 11, 1937, Major General Hiroshi Oshima, military attaché to Berlin, and intelligence chief Admiral Wilhelm Canaris signed an agreement for German–Japanese exchange of information about the Soviets, but the agreement did not provide Japan with any really useful information. Nevertheless, a German–Japanese Information Exchange Agreement on signals intelligence was signed in 1941 and a communications agreement was also signed between the German and Japanese navies in September 1942.

2

JAPANESE ARMY INTELLIGENCE

CODEBREAKING ACTIVITIES AGAINST THE US AND BRITAIN

In the IJA, all intercepted signals communication of the enemy was called *Toku-jo* (Special Information), and was placed in one of three categories: *A-jo* (A information) obtained by codebreaking; *B-jo* (B information) by tapping telephones; and *C-jo* (C information) by direction finding and mapping activities.[41] According to the report of ex-Lieutenant Colonel Yukio Yokoyama, specialist in breaking Chinese codes and senior SIS staff officer of the Army General Staff, the origin of the IJA's codebreaking activities was the establishment of a study group that met at the branch office of the Signals Traffic Department of the Foreign Ministry in 1921, a meeting held jointly by the IJA, the Foreign Ministry, and the Ministry of Communications.[42]

The participants at the meeting were experts in cipher intelligence from each organization, and the focus of the meeting was mainly toward cracking US and British ciphers. At this time, the IJA gave relatively low priority to codebreaking, and its main target was the Soviet Union. In the field of codebreaking against the United States and United Kingdom, therefore, the IJN was superior to the IJA. In the mid-1920s, this study group had developed into an official body under the agreement of the four ministries.

It was the dispatch of the troops to Siberia from 1918 to 1922 that caused the IJA to attach a deeper importance to codebreaking activities. In the summer of 1922, when the Japanese delegation negotiated with the Soviet Union about withdrawal from Siberia, Lieutenant Colonel Kazuo Mike of the Japanese Expeditionary Army to Vladivostok, was dispatched to Dairen to gather information for the negotiations. He found that the Soviet delegation was staying at the Daiwa Hotel in Dairen and asked the Military Police to monitor the delegation's activities, collecting tons of waste paper everyday.

On one occasion, the Military Police officers found a ciphered document among the waste paper and sent it to the Army General Staff in Tokyo, but they were unable to decrypt the Soviet cipher at that time. Around this time, however, Lieutenant Colonel Naozaburo Okabe, the military attaché to Poland, was informed that the Polish Army had broken the Soviet cipher, and the ciphered document obtained in Dairen was decrypted by the Polish.[43] The Polish Army had smashed the Soviet Army by breaking its cipher in the war against the USSR from 1919 to 1920, and the significance of this achievement was not lost to the Japanese Army General Staff.

Fully realizing the importance of codebreaking, the IJA General Staff invited Captain Jan Kowalewski of the Polish Army to Tokyo in 1923 for help in breaking the Red Army's cipher system. Captain Haruyoshi Hyakutake (who studied Russian intelligence), Captain Yoshihisa Inoue (British), Captain Naotomi Mikuni (French), and Captain Kaoru Takeda (German) were members of the cipher studying course, and Commander Hisajiro Nakasugi, IJN, also joined the group.[44] Once the program was complete, the codebreaking team headed by Hyakutake was allocated to the 7th Section of the 3rd Department (Communication) of the Army General Staff.[45] This was the birth of the Army General Staff's official codebreaking apparatus.

During this period, a US diplomatic code that utilized five alphabets began to be used between the State Department in Washington, D.C., and the US embassy in Tokyo. Hyakutake and Commander Risaburo Ito, the senior staff officer of the Traffic Section of the IJN, were assigned to decode it together. Based on the assumption that the word "NADED," which was frequently used in the code, meant "period" in English, they were able to break the rest of the code.[46] The code was called the "Gray Code" in the US Department of State (DoS), "N Code" in the IJA, and "AN2" in the IJN. The Gray Code, however, was not a high-grade system, and the British codebreaking apparatus at the Government Cipher and Code School (GC&CS) also cracked it. As the US DoS paid poor attention to their security, the code was nevertheless used often during the 1920s and 1930s.[47]

In July 1930, the IJA began systematic codebreaking activities, assigning the 5th Section of the 2nd Department of the Army General Staff to breaking foreign ciphers and to developing its own military cipher system.[48] Codebreakers such as Hyakutake and Captain Shunjiro Okubo had already been breaking the cipher of the Chang Hsueh-liang government in mainland China at this time.[49] The 5th Section turned into the 8th Section in 1934 and then the 18th Section, with 135 staff in 1936.[50]

In 1934, the DoS introduced a new code system called the "Brown Code," and used it together with the Gray Code. However, as the department informed the US embassies abroad of the change by using the already broken Gray Code, the introduction of the Brown Code was known to other countries in advance. Watching for their opportunity to obtain the new code book, the Military Police succeeded in taking photographs of it at the US consulate in Kobe, targeting the DoS courier who called at Kobe with the code in his possession.[51] Thanks to this achievement by the Military Police, the IJA easily broke the American Brown Code. In 1938, the IJN also broke this code, which they called "AF6."[52]

Now came the problem of the "Strip Ciphers," which were known to be the most secure diplomatic ciphers used by the United States. To obtain these codes, the Military Police succeeded in raiding the poorly guarded US consulate in Kobe and opening the depository with the assistance of a Japanese employee. Inside, however, they found only some strips of celluloid instead of a code book. The Strip Ciphers were sophisticated – not based on a code book but on strips that could alter the code by changing their combination. Simply photographing the strips, therefore, did not crack the code, and the last means for the 18th Section was to break the Strip Ciphers through a scientific decoding, which was a highly laborious operation.

Yet it does appear that the section eventually broke the Strip Ciphers. Atsushi Moriyama proved this by comparing deciphered records of SIGINT in Japan with the original records of the American cables, and he also broke the Strip Ciphers himself through mathematical methods.[53] Furthermore, a wartime report from British intelligence concluded that Japan had already succeeded in breaking the Strip Ciphers in 1943.[54] The British knew this because there was some information among the deciphered records of Japanese military cables that seemed to come from American Strip Ciphers cables. The Strip Ciphers were so sophisticated that it was a difficult system to break. At the same time, it required high degrees of skill and attention to compose and send such a message. The telegraphers committed inevitable simple mistakes in the ciphering process, which gave the Japanese a hint how to break it.

In summary, the IJA had broken the diplomatic codes of the US DoS, the Gray Code, the Brown Code, and the Strip Ciphers. The best British and German codebreaking apparatus at that time had not cracked the Strip Ciphers, so Japanese codebreaking ability must have been considerable.[55] The breaking of the Strip Ciphers also resulted in the conclusion of the German–Japanese Traffic and Information Exchange Agreement in 1941, which led to the exchange of SIGINT between the two powers.[56] The IJA SIGINT section also broke US diplomatic ciphers in China, which revealed Chinese political and diplomatic intentions towards Japan. Until 1941, therefore, the IJA could decrypt a large number of the US diplomatic cables. With this capability came embarrassing revelations about problems with Japan's own security. On August 31, 1940, Japanese War Minister General Hideki Tojo complained that "According to the [US] ambassador's report to Washington, I have realized that he knows much more about Japanese internal affairs than I do ..."[57]

Regarding the British ciphers, however, Japanese codebreaking activities progressed only slowly. The Japanese had broken part of the British diplomatic code, specifically the "Interdepartmental Code," as there are some decoded British diplomatic cables kept in the Diplomatic Record Office of the Ministry of Foreign Affairs. According to ex-Major Eiichi Hirose, who had served in the 18th Section, by decoding a cable from the head of the Far Eastern Combined Bureau (FECB) in Singapore in January 1941, the section discovered that the British defense of Malaya was highly vulnerable.[58]

The IJA steadily continued the interception of British traffic, with occasional decoding successes. It was only after the war that Japanese codebreaking activities against British cables became known to British intelligence. The clues were in reports from the Japanese attachés in Berlin and Helsinki to Tokyo, which indicated that the Japanese decrypted part of the British code, and in some German official papers confiscated by the British, among which were British ciphered documents decrypted by the Japanese and sent to Germany. The British Security Service conducted a narrow investigation, fearing a leak of information from the inside, but then discovered that the Japanese had broken some British code and ciphers. The record of these investigations was concealed for a long time after the war.[59]

Up until the outbreak of the war against the United States in December 1941, the 18th Section made major efforts to break code and ciphers, and hence had little interest in creating code systems of its own for the Army. After the Pearl Harbor attack, however, they came to regard the creation of their own codes as essential, but made quite a slow start. Major Morio Tomura, who engaged in signals traffic operations at the outbreak of the war, stated that they considered their signals traffic was safe because it was a supposedly highly secure, infinite random numbered cipher.[60] Thus, the Japanese took almost no cipher traffic safety measures until the IJA established the Cipher Security Committee, in association with the IJN and the Ministry of Foreign Affairs, in late 1943.[61]

For the decryption section of the IJA, codebreaking activities against the United States and Britain were actually only secondary work, for their principal target was the Soviet Union. That priority finally changed in 1943 after the battle of Guadalcanal. In July 1943, the Army General Staff formed the *Chuo Tokushu Jo-ho Bu* (Central Special Intelligence Section; CSIS) and began to make real efforts to decrypt the US ciphers. The Extraordinary Establishment Order of the Special Intelligence Sections listed its objectives as:

> 1) create the Central Special Intelligence Section in Tokyo, assigning it to gather international signals information.

2) form the Research and Educational Section within the Central Special Intelligence Section, in light of the situation where enemy cipher systems are becoming increasingly fortified and hard to break, especially as codebreaking activities against the United States and United Kingdom are extremely inadequate, with few qualified staff.

3) invest the chief of Central Special Intelligence Section with authority to control the directors of the Special Intelligence Sections of each army in areas concerning the technical matters of codebreaking.[62]

At this point in 1943, the number of staff within the CSIS was 301, including 63 senior officers, but it grew to more than 1,000 staff at its peak in 1945.[63] There were also the secondary Special Information Sections: the Kwantung Army had 548 Special Information staff in 1943; the Japanese China Expeditionary Army had 688; the Second Air Force had 303; the 3rd Flying Squadron had 228; the Japanese Southern Army had 360; the Eighth Field Army had 287.[64]

According to the memoir of Lieutenant Colonel Yukio Yokoyama, the senior staff officer of the CSIS, the section mobilized university students who majored in mathematics and foreign languages in May 1944, and introduced the statistical machines of IBM to break the American military codes. These efforts resulted in 80 percent success in decryption.[65] This achievement enabled Japan to deduce the movement of the B-29 Superfortress bombers flying over Japan, and consequently the IJA managed to shoot down some B-29s over Japan and Hong Kong.

The CSIS could also follow the movement of B-29 *Enola Gay*, which dropped the first atomic bomb on Hiroshima on August 6, 1945, though they could not know about the ordnance carried by traffic interception only.[66] Lieutenant Colonel Eizo Hori, senior staff officer of the Army intelligence section, wrote:

At 4:00hrs on the morning of August 6, we caught a call sign for B-29s. They sent a message, "we are going off the mission." We had known the B-29s had a special mission and we alerted the air defense group to "some B-29s approaching Japan," but we could not follow them after that because they kept signal silence. At 7:20hrs we caught a signal from a B-29 flying over Hiroshima. We lost other signals. While we were trying to find the lost B-29s around the Hiroshima area, suddenly one of them dropped the atom bomb on the city at 8:15hrs. Oh, my God ... We had read foreign press before that said "A new experiment was conducted on July 16," but we were unable to know what kind of experiment it was ... On August 11 we found the word, "nuclear" in decrypted US documents sent by the M-209 ciphering machine, but it was too late ...[67]

In the southern theater of the Pacific, the Japanese had temporarily broken US codes by obtaining information about the coded traffic from American POWs, but the Americans soon noticed the fact and changed the code.

After 1943, the SIS of the Southern Army began to intercept and decode US coded military communications with notable results, such as predicting the size of the Allied force that invaded Wake Island and the Philippines. However, the British and Americans were aware of this activity – British intelligence warned that the top-secret information was compromised by the Japanese interception and decoding of US and British traffic, based on an investigation during the war.[68] Nevertheless, the evidence demonstrates that the IJA had significant success in breaking Allied codes, although such information often came too late in the war to have military significance.

CODEBREAKING ACTIVITIES AGAINST CHINA

It was the Mukden incident that prompted the IJA to begin codebreaking activities in mainland China. On September 18, 1931, a section of Japanese-owned railway in southern Manchuria was dynamited, the Japanese claiming that the sabotage was performed by Chinese dissidents. Whatever the true cause, the incident proved to be the catalyst for the Japanese invasion of Manchuria. Back in 1928, the IJA's Signal Intelligence Section had already broken the traffic code used by the army of Chang Hsueh-liang.[69] When the Mukden incident occurred, the Army General Staff dispatched Captain

Katsuhiko Kudo to the Kwantung Army to engage in interception and codebreaking activities. He obtained genuinely useful information – including material used by the Japanese in the Tangku Agreement, by which Japan tried to settle the Mukden incident diplomatically – and became the first intelligence officer to win the *Kinshi Kunsho* (Golden Kite Medal).

In 1934 the SIS was established in the Japanese forces based in Tientsin, headed by Major Tomio Tsuruta with 12 staff members. The number of staff doubled in the next year and the section had Chinese, British, US, and Soviet groups. After the outbreak of the Sino-Japanese War in 1937, signals intelligence sections were established in the Japanese Army to North China (Peking), the Japanese Army to Central China (Nanking), the Japanese Army to South China (Canton), and III Air Corps (Nanking). These sections were combined as the Special Intelligence Section (covert name: *Sakae 9440 Butai*) in August 1943, which was based in Nanking and engaged in codebreaking missions against Chinese forces until the end of the Pacific War.[70]

As the Chinese military code, called *Mi-ma* at that time, was basically composed of four-digit numbers and often repeated the same words, it was not difficult to break. So, the Japanese Kwantung Army could break most of the code used by the Kuomintang (KMT) forces and gather information about the formation and movements of the armies of Song Zheyuan, Chang Hsueh-liang, and the others allied to Chiang Kai-shek. Such information enabled the Kwantung Army to forestall the objectives of the Chinese armies. For example, an officer who engaged in codebreaking activities in the SIS of the Japanese North China Expeditionary Army recollected that "during the Yichang operation in May 1940, we intercepted 120 Chinese telegrams. The great satisfaction that we felt when the operational movement of 54 Chinese divisions was detected ... makes me excited even today."[71]

A further example occurred in July 1937. When Prime Minister Fumimaro Konoe dispatched Ryusuke Miyazaki and Teisuke Akiyama to Nanking as couriers for peace negotiations, the IJA came to know about Konoe's political maneuvers by decoding Chinese communications with the Japanese Foreign Ministry. The Army's Military Police consequently arrested the couriers on their way to China.[72] Evidently, the IJA tried to monitor Japanese political activity by eavesdropping, then acted to shape events according to its own desires. On May 13, 1939, the Minister of Foreign Affairs Hachiro Arita stated in an anxious voice:

> In Japan, it seems that we are in a very difficult position for conducting real diplomacy, because Japanese politicians are always watched by the military. I cannot make good use of flattering nor diplomatic language, so people such as the US and UK ambassadors may feel alienated. But if I say something wrong on the cable, the Japanese Army and Navy intercept it and immediately criticize me for my slip of the tongue … It is impossible to ask foreign ambassadors not to send telegrams because the Japanese Army and Navy intercept them. The situation is so awkward.[73]

The IJA exploited its internal eavesdropping as a useful tool to enhance its political and diplomatic clout with the Japanese government. Such monitoring severely restricted the efforts of moderates in the Japanese government, who sought a diplomatic compromise with the United States and Britain during the run-up to the Pearl Harbor attack.

The IJA had already broken the KMT's diplomatic code by 1936. For instance, after the Sino-Japanese incident in July 1937, the IJA intercepted and decoded a telegram sent by Chiang Kai-shek to the Chinese ambassadors in the United States, Britain, France, and the Soviet Union, which asked what support the powers would provide in case of outright war against Japan.[74] According to Yokoyama, the IJA could divine the intentions of the United States and Britain during the Pacific War through the Chinese coded cables,[75] even though the Allies also recognized the extremely poor level of the Chinese security.[76] Barbara Tuchman has explored the inadequacy of Chinese information security, writing that "the Americans had learned through their access to Japanese code that the Japanese in their turn had broken Chinese code. Chinese security, already a sieve, now had large holes in it." [77] The British themselves also intercepted and decrypted the Chinese coded cables, so they knew the weakness of the Chinese system. According to the investigations of British intelligence, the Japanese intercepted and decoded the signals traffic between China and its attachés in London, New Delhi, Ceylon, Sydney, Melbourne, Washington, D.C., and Ankara.[78]

On August 29, 1944, the Americans and British intercepted and decoded a telegram from the Army General Staff in Tokyo to the commanders of area armies, informing them that: "According to the report from the Chinese attachés to Chongqing [Chungking], the US and UK have recognized that Japan has broken the code of the Allied force."[79] This sentence revealed that Japan had in some way broken the code used among the Americans, British, and Chinese. The Japanese cables intercepted and decoded by the United States on March 9, 1944, also indicated that Japan decrypted the telegram from the Chinese ambassador in Britain to Chungking regarding the discussions with the British Foreign Minister Anthony Eden. Richard Aldrich explains: "In April 1944, as the preparations for D-Day placed Britain under a tight cloak of security, the Chinese embassy in London was summarily deprived of its cipher and diplomatic bag privileges, resulting in vigorous protests. Eden assured Churchill that in the circumstances they had no choice."[80]

For the United States and Britain, the leaking of important information from China to Japan was serious problem. An improvement in Chinese security, however, would give the Americans and Britain difficulty in their own codebreaking against China. The only solution was to keep important information from China.

Regarding the code of the Chinese Communist Party (CCP), this was quite tough to break because it originated in the Soviet Union. The Japanese SIGINT section made serious efforts to break the code and finally, on February 28, 1941, they broke it for the first time.[81] However, the CCP had a relatively high awareness of security issues and changed the code frequently. Therefore, the IJA could only intermittently read the CCP code, although the Chief of Staff of the North China Expeditionary Army stated that the Japanese were able to gather information about a number of offensives by the CCP.[82]

CODEBREAKING ACTIVITIES AGAINST THE SOVIET UNION

As mentioned above, the IJA had invited Polish instructor Captain Kowalewski to Japan in 1923 to provide training in basic codebreaking. After that, the Army General Staff dispatched six officers to Poland to take a one-year codebreaking course: Lieutenant Colonel Haruyoshi Hyakutake and Captain Katsuhiko Kudo in 1925, Majors Naoji Sakai and Toshijiro Okubo in 1929, and Majors Shinta Sakurai and Eiichi Fukai in 1935. According to Hyakutake, the Polish Army General Staff allocated between 260 and 270 staff to codebreaking against the Soviet Union and Germany.[83]

In 1928, the IJA also obtained a couple of tables of random numbers for the Soviet diplomatic ciphers, acquiring these from the Soviet consulate in Harbin through the Chinese authorities, an essential source of information for breaking the Soviet ciphers.[84] The officers involved became core members of the SIGINT section when it was established in the Kwantung Army in 1934; it was officially called the Study Section of the Kwantung Army, headed by Colonel Toshijiro Okubo in the 2nd Section (Intelligence) of the Army General Staff of the Kwantung Army. The HQ of the organization was located in Hsinking, Manchuria. The main mission was decrypting the Soviet military ciphers and the Study Section succeeded in breaking the Soviet Red Army's four-digit code by around 1935.

In April 1940, the SIS of the Kwantung Army invited former Polish Army General Staff codebreaker "Michel" to improve the methods of cracking the Soviet code. Owing to his cooperation, the section succeeded in breaking the four-digit code of the Soviet Air Force, which enabled them to follow the deployments of the Soviet Air Force to the Zabaikal area in the same year.[85]

As for non-coded Soviet radio traffic, the Chief of Staff for railways in the 1st Department of the Army General Staff of the Kwantung Army requested an investigation by the Research Section of the Manchurian Railways. In 1936, the Kwantung Army was particularly interested in the 2nd Siberian Railways being built by the Soviet Union, and attempted to collect information about the progress of the construction. The Research Section established a branch office of the North Section in Harbin and began intercepting the Soviet non-coded radio traffic. Meanwhile, the SIS of the Kwantung Army established the East Asian Traffic Research Group in Hsinking, Manchuria, in order to tap public telephone conversations and collect the non-ciphered communication. The group was a semi-official organization with 320 staff, whose traffic information was sent to the intelligence section of the Army General Staff.[86] Another example of interception activities is Operation *Akizuki*, in which the IJA tapped the Soviet cables. To tap the Soviet military phone network, the Japanese needed to pass across the Soviet border. By trial and error, the IJA finally succeeded in picking up a slight electrical current that came from a Soviet phone line at a spot about 1,000 yards from the border, and hired some Russians to tap the phone.[87]

The IJA also established the Sakhalin Army Communication Site headed by Colonel Gunzo Ota in Shikika (now Poronaisk), Sakhalin. The intelligence staffs conducted further codebreaking activities against the Soviet Union, especially of the Soviet Air Force's four-digit and five-digit codes. On June 23, 1941, the day after the outbreak of the Soviet–German War, Ota recorded that "information about the Soviet–German War came out constantly."[88] Through their codebreaking activities, they collected information about the Soviet troop dispositions, education and training, personnel transfers, and supply conditions.[89]

According to the memoir of Eiichi Hirose, as the Soviets limited the use of radio traffic as much as possible, the interception results in Sakhalin made hardly any progress. Therefore, Hirose asked a Japanese policeman to pass in front of the Soviet border guards in order to provoke them to send signals that the IJA could intercept. Then they changed the number of policemen and the timing of his movements, so that they could pinpoint the words that varied among the coded sentences. It was these words that gave the IJA the ability to break the Soviet border guards' code, "LK2."[90]

In 1943, the SIS of the Manchurian Second Air Force decrypted a communication that revealed that the United States would supply the Soviet

Union with strategic materials by air from Fairbanks, Alaska. Once they even discovered that the US Vice President Henry Wallace would visit Chungking by the air route, and made a plan for shooting down the aircraft over Manchuria.[91]

Even if codes could not be broken, just intercepting telegrams and monitoring their volume enabled the IJA to collect information to a certain extent. This information was called "C-jo," as mentioned above. For instance, on August 2, 1941, facing sudden Soviet signal silence, the SIS of the Kwantung Army was charged with tension. The information was reported to the 2nd Department of the Army General Staff, Tokyo, through a direct telephone line by Lieutenant Colonel Etsuo Koutani, the staff officer of the Kwantung Army in charge of intelligence. As the situation developed, Lieutenant Colonel Masanobu Tsuji even insisted that the Japanese should go on a diplomatic offensive by suggesting to the Soviets the purchase of Northern Sakhalin, though in actual fact it was atmospheric conditions that prevented interception of the Soviet signals traffic.[92] On the other hand, in May 1945 changes in the quantity of signals traffic enabled the SIS of the Kwantung Army to perceive the concentration of the Soviet Army on the border between Manchuria and the Soviet Union, which was reported to the Army General Staff.[93]

During World War II, the IJA's codebreaking activities against the Soviet Union were developed by allocating Colonel Tahei Hayashi to Germany (and to Hungary as military attaché in 1943), Lieutenant Colonel Shinta Sakurai to Hungary, and Major Eiichi Hirose to Finland. In 1944, Sakurai established codebreaking operations against the Soviets in Budapest, efforts that became the forefront of the IJA's codebreaking activities against the Red Army.[94] In addition, some Polish exiles were hired to break the Soviet code at the attaché office in Romania.[95]

In Berlin, thanks to the German–Japanese Traffic and Information Exchange Agreement, the British and US codes decrypted by the IJA were exchanged for Soviet codes decrypted by Germany. In March 1945, the Japanese ambassador to Germany, Hiroshi Oshima, was informed of the contents of the Yalta Conference by German Foreign Minister Joachim Ribbentrop. The information was obtained from the communications of the Polish government in exile, which the German intelligence intercepted and decrypted.[96]

In January 1943, Hirose, who engaged in codebreaking against the Soviet Union by cooperating with Finnish SIGINT, reported that: "Finland has succeeded in codebreaking against the USSR, United States, and Turkey. Now they are trying to break the French code. Moreover, it seems that they are decrypting the Swedish and German codes as well."[97] The Finnish apparatus gave Hirose the decryption records of the US Strip Ciphers, which implied that the Japanese codes were broken by the United States and Britain.

Hirose cooperated with codebreakers in Finland, Poland, and Hungary to break the Soviet codes, and is likely to have broken the Soviet merchant ship code, diplomatic four-digit code, and a part of the Red Army's five-digit code by 1944 at the latest, primarily through cooperation with the Finnish SIGINT apparatus.[98]

In the Army General Staff, although they recognized that SIGINT was the best way to monitor the deployments of the Soviet Army, their efforts to increase the staff numbers were not enough. After the war, Lieutenant Colonel Saburo Hayashi, chief of the Russian Section in the 2nd Department of the Army General Staff, recollected "we should have allocated more staff to this field [SIGINT], as well as given preference to the staff in promotions and pay raises."[99] Compared to the large-scale and systematic US and British SIGINT activities, the Japanese SIGINT service seems clearly inferior. Nevertheless, the large amounts of SIGINT obtained by the Japanese required a massive effort from excellent staff. Considering the Soviet Border Guards only, the IJA had eight SIGINT sites in Manchuria, each one of which intercepted an average of 20 cables a day, thereby acquiring more than 50,000 cables a year.[100] The IJA had considerable codebreaking abilities for all its shortages of staff and funds. It seems that the Japanese SIGINT competence could have been equal to that of the United States and Britain if they had urgently increased the staff to cope with the enormous volume of signals traffic.

There are some stories that clearly indicate the skill of the Japanese codebreakers. Ex-Lieutenant Colonel Hisashi Hara and ex-Captain Kazuo

Kamaga, specialists in US codes, demonstrated their ability in solving US ciphers during Allied interrogation in 1948.[101] Ex-Colonel Shunjiro Okubo and ex-Lieutenant Colonel Yukio Yokoyama, who had decrypted the Chinese and Soviet codes, were asked by the KMT to continue their codebreaking activities against the Soviet Union after the Pacific War. They subsequently succeeded in collecting information about the deployment of the Soviet Far East Army and about the Soviet research into nuclear power in mainland China and Taiwan.[102]

JAPANESE ARMY HUMINT

Though the term "HUMINT" suggests a kind of espionage-based collection of information, it is conducted by attachés dispatched to embassies and consulates abroad. The Japanese attachés usually exchanged information with their counterparts such as foreign attachés and military officers, and collected information through open sources such as newspapers. They also hired locals and manipulated them to gather information as agents. In 1941, the IJA spent 40 million yen (32 billion yen today) of secret funds a year, which expanded to 400 million (320 billion today) at the end of the war in 1945.[103]

The IJA's HUMINT can be divided into three categories: 1) against the Soviet Union in the "Northern Area" (Manchuria); 2) against China in mainland China; 3) against France and Britain in the "Southern Area" (southern Asia). The IJA had its interest in the northern area and less in the south, so they turned their most intense efforts to intelligence activity against the Soviet Union.

Before the war, the Japanese foreign intelligence apparatus was the Special Duty Agencies (SDAs), which were classified as part of the Intelligence Department from 1940. In 1919, the year of the Siberian intervention, SDAs were placed in the cities of Far Eastern Russia such as Vladivostok, Khabarovsk, Blagoveshchensk, Nikolaevsk, Chilin, Harbin, Chita, Irkutsk, and Omsk. The name *Tokumu kikan* was introduced by Major General Yasutaro Takayanagi, a staff officer of the Japanese Army in Vladivostok and the head of Omsk Section, in February 1919.[104]

The IJA's intelligence activities were not controlled by the Army General Staff but left to the autonomy of intelligence departments under each area army.[105] According to Captain Masatane Kanda, officer of Heihe SDA in the early 1920s, while Special Duty Agencies were under the control of the Kwantung Army, they had connections with the Russian Section of the Army General Staff in Tokyo. The fund for intelligence was 100 yen (80,000 yen today) a month, which caused a shortage of money in information gathering, even considering local prices.[106]

In the Kwantung Army, intelligence collection was the responsibility of the 2nd Section, which developed into the Intelligence Department of the Kwantung Army under Major General Genzo Yanagida in 1940. It had a Harbin Section with 200 staff forming an intelligence center and 12 branches with 45–70 staff each as organs for information gathering. The number of staff in the Harbin Section expanded to 400 at its height in 1944, under the Chief of the Intelligence Department Akio Doi, while the total number of staff in each branch reached almost 2,000.

The Harbin Section had various missions, such as information collection, political plotting, propaganda, and security, focusing mostly on perceiving the movement of the Soviet Army by HUMINT sources – operatives who graduated from the Nakano School, local cooperators, exiles from the Soviet Union and so on.[107]

The Kwantung Army established the training division for the Russian language in Harbin in 1939 and educated officers in the Russian language and the Soviet military situation. The division delivered three-month and one-year courses and 300–350 officers learned Russian, with 25 native Russian speakers providing instruction support. Almost 100 students graduated from the two courses and 20 of them were assigned to the Kwantung Army every year.[108]

It was natural that the IJA reinforced intelligence activities in Manchuria and Russia, because the interest of the Army General Staff was focused on those areas. Although the Soviet Union was an imaginary enemy of the IJA for much of the war, the Japanese nevertheless invested considerable effort on anti-Soviet intelligence. Yet the Japanese intelligence activities in the Far

East were a serious threat to the Soviet Union. Except for the late 1930s, when Germany was gaining its power, Soviet security centered on battling Japanese intelligence during the inter-war period. Japan and the Soviet Union came to have adjacent spheres of influence after the foundation of Manchukuo in March 1932. Ex-Colonel Yukio Nishihara, the intelligence staff officer of the Kwantung Army, classified tensions in the border dispute between Manchukuo and the Soviet Union into three periods: small-scale clash period (1932–34), middle-scale clash period (1935–36), and large-scale clash period (1937–39), with the Nomonhan incident from May 1939 as its climax.[109]

The Soviet Union reinforced its counter-intelligence via the Border Guards and the *Narodnyi Kommissariat Vnutrennikh Del* (People's Commissariat for Internal Affairs; NKVD) on the occasion of its second Five-Year Plan (1932–37). The Border Guards started to expand rapidly from three or four corps (1,000 to 2,000 soldiers each) to 18 or 19 corps during the early 1930s.[110]

Stalin himself demanded an iron control of the intelligence apparatus to underpin his power. For that purpose, he needed a conspicuous external enemy, and Japan was chosen because of the strong possibility of clashes in the Far East. Moreover, he was pessimistic about Japanese intentions in Manchuria. He wrote to Commissar for War K.Y. E. Voroshilov: "Japan plans to seize not only Manchuria but also Peking. It's not impossible and even likely that they will try to seize the Soviet Far East and even Mongolia to soothe the feelings of the Chinese clients with land captured at our expense."[111]

The NKVD conducted fervent investigations through vast intelligence sweeps, reporting almost all the information gathered, including subversive activities and perceived Japanese conspiracies. In this way, Japanese operations in the Far East were exaggeratedly reported to Moscow. On insufficient evidence, these investigations led to the monitoring, arrest, and imprisonment of those Russians who had contact with the Japanese, and also of Asian nationals who physically resembled the Japanese.

Faced with the Soviet reinforcement of counter-intelligence activities, the IJA responded with a new plan in 1936. It was a plan "to strengthen our intelligence activities in the USSR, oppose the Soviet reaction operations, and pursue swift and perfect information gathering," backed by an expansion in funding for intelligence activities against the Soviet Union, including the reinforcement of SIGINT. The budget required by the Intelligence Department of the Kwantung Army in the year was 926,265 yen (about 800 million yen today).[112]

IMPROVEMENTS IN INTELLIGENCE APPARATUS

In the late 1930s, the Army General Staff had been reconsidering intelligence activities against the Soviet Union, and working out a plan for strengthening open source and signals intelligence. The person who led the program of improvements was Lieutenant Colonel Shun Akikusa, chief of the 5th Group of the 2nd Department (Intelligence) of the Army General Staff at that time. Akikusa specialized in intelligence against the Soviet Union, and worked for the Harbin SDA for three years from 1933. He manipulated the Russian Fascist Party (RFP) through Constantine Rozaevskii, chief of the Far Eastern branch of the RFP, still in his 20s. Although the then RFP was a small party with fewer than 10,000 members, it was suitable as an operational tool for Akikusa because the party had professed that it would defeat the Soviet regime with the assistance of Japan and Germany. Rozaevskii met General Sadao Araki, Minister of Education, and Kuniaki Koiso, Minister of Greater East Asia, and succeeded in gaining Japanese support for the RFP.[113]

Akikusa's mission in Harbin impressed upon him the importance of intelligence activities against the Soviet Union as well as the lack of personnel to conduct them. He required highly educated intelligence officers plus the intelligence apparatus to support his activities.

In the same period, staff officer Lieutenant Colonel Hideo Iwakuro, chief of military affairs in the War Ministry, drafted his idea for the "scientification of intelligence." He was trying to revise the Military Secret Act, which had been established after the First Sino-Japanese War in 1894 and had remained unchanged since then. The late 1930s were a period of drastic change for the IJA's intelligence system legally and practically. The major factors in the improvement of the intelligence apparatuses were the reinforcement of the Soviet counter-intelligence against Japan mentioned above, and the reorganization of the IJA after the "2.26 incident." (On February 26, 1936, a group of young army officers backed by over 1,000 troops attempted a coup in Tokyo, killing several ministers during their unsuccessful bid to overthrow the government.)

First of all, the Russian Section was founded in the 2nd Department of the Army General Staff in August 1936. By then, the European and American Section of the 2nd Department was covering Soviet intelligence, and the separate section was organized to intensify information gathering against the Soviets. A Conspiracy Section was established headed by Major Sadaaki Kagesa. The Military Service Bureau (MSB) was also formed within the Department of the Army. Major General Korechika Anami directed the head of the Military Service Section, Shinichi Tanaka, plus Iwakuro, Akikusa, and Military Police major Kameji Fukumoto to develop the counter-intelligence apparatus.

In December 1937, "Rear Staff Training School" (later the Nakano School) was established in the MSB, with Fukumoto, Iwakuro, and Akikusa at the core. In 1939, when the Nakano School was formally established, the budget was only 625 yen (about 500,000 yen today) as the first year fund for conspiracy material and 200 yen (160,000 yen) a month for conducting research into conspiracies. The number of enrollments in the first year was 19, 18 of which became the first graduates in August 1939.[114]

There were two reasons why the IJA established the school. First, the Army Intelligence Department had employed officers who graduated from the Army Staff College or foreign language college. The latter had acquired foreign languages, but not intelligence-gathering and intelligence-processing skills, because the college did not have a course for intelligence officers. They were obliged to acquire such skills through their daily work. Second, the number of such graduate officers was very limited. For example, the Army

Intelligence Department could hire at most five officers a year, and Japanese intelligence suffered a chronic shortage of manpower.

The objective of the Nakano School was the rapid training of officers who, mainly engaging in counter-sedition work and information gathering, would fight in the covert war, which the school defined as consisting of espionage, propaganda, security, and plots. With this aim, they had four objectives: 1) develop the intelligence organization, since Japanese intelligence had fallen behind the central intelligence apparatus of Europe and the United States and relied too much on individual ability; 2) make use of advanced technology, especially SIGINT but also including scientific and logical analysis; 3) fully exploit the special knowledge and qualification of each staff member; and 4) nurture the personality of the members.[115]

The *Himitsu-sen Gairon* (Introduction to Covert War) produced by the school defined the covert war (the focus of its education) as "external activities, measures against international struggle, defensive actions, secret operations whose objectives are concealed at all time, and mental conspiracy."[116] The text also described the aim of information gathering as intelligence to support the economy, intellectual activities, politics, the military, finance, and diplomacy, and its means as intelligence derived from observation, society, documents, evidence, and the wireless. In those days, both the IJA and IJN had no full-scale training apparatus for intelligence; therefore the intelligence education provided by the school was epoch making for the IJA.

The other elements of its education were as follows: "knowledge" subjects such as foreign languages, war studies, conspiracy, and intelligence; practical subjects such as fencing, judo, and ciphers; field work etc. Students had to complete all the curriculums in a year.[117] The Nakano School offered specialist subjects such as lock-picking, ninja martial arts, and so on, among which the *Kokutai-gaku* (Study for National Structure and Mind) is especially worth mentioning. This subject presented the imperial view of history based on *Jinno Shoto-ki* (Record of the Legitimate Succession of the Divine Emperors) by Chikafusa Kitabatake, a court noble in the 14th century, which became a mental and spiritual "Bible" for the students. By investing in ideological education, the school could nurture intelligence officers who would be resistant to bribery or honey traps and would fight through the Pacific War under terrible conditions, especially in the hopeless defensive battles in the late period of the war.

The school's underlying principle of education was realism, and it contrasted in many ways with other martial Japanese schools. For example, most Japanese students of military schools were usually educated to die rather than surrender on the battlefield, an attitude that led to the *Banzai* or *Kamikaze* attacks in the Pacific War. On the other hand, the Nakano School emphasized that students should attempt to survive even in extreme conditions. Lieutenant Hiroo Onoda, a graduate of the Nakano School, continued to engage in his mission of espionage activities with his subordinates on Lubang Island, Philippines, until 1974, 29 years after the Japanese surrender of 1945. The school sent a total of 1,900 graduates to the Pacific theater.

From the perspective of Japanese intelligence history, the foundation of the school seems to have plugged weak points in the IJA's intelligence, as well as contributed to preparations for war against the Soviet Union. Thus had the IJA improved its intelligence against the Soviet Union from 1936, reacting to the Soviet investments in counter-intelligence. The question was to what extent the improvements were effective, and also how much effort could be apportioned to the impending war against Britain and the United States.

HUMINT ACTIVITIES AGAINST THE SOVIET UNION

After the war, Lieutenant Colonel Saburo Hayashi, left valuable material about the HUMINT information gathering against the Soviet Union. According to this material, the intelligence operations against the Soviets were extremely laborious and "like searching for very fine gold dust in mud."[118] As mentioned above, Soviet counter-intelligence was run by the NKVD, the existence of which hindered collection of Japanese intelligence within the Soviet Union. The NKVD also guarded the Soviet–Manchurian border thoroughly, so that trained staff could only with difficulty escape if they were followed.

In those days, the IJA's intelligence activities against the Soviet Union were covered by the 4th Group in the 2nd Section of the Kwantung Army (intelligence and plots) and each Special Information Section under the HQ of the Kwantung Army. In terms of HUMINT gathering, the first method was asking cooperation from Japanese civilians who formally entered the Soviet Union, though this source bore no fruit because of the NKVD's impregnable counter-intelligence. Japanese attachés to Moscow also attempted to collect information, but rarely succeeded – the attachés dispatched from Japan received strict security checks at first entry to the country, then were confined to the Savoy Hotel. Their phone calls and letters were intercepted and they were followed when they went out. Although the authorities restricted domestic travel, the attachés tried to grasp the actual conditions within the Soviet Union by traveling around the country at every opportunity. They ordered German-made reconnaissance cars and toured around the Soviet Union, sleeping at night in the cars. Through these reconnaissance missions, they reported, for example, that aviation divisions near Moscow were supplied with 200 aircrafts whereas ones in the provinces had only about 50 aircraft.[119]

About counter-intelligence activities in the Soviet Union, Hayashi recollected:

> The shadows seemed to be trained proficiently. They were not only men but also young ladies, and they usually changed every one or two weeks so we could not remember their faces. They also showed versatility by reversing their coats or wearing false mustaches during a chase. Moreover, they seemed to be allowed special rights. For instance, we frequently saw them taking taxis by showing a red card … when they suddenly needed a car in a chase, and could easily eject guests from a hotel room. Therefore, once closely followed by them, it was almost impossible to shake them off.[120]

It was also extremely difficult for Japanese to make contact with local Russians, for the consciousness of counter-intelligence penetrated even civilians in those days. Besides, during Stalin's purge merely being asked the way by foreigners could be regarded as spying. Lord Chilston, British ambassador to the Soviet Union, also pointed out that diplomats stationed in Moscow were "deprived of almost all personal contact with those whose tendencies and reactions he is to estimate ... Soviet officials and officers did not speak to foreigners on sensitive subjects."[121] The situation was much more serious for Japanese attachés in Moscow, because Japan was Russia's arch-enemy in the Far East.

Even if the Japanese personnel did make contact with the Russians, it was almost impossible to obtain significant information, since Soviet secret information was shared among strictly chosen party members, so that the others could know only fragmentary information. In 1938, General Genrikh Lyushkov of the Far Eastern Regional NKVD directorate, defected to Japan. After Japanese Manchurian Police detained Lyushkov on the border of Manchuria, he was sent to Tokyo, where he was debriefed by the Russian Section of the Army Intelligence Department. Lyushkov lived until 1945 in Tokyo, more or less under house arrest, working for the Japanese Army's intelligence and propaganda apparatus. In 1945, the Japanese military sent him back to Manchuria to advise the Kwantung Army, which faced a massive Soviet assault in August 1945.

Lyushkov provided the Japanese with information about the politics inside the NKVD, the number of executions during the "Great Terror" from 1936 to 1938, and Soviet military dispositions. Only two months after Lyushkov's exile, the Japanese forces in Manchukuo launched an offensive against Soviet troops in the disputed territory around Lake Khasan, in what became known as the battle of Changkufeng. It may well be that Lyushkov's information contributed to the outcome of the battle, but unfortunately there is no surviving documentary record on Lyushkov in Japan. It was clear that the IJA did not obtain as much information from him as they had expected. An ex-officer of the IJA Intelligence Department later explained: "Lyushkov knew some details but not all. He was just a member of the NKVD after all ... [I]n a country such as the Soviet Union, information ... was distributed among the minimum group, limited to its need."[122]

To obtain crucial information by HUMINT in the Soviet Union, therefore, was difficult. Lieutenant Colonel Etsuo Koutani, senior intelligence staff officer of the Kwantung Army, remarked: "as far as intelligence against the Soviet Union was concerned, you could not expect a series of coherent information. If you had such information, it was dangerous to believe it."[123] Hayashi also wrote: "When the informant or 'walk-in' knew quite a lot about the Soviet Union, you needed to suspect him or her at first. It was impossible to obtain much information about the Soviet Union, which conducted strict counter-intelligence operations."[124] Making contact with informed persons of military or intelligence departments was so difficult that the Japanese invented new measures, such as taking Russians who had exiled themselves to Manchuria from the Soviet Union and then bribing them to infiltrate back into the Soviet Union. The Intelligence Department of the Kwantung Army had framed a plan for training Russian agents for espionage and sending them into the Soviet Union. The plan was barely realized, since most of the agents were arrested by the NKVD or the Border Guards and many of them came back as Soviet double agents after brainwashing. Around 1943, the Harbin SDA again schemed to send bribed Russian agents back into the Motherland, but the SIGINT from the Special Information Section of the Kwantung Army revealed that the plan had already leaked to the Soviet side.

According to the information from an ex-intelligence officer, the Soviet Union guarded its Far East border so strictly that it was almost impossible to send spies from Manchuria along it. Koutani recollected that in 1934 the NKVD had already fortified the Soviet–Manchurian border with 20,000–30,000 Border Guards and military dogs.[125] The Intelligence Department of the Kwantung Army was annoyed at having to cope with the dogs, and to make them less effective, attempted to invent chemicals for paralyzing the animals' powers of scent while also stimulating their sexual desire (to make them less manageable). (For this task they requested the help of the Army Institute for Scientific Research, Noborito.[126])

Even if spies succeeded in penetrating across the border, most of them were arrested immediately. According to Koutani's note, the record for duration of penetration over the border was just a week.[127] In terms of the quality of spies, those provided by the Military Police seemed superior to those of the Kwantung Army. Statements of the Military Police seem to indicate some successful operations, and the staff intelligence officer of the Kwantung Army even requested that the Military Police send agents to the Soviet Union.[128] Yet no SDA had enough money for extended or advanced operations. For instance, a Soviet agent arrested by the Military Police had the then most expensive Leica camera and 5,000 yen (4 million yen today) in cash. The IJA simply could not afford to spend such money on an agent.[129]

After the outbreak of war between the Soviet Union and Germany in June 1941, deserting Soviet soldiers passed across the border, one every two days or so, and the IJA accumulated information from this source. Arrested Soviet soldiers numbered 130 by the end of the year.[130] However, the NKVD also disguised spies as runaways, so that considerable numbers of Soviet agents penetrated into Manchuria. In those days, the Security Bureau of Manchukuo detained these "deserters" for a while and then released them, providing the spies with a liberty of which the Soviet Union took advantage.

Manchurians, Koreans, and Mongols were also chosen as spies, but most of them tended to be Soviet agents. There were many cases in which Russians whom Japanese SDAs employed for many years, and trusted deeply, turned out to be Soviet agents after the war. Such was proved by the fact that SDA personnel such as Shun Akikusa, the chief of the Intelligence Department of the Kwantung Army, were readily identified and arrested one after another when the Soviet Army marched into Manchuria on August 9, 1945.

A rare example of success occurred when the IJA bribed "Mikhailov," telegrapher of the Soviet consulate to Harbin, and acquired copies of secret telegrams between Khabarovsk and Moscow through the operation of Major Hayashi Yamamoto of the Harbin Agency (future principal of the Nakano School) in 1936.[131] The Japanese Army paid 5,000 yen monthly to Mikhailov (this is almost equal to 3 million yen today), and obtained secret information. The Soviet Union came to know about Mikhailov, and began sending false information mixed in with genuine facts. The IJA pretended not to notice that their source had been unmasked – collection of false information had a value all its own, because even knowing that the information was false told intelligence officers something about the sender's intentions.[132]

The information obtained through Mikhailov appeared frequently as *Ha-toku-cho* (Harbin Special Intelligence) in the IJA's coded traffic decrypted by the Americans and British. British intelligence even doubted that the Japanese decrypted the Soviet coded traffic.[133] However, these successful intelligence operations were rather exceptional – the other HUMINT activities seemed to produce poor results.

As to other means of information gathering, the IJA could only take rudimentary measures, such as the "border watch" – intelligence staff raked the Soviet side with their binoculars on the Manchurian–Soviet border – and the field watch, for which couriers dispatched to Moscow by the Ministry of Foreign Affairs took the Siberian Railways, observing the landscape either side of the track. These steady missions, however, also had their importance in accumulating data. For the border watch, a reconnaissance that consisted of 700–800 soldiers with good eyesight watched the Soviet border all day and night with 24- to 150-power binoculars. They recorded minute details, mentioning every soldier, horse, and car, and in Vladivostok they watched the comings and goings of shipping.[134] Although these were painful efforts, these steady fixed-point observations are often the basis of information gathering.

The accumulation of these observations revealed that the Soviets had started large-scale construction and were building *tochkas* (military positions, pillboxes) along the River Amur in 1933. In the same period, the Kwantung Army had acquired information about the *tochkas* under construction along the Soviet–Polish border, so it flew an airplane chartered from Manchurian Airlines along the border to conduct aerial reconnaissance. The detailed analysis of the Soviet *tochkas* produced the report entitled *So-gun Kokkyo Chikujo Joho Kiroku* (The Record of Information about the Soviet Construction of Tochkas along the Border).[135]

The Ministry of the Army entered into discussions with the Ministry of Foreign Affairs and decided to dispatch two reconnaissance officers to Moscow and Berlin who specialized in train, air, and military observation, disguised as couriers. Graduates from the Nakano School were chosen frequently for this mission. The main task was to investigate the transport capability of the Soviet military railways by deducting the length of bridges from the speed of trains, studying headway and structure of bridges, and so on.[136] During the 1930s, Japan exchanged Soviet information with Poland once or twice a year. Poland was eager to obtain observations on the Soviet military railways and offered considerable information in return.[137] In the records of Major General Seizo Arisue, who worked as the Intelligence Department Chief of the Army General Staff, these courier reports are regular finds.[138] They included detailed information about the Soviet transportation toward the Far East during the Nomonhan incident in 1939, which enabled the Kwantung Army to calculate the scale of the Soviet operating force to the Far East. This kind of information about military transportation was also reported just before the Soviet entry into the war against Japan in 1945.[139]

The Intelligence Department of the Kwantung Army had accumulated vast amounts of data (whatever its quality) by border watch, information from the agents sent into the Soviet Union, and reports by the reconnaissance officers. Captain Kenji Okoshi, alias 'Saburo Yamamoto', who served as vice consul to Chita, acquired Russian agents and collected detailed information of Soviet military trains passing Chita station. The Intelligence Department integrated and analyzed the information, then succeeded in completing a diagram of the Siberian Railways.[140]

The Chita information gathered in April 1945 is a good example of how accumulated information on Soviet railroad transportation and fixed-point observation could provide decent results. Intelligence officers who graduated from the Nakano School worked for the Japanese consulates in Vlagobeshchensk and Chita as diplomats. They conducted fixed-point observation there almost every day, overlooking the Siberian Railways from hatches in the consulates.

From March to April 1945, they monitored a large increase in Soviet train transportation to the Far Eastern area, and the consulate reported this to the Army General Staff. The *Kimitsu Senso Nisshi* (Secret War Record) of April 16 mentioned that:

> According to the report of consulate staff in Chita on May 1 and the observation of couriers in early April, the Soviet Union seems to have begun transportation of snipers and a large number of combat planes and tanks to the Far East. The 2nd Department (Intelligence) concluded that the USSR has already started to prepare for a war against Japan, based on the situation of the Soviet–German war. If it comes true, it will be a serious problem, and we have to be highly concerned about the timing of a Soviet Union war against Japan and to complete preparation for it rapidly as the vital key to success in the Great East Asian War.[141]

Regarding open source information, full analysis was started when Captain Hiroshi Onouchi established the Document (Open Source) Intelligence Group in the Harbin Agency in March 1935. Though the group was small at the beginning, it was expanded to one with 37 Japanese Army officers and 52 Russians, the latter chosen from intellectuals such as ex-military officers of Imperial Russia.[142] The group collected publications in the Soviet Union as much as possible and analyzed open sources, sharing with the Army General Staff. Broadly speaking, the Army General Staff dealt with information about the Soviet Union as a whole, while the Intelligence Department of the Kwantung Army coped with information about the Soviet Far East.

The Document Intelligence Group (DIG) mainly collected and diligently analyzed central institutional journals such as *Pravda* and *Izvestiia*, local newspapers such as *Tikhookeanskaia Zvezda* and *Zabaikalskii Rabochii*, and the military journals such as *Krasnaia Zvezda* and *Voennaia Mysl*. The group also tapped the phones and radios, providing information called *Nehi* (secret voice) and *Nejo* (voice information).

The DIG developed a card index of 4,000 commanders of the Soviet Far East Army and concluded the formation and deployment of each military formation quite correctly based on the cards. Also, when a Soviet postal airplane made an emergency landing in Manchuria around 1938, they opened, sorted, and copied the mail, then return the delivery to the Soviets.[143]

It seems that the analysis of information based on open sources was the most reliable for the Army General Staff, and the Russian Section had 20 staff devoted to open source material. The military attaché in Moscow predicted the Soviet invasion of Poland in September 1939 purely by reading Soviet newspapers. The Kwantung Army also asked the Research Department of the Manchurian Railways to collect the open source information, which was reported monthly as the form of *So-ren Chosa Siryo Geppo* (Monthly Soviet Research Reports).[144] Yet in the Soviet Union, publications were strictly censored and it was often difficult to obtain them because of the obstruction of the NKVD. As most Soviet publications were sold to known recipients, the subscribers were under the NKVD's observation. Hayashi recollected: "Although we subscribed to many local papers in Moscow every year, almost all the subscriptions of papers concerning far eastern Soviet territory were cancelled after their reception."[145]

In addition to the HUMINT intelligence activities against the Soviets from the East by the Kwantung Army and the Army General Staff, there were those conducted in the West by military attachés placed in each European country. Regarding the latter, the Vice Chief of Staff issued concrete requirement for information gathering, and the Army General Staff collected the information about the Soviet Union by cooperating with the intelligence apparatuses of Germany, Poland, Sweden, Finland, Estonia, Latvia, and others.

As mentioned previously, Colonel Makoto Onodera was dispatched to Sweden, where he collected and analyzed the information from open sources and HUMINT, then reported his information to Tokyo. In Sweden, as a neutral country, he could read foreign newspapers, journals and so on, which were sent to Tokyo through the *Domei* press agency.[146] A key information source for Onodera in Sweden was ex-Polish officer Peter Ivanov. While his role was to collect information about Germany and the Soviet Union and report it to the exiled Polish government in London, he seems to have supplied considerable information to Onodera as well. Onodera also eagerly collected information about the Soviet Army by socializing with officers such as Major Kemp of the Swedish Ministry of Army, Major Petersew of the Swedish Intelligence Department, and Major Vickengie of the Hungarian Army. The information about the Soviets gathered by Onodera was exchanged for the information about the United States and Britain collected by Karl Heinz Kraemer of the German Abwehr.

During the war, it seems that the Army General Staff sent Onodera money for the operations, but it did not reach him, so Kraemer had to raise the money. According to Kraemer's statement, the money amounted to about $20,000 (40 million yen today).[147] Onodera and Kraemer not only exchanged but also gathered information cooperatively. These efforts meant Onodera was regarded by the Allies as the key person of the Japanese intelligence network in Europe – he was cast into Sugamo Prison after the war. His accomplishment nevertheless shows a part of the IJA's HUMINT activities in Europe.

There were Japanese HUMINT activities in other European countries too. The military attaché to Turkey, for example, conducted fixed-point observation against Soviet fleets passing through the Bosporus Strait. Further afield, Major Giichi Miyazaki gathered information about the Soviets in Afghanistan and was banished as *persona non grata* in November 1936.[148]

After the war, Hayashi reflected as follows upon the information gathering against the Soviet Union:

Actually, most of information we collected was fragmentary … it came to be a serious matter how we should digest such information. In other words, how could we perceive the iceberg under water, seeing only the tip of it? … I suppose that it is important to study information from various points of view, analyzing opinions or evaluations every time you get them. Through analyzing and studying information constantly, the core issue can be made clear by narrowing the range of focus after acquiring second and third levels of fragmentary information.[149]

Hayashi's reflection about the intelligence activities against the USSR can be instructive even today. That is to say, in a situation without decisive information, the only possible way is to rely on fragmentary information buried in open sources, assembling these pieces of information patiently. Then once new information is obtained, it must be compared with the half-done puzzle of information to check the unity. If a large piece of important information can be obtained, the puzzle can be completed more quickly, though this is not likely to occur. Koutani also described the patient collection of fragmentary sources in the intelligence activities against the Soviet Union.[150]

HUMINT ACTIVITIES IN MAINLAND CHINA

It was the 7th Section (China) of the Intelligence Department of the IJA that engaged in Chinese intelligence. They gathered information through frontline troops, the IJA's special agencies, signals intelligence services, and local Military Police officers. On December 1, 1939, the IJA North China Army held a meeting that discussed the army's policy for intelligence activities in China. Colonel Taira Hamada, staff officer of the Army, spoke as follows:

> We have the signals intelligence service in the area army. We can get details of our enemy through signals intelligence, which has contributed to our operations in the past battles. But it is difficult to know everything using only SIGINT...We also need human sources to fill the deficit of signals intelligence ...We also need military, political and economic information through counter-intelligence activities ...[151]

Japanese intelligence activities in China can be separated into the north, central, and south sectors. The IJA emphasized counter-insurgency in the north, counter-terror and covert activities in the central sector, and information gathering on British and French colonies in the south. In China, information was collected by military attachés of the consulate (which became an embassy in 1935) in China dispatched by the Army General Staff and military attachés placed in major Chinese cities. From the Meiji

(1868–1912) to the end of the Taisho period (1912–1926), military attachés were posted to Shanghai, Chinan, Nanking, Fuchou, and Hankow.

The specialists for Chinese affairs were called *Shina-tsu* ("China hands" or "China specialists"), taking their place alongside *Manmo-tsu* (Manchurian and Mongolian specialists), *Canton-tsu* and so on.[152] They also exchanged information with Italian military attachés and diplomats, but the Germans in China were generally pro-Chinese. (The Chinese also preferred to give information to influential foreign military personnel rather than to diplomats.) The *Shina-tsu* increased in importance as Japan intervened in mainland China more deeply, and there appeared famous China hands such as General Kenji Doihara, known as "Lawrence of Manchuria" for his espionage activities in Manchuria and China, General Seishiro Itagaki, who plotted the Manchurian incident, Colonel Daisaku Kohmoto, who led the killing of Chang Tso-lin (a ruler of Manchuria) in 1928, and Colonel Sadaaki Kagesa, who assisted in the establishment of the Wang Jingwei government.[153] (Wang Jingwei was a nationalist rival to Chiang Kai-shek, and in 1940 was appointed head of Japanese-controlled territory in China.)

Yet as Tobe points out, the weakness of the *Shina-tsu* was the shortage of expertise on Chinese affairs as a whole, for their information was too centered on specific areas and too limited – in other words, their knowledge was distorted.[154] Having a puzzle with lots of small pieces, there didn't appear to be anyone who could assemble the pieces into an entire picture, although to be fair the assembly work was really the responsibility of the China Section of the Intelligence Department of the Army General Staff.

On August 31, 1937, the IJA North China Army established the 2nd Section for Chinese intelligence and the North China Military Police headed by Lieutenant General Toichi Sasaki, Chinese specialist in the IJA.[155] The IJA occupied most parts of northern China, but they had to tackle Chinese insurgent activities against Japan; hence Japanese intelligence in the north focused mainly on counter-insurgency. There were mainly two Chinese insurgency groups in the area: the Chinese Blue Shirts Society (a military intelligence service under Colonel Dai Lin, intelligence officer for Chiang Kai-shek) and the CC Clique (anti-communist branch of the KMT). The North China Military Police handled the counter-insurgency war, and in the case of battles with the KMT army, the IJA's intelligence troops cooperated with the Military Police. The officers of the Military Police hired local Chinese and sometimes infiltrated into the Chinese guerrilla groups and collected information. Some officers were captured and executed during their missions.[156]

The Blue Shirts Society had 3,000 members in Peking and was headed by Ma Hansan. In July 1939 the Military Police Peking branch scented the information that Ma was planning a bomb plot against the Japanese.[157] The KMT government sent a field agent, Li Xi-meng, from Chungking to Peking to support the plot. Li concealed himself in a French church in Peking, but the Military Police uncovered him. They negotiated with French officials in Peking and were finally allowed to capture Li. But Ma was only one step away from the Military Police's hunt in the French area. The interrogation of Li revealed that Chiang Kai-shek had asked the Italian government to mediate between China and Japan. It was also revealed that the Blue Shirts Society was planning some assassination plots in Peking.[158] The arrest of Li damaged the Society's covert activities in the area. The Peking Military Police made a report in December 1939 that stated: "We have captured many activists of the Blue Shirts Society and the CC Clique and damaged their conspiracies."[159]

There were also Chinese communist anti-Japanese activities in North China, but the IJA North China Army had no specialist on the CCP. The Army set up the "Committee of Anti-Communist Countermeasures in North China" in Huang Chen, Peking, and started to study the CCP in November 1937. The committee gathered Chinese specialists from the Military Police, Ministry of Foreign Affairs, Interior Ministry, and Japanese communist groups for their research.[160]

The "Hundred Regiments Offensive" by the Chinese communist Eighth Route Army in July 1940, however, deeply shocked the IJA. The Eighth Route Army was held in low esteem by the IJA, but more than 20,000 Japanese soldiers were killed by sporadic battles. In the North China Army operational record it states: "the sudden Chinese attacks were unexpected and we were heavily damaged ..."[161] Major Yukio Yokoyama, intelligence staff officer of the Army, recollected: "We have achieved certain results in gathering information on the KMT group, but no information on the CCP. We began to realize that their conspiracy would be a large obstruction to our intelligence activities. However, they forestalled us and we seriously started to study them after the Hundred Regiments Offensive ..."[162]

There was a difference in the levels of interest concerning the CCP between the North China Army and the General Staff in Tokyo. The former seriously tried to bear down on the communists' insurgency activities, but the China Section of the latter was indifferent to such activities. China specialists in Tokyo regarded the KMT as their main target, not the CCP.

In central China, the IJA Central China Army, which was established in February 1938, covered intelligence duties centered on Shanghai. Shanghai was an international city in those days and much of the IJA's political plotting focused on the city. There were numerous Japanese special agencies, such as *Ume* (plum), *Matsu* (pine tree), *Sakura* (cherry tree), *Take* (bamboo), *Fuji* (wisteria), *Doihara* and so on.[163] The basic role of these agencies was political operations, information gathering, policing, and delivering propaganda, and each consisted of dozens of staffs.

Among these special agencies, *Matsu Kikan* and *Ume Kikan* conducted aggressive operations within Shanghai. The *Matsu Kikan* was headed by Lieutenant Colonel Yoshimasa Okada, staff officer in charge of field intelligence operations in the Japanese China Army. The agency conducted *Sugi* (cedar) operations, in which they circulated a large quantity of phony banknotes produced meticulously at the Army Institute of Scientific Research, Noborito, with the aim of destabilizing the Chinese economy. It required considerable skill to produce the notes authentically. Therefore the staff of the Noborito Institute analyzed the print of the original notes and the IJA imported two German-made high-speed rotary presses called "Iris," only one of which had existed in Japan before, to print the counterfeit notes. The notes were then shipped in July 1941.[164] Ultimately, the IJA transported to China phony notes with a value of 100 to 200 million yuan every month.[165]

In May 1939, the *Ume Kikan* was established by Colonel Sadaaki Kagesa of the Army General Staff to receive Wang Chao-ming, the Japanese puppet ruler, in Shanghai. The agency invited Military Police officers and graduates of Nakano School to conduct related intelligence activities. After 1942, the agency also carried out information gathering about the US Army in China, plus subversive operations, counter-intelligence activities against operations out of Chungking, collection of military supplies, and so on.[166]

The special agencies collected information from both government and private organizations. These included the *Koa-in* (East Asia Development Board), the Japanese police in foreign settlements of Shanghai, the consulate in Shanghai, Shanghai customs offices, the Shanghai bureau of Manchurian Railways, the Shanghai branch of Mitsubishi Corporation, Mitsui & Co. Ltd, and the Japanese mail steamship company.[167] In addition, the Onodera Agency (the future Shanghai Agency), established by Onodera, is well known for its activities. Unusually for an IJA organization, the agency assembled 20 staff who were specialists in the Chinese language, recruiting them from Japanese universities and from among the locals, and collected and analyzed documents.[168] Exploiting the international characteristics of Shanghai, the agency also conducted broad intelligence activities against China, the Soviet Union, the United States, and European countries. They produced the "Estimate of Resistance Power of Chungking" and "Who's Who within Each Organization in the Chungking Government," cooperating with the Shanghai bureau of Manchurian Railways.[169] The chief of the agency, Koji Urano (who succeeded Onodera), was officially called by his cover name "Sasahara," hiding his status as a military officer and living in the agency building. His low profile made a sharp contrast with Harry Steptoe, who was the Chief of the British SIS Shanghai Bureau in the same period. Steptoe was decidedly high profile and broadcast his status as an SIS officer. He was a remarkably colorful character, with an odd gait that gave an air of ostentatious subterfuge to everything that he did.[170]

In July 1940, Kiyota Izaki, deputy of the Shanghai Agency, visited Shanghai, Hong Kong, Canton, and Taipei for a month under the cover name of "Yasuyoshi Fukuhara." Pretending to be a Japanese trader, he closely observed the British forces in Hong Kong in particular and reported the results to the military attaché there.[171] In September 1942, the Shanghai Army Department was established under the direct control of the Army General Staff and took over the intelligence and operational activities in Shanghai. The department consisted of about 20 officers and 100 agents who collected all manner of information except for SIGINT.

As far as counter-intelligence was concerned, the Shanghai Military Police of the Central China Army engaged in counter-intelligence operations under Colonel Shigeru Ohki. They were stationed at the Bridge House in Shanghai, with 1,500 staff.[172] The Shanghai Military Police also struggled with the anti-Japanese terror campaign by the CC Clique and the Chinese Blue Shirts – both organizations regularly assassinated Chinese collaborators. Wang Jingwei, also had a secret service group called the "76th Jessfield Road," which comprised 50 operative agents and 20 codebreaking staff in Shanghai.[173] In June 1938, members of the group Li Shi-gun and Ding Mo-cun called on Lieutenant General Kenji Doihara, head of the *Doihara-kikan*, and his subordinate, Major Yoshitane Haruke. Li and Ding were former members of the CC Clique, but they escaped and joined the 76th. They knew much about the KMT's covert activities and persuaded Doihara and Haruke to change their counter-terror activities in Shanghai. According to their arguments, the defensive Japanese counter-insurgency activities were not effective in containing the KMT, and they insisted that the Japanese take more preemptive action.[174]

Haruke returned to Tokyo and recounted Ding's plan to Colonel Kagesa, chief of the Chinese Section, Army General Staff. On February 10, 1939, the Army General Staff officially ordered Haruke and the Shanghai Military Police to cooperate with the 76th's plots against the CC Clique and Chinese Blue Shirts in Shanghai. They were supplied with 500 guns, 50,000 bullets, and 300,000 yen (24 million yen today) from the IJA.[175] Heavily armed, the 76th now started to make bloody counterattacks against the KMT groups. They killed and captured numerous insurgents and destroyed some press organizations that published anti-Japanese papers. The 76th also succeeded in capturing Wang Tian-mu, head of the Blue Shirts in the Shanghai area, and persuaded him to join the 76th. With collaboration from Wang, the 76th changed its method of operations from guns and bombs to infiltration into the KMT. The Shanghai Military Police and Haruke secretly assisted the plots.[176]

In South China, the IJA's intelligence was against British and French assistance to China rather than the Chinese themselves. The IJA was anxious about the supply routes from French Indo-China and British Burma and repeatedly tried to sever the lines. After the Japanese advance into north French Indo-China in September 1940, the IJA focused on information gathering on British garrison forces in Malaya and Singapore. For example, the IJA established a special agency at the beginning of 1941, known as the *Koa Kikan* (Asia Development Agency).

The *Koa Kikan* was established by Lieutenant Colonel Yoshimasa Okada on December 16, 1941, and engaged in information gathering and subversive activities to support the Japanese advance into Hong Kong at the end of 1941. At the beginning of the year, the *Koa Kikan* was actually a nameless body, but during the battle of Hong Kong in December 1941, Major General Tadamichi Kuribayashi, Chief of Staff, the Twenty-Third Army (later commander of the garrison army on Iwo Jima), gave it the name of *Koa Kikan*.[177]

Okada was a specialist in Chinese affairs, especially the Chinese underground organizations *Qing-bang* (the Green Gang) and *Hong-bang* (the Red Gang). He had studied Chinese underground movements in the 8th Section (Intelligence and Subversive Activities) of the Army General Staff, and commanded the *Matsu Kikan* in Shanghai for passing forged Chinese notes. According to Okada's memoir, it was at the beginning of 1941 that the 8th Section ordered him to study the possibility of subversive activities in Hong Kong. In December 1940, Rear Admiral Paul Wenneker, the German naval attaché, handed over a captured document from a British Blue Funnel cargo ship, S.S. *Automedon*, to Japanese authorities.[178] The document, which was addressed to Air Marshal Robert Brooke-Popham, the British commander-in-chief in the Far East, indicated that the British Chief of Staff regarded both Thailand and Hong Kong as indefensible against Japanese attack.[179] There is no doubt that the document encouraged the Japanese war planners in their decision to advance into Southeast Asia.

The 8th Section was ordered to: 1) organize a sabotage group using native Chinese in Canton area; and 2) organize subversive activities in Hong Kong. Okada secretly contacted the Chinese underground organization *Sanhehui* (the Triad Society) through his colleague, Shigemori Sakata, who led the Sakata Agency in Shanghai. He could speak fluent Chinese and joined the Triad Society using the Chinese cover name "Tian." The British Hong Kong police arrested him at the Hong Kong Grand Hotel on May 12, 1941. The British HUMINT and SIGINT revealed Japanese covert activities in Hong Kong, but Sakata finally succeeded in breaking out of jail with Chinese help.

On October 12, 1941, Major General Jun Ushiroku, Chief of Staff of the Japanese Expeditionary Army to China, gave the following specific orders to Okada:

(1) prevent British destruction of the main roads into Hong Kong

(2) direct Japanese troops to Hong Kong

(3) interrupt British troop movements

(4) destroy electric powerplants and water sources in Hong Kong

(5) execute subversive activities in Hong Kong.

For these operations, the Army Noborito Institute developed a suitcase bomb, but it was too difficult a device for the native Chinese to operate. Okada ordered the Shanghai army police to develop an alternative easily handled bomb, whose instructions were nothing more than "open the suitcase, turn a clock screw, and close the case." The "cigarette can bomb" was also developed by the army police.

Okada and Sakata prepared uniforms for fake employees of the power plant, telephone exchange, water supply agency, and train station, and printed thousands of anti-British leaflets. They gave tons of grenades and guns to Chinese underground operatives. Okada was granted monthly

10,000 yen (about 71 million yen today) by the IJA and acquired additional funds through counterfeit money and drug trafficking. On November 3, Sakata scattered the anti-British leaflets throughout Hong Kong. They secretly dug a tunnel from the Chinese mainland to Hong Kong and came and went through the tunnel without drawing any attention from the British.

On December 8, Okada launched the operation. The first mission of the *Koa Kikan* was to prevent British destruction of the main roads to Hong Kong. The agency had suborned Indian soldiers not to execute the bombing, but three out of ten roads were destroyed by the British. Chinese groups that had infiltrated into Hong Kong began subversive activities, bombing the British Army camp, Kowloon power plant, train stations, and also a movie theater to frighten civilians in Hong Kong. They failed to destroy the telephone exchange, because the suitcase bomb was removed by the officials. The agency succeeded in taking control of the water supply from Kowloon to Hong Kong on the 13th, which forced the British to surrender.

Okada had also planned to capture VIPs of Hong Kong's political and business circles.[180] He obtained a passenger list of Hong Kong airport arrivals and departures and found the name of Song Meiling – Madam Chiang Kai-shek – who was in Hong Kong for dental treatment. He tried to catch her, but she succeeded in escaping from Hong Kong at the last minute.

On December 16, Okada established the agency's HQ at the Hong Kong Hotel and housed a hundred captured VIPs there. He interviewed each person and gathered information. Some of them were transported to Shanghai for the IJA's political maneuverings in China. Major General Sadaaki Kagesa, military adviser to Wang Jingwei's Nanking government, was interested in exploiting the VIPs.

After the fall of Hong Kong, Okada dissolved the Chinese group and the *Koa Kikan* was moved from Hong Kong to Chungking, capital of the KMT government. The agency had connections with the Showa Trading Company, which was founded by the IJA with combined funds from the Mitsui and Mitsubishi corporations. It seems that through the Showa, the agency also raised funds through opium trafficking and trading military supplies.[181]

Compared to the operations in the Soviet Union, the IJA's HUMINT activities in China were relatively easy. They could obtain newspapers and magazines published in China, which brought important OSINT. Many IJA officers studied the Chinese language at a rudimentary level during the IJA academy or staff college days, and they could deal with vast amounts of Chinese documents, gaining the cooperation of the *Toa Kenkyujo* (Institute of East Asian Studies), the *Mantetsu Chosa-bu* (Investigative Department of the Manchurian Rail Service) and the *Domei* press agency. However their analysis was sometimes biased because they did not acquire appropriate analytical skills. The intelligence officers of the China Section tended to duplicate Chinese sources in their analysis, and also relied heavily on Western academic studies of China, such as those of Edgar Snow and Owen Lattimore, who were famous for their books on Chinese affairs in those days. A Japanese communist, who was hired by an intelligence officer of the Shanghai legation, frequently sent copies of Agnes Smedley's book *Red Star over China*. The officer did not realize the source of the information and sent it to the Army General Staff in Tokyo, sealing it as "Top Secret."[182]

The IJA collected HUMINT, SIGINT, and OSINT on China and used the information gleaned both for their operations and also for counter-intelligence. However, the intelligence staff of the Japanese China Army and the Army General Staff directly passed such information to operations staff or frontline unit without analyzing it in the process. This was mainly because the IJA officers would gather excessive information on China and also tended to think that it was a waste of time to evaluate what they judged to be inferior Chinese troops. Moreover, they had ignored the Chinese communist army for a long time.[183] Lieutenant Colonel Etsuo Koutani, senior intelligence staff of the Russian Section, said: "We [Russian Section staff] understand the Chinese Red Army in more detail than China Section staff."[184]

In addition, the IJA did not realize that the war with China was also a propaganda war. The IJA's intelligence specialized in the operational and tactical use of intelligence. They could overcome the Chinese in this field, but they failed to handle unconventional war. Lieutenant Colonel Shigesaburo

Yamazaki, an officer of the Chinese Intelligence Section of the IJA, reflected: "We failed to realize that we were fighting the Chinese not only in the military field but also in political, economic, and cultural fields. We were almost blind in the latter fields ..."[185] Yamazaki's observation illustrates the limit of the IJA's tactical use of intelligence in the battle with the Chinese.

INTELLIGENCE ACTIVITIES IN THE SOUTHERN AREA AGAINST BRITAIN AND AMERICA

In 1939, the Southeast Asia Group, which engaged in information gathering on French Indo-China, Thailand, British Malaya, and the Dutch East Indies, was established in the 6th Section (dealing with European and US affairs). The IJA began to plan an advance into Southeast Asia, because the area was considered to be a supply route to southern China, with whom Japan had now been fighting for two years. The area was also considered to be abundant in natural resources. The group's duty was to explore several possibilities that the IJA could advance into the area, and they sent military attachés and intelligence officers to Australia, the Dutch East Indies, Malaya, the Philippines, and French Indo-China for intelligence purposes.

In Southeast Asia, the military attaché to Thailand was responsible for strengthening information gathering in the Malaysia and Singapore area. He collected information about the Southern Area along with the Japanese Taiwan Army and military attaché to Indochina.[186] Thailand was the only independent country before the war in this area; therefore Japanese intelligence efforts tended to be focused in Bangkok in organizations such as the *F Kikan* and *Minam Kikan*. It was Colonel Hiroshi Tamura, the military attaché to the consulate in Bangkok, who was at the center of the intelligence network in Southeast Asia. In an area of strong anti-Japanese feeling, he thoroughly investigated topographical information, the deployment of the British and Thai armies, and other information in order to prepare for the war.[187] In particular, he investigated the routes through Thailand for the future invasion of Malaya, and also Kota Bharu as an amphibious landing point in the Malay Peninsula.

Information-gathering efforts in the area increased after the summer of 1940, when the IJA began to consider war against Britain. The Army General Staff dispatched a staff officer of the 1st Department, Lieutenant Colonel Kazuo Tanigawa, and Captain Teruhito Kunitake to the Malay Peninsula and had them investigate the peninsula for two months from January 1941.[188] The results were circulated in the IJA as "Intelligence Record of British Malaya." The record of the investigation contained minute information on topography and military dispositions from the Malay Peninsula to Singapore, including the number of the guards, tanks, and batteries and the position of emplacements. For example, about an emplacement in the city of Singapore, it says: "The wall is so thin that it is vulnerable to shell fire. Blind corner is extremely large because of its structure. The location is exposed. The foundation work is not perfect." The two officers also closely mapped the deployment of the guard in the city of Singapore. This data was utilized in the invasion of Malaya.[189]

As the *Koa Kikan* supported the Japanese advance into Hong Kong, the *F Kikan* encouraged the Indian independence movement to break down the British garrison in Malaya and Singapore. On September 18, 1941, General Hajime Sugiyama, Chief of Staff of the IJA, ordered Major Iwaichi Fujiwara to engage in covert operations under Colonel Hiroshi Tamura, military attaché to Bangkok.[190] In particular his mission was to contact Indian and Malayan independence groups and secretly support their movements against British colonial rule. In October he joined the Japanese embassy in Bangkok and established the *F Kikan* with 11 personnel.

In Bangkok, Fujiwara contacted two key persons – Pritam Singh and "Harimau" (Tiger) Yutaka Tani. Singh was a member of the Indian Independence League (IIL) in Thailand and hoped for Japanese support for his independence movement. Fujiwara negotiated with Singh on several occasions and finally they reached an agreement on December 1, 1941. According to the agreement, in the event of an Anglo-Japanese war the IIL would attempt to draw away Indians in British Indian Army service through propaganda activities in exchange for Japanese mediation between the IIL and Subhas Chandra Bose, who at that time was in Berlin.[191] (Bose was an Indian nationalist politician and later leader of the Indian National Army.)

Yutaka Tani was born and grew up in Malaya and he converted to Islam in the 1930s. He hoped to join the IJA, but his Muslim beliefs were opposed to the IJA's worship of the Emperor. He gave up the idea of joining the IJA and engaged in illegal activities, leading a 3,000-strong band of thieves in Malaya. Fujiwara focused on his knowledge of Malayan affairs and organizations and hired him as an *F Kikan* agent. He died of malarial fever on March 17, 1942, but his espionage activities were propagandized in the film *Tiger in Malaya* during the war.

After the outbreak of the war, Fujiwara organized IIL propaganda teams led by *F Kikan*'s officers and sent them to the frontline. Fujiwara and Singh also chose Indian troops from among captured British Indian Army personnel in Malaya, persuading them to join the IIL movement. During the operations, Fujiwara contacted Captain Mohan Singh, who later fought for Indian freedom as commander-in-chief of the Indian National Army (INA).[192]

F Kikan's mission came to a climax with the British surrender of Singapore on February 15, 1942. On the morning of February 17, 45,000 Indian POWs gathered at Farrer Park, where Fujiwara addressed them. He told them of "the Great East Asian Co-prosperity Sphere" under the leadership of Japan, and of the Japanese intention to help raise a liberation army for the freedom of India. He invited the troops seated in the park to join this army. He also told the troops that they were going to be treated not as POWs, but as friends and allies. Fujiwara ended his speech by stating that he was passing on responsibility for and command of the troops to Mohan Singh.[193]

In March 1942, the *F Kikan* was dissolved and taken over by the *Iwakuro Kikan*, which worked for the independence of India. The *Iwakuro Kikan* placed the Malay branch in Singapore, Burma branch in Rangoon, and branch offices in Hong Kong and Saigon, with a total of 500 staff at its height. In the next year, the agency turned into *Hikari* (Light) *Kikan* under Colonel Hayashi Yamamoto and continued supporting Indian independence movements from behind the scenes, helping the Bose family, for example, visit Japan in 1943.[194]

Meanwhile, in February 1941 *Minami* (South) *Kikan* was founded under IJA Colonel Keiji Suzuki as a joint special service agency of the Army and Navy, aiming at the interception of the Burma Road, which was the primary British route for supplying materials to China, and supportingindependence movements in Burma, which was British territory at that time. Information gathering in Burma was not advanced when compared to that in the Philippines and Malaya. The IJN was concerned about this situation and proposed establishing the joint organization, though this kind of special service agency was quite rare.[195] The *Minami Kikan* officially used the name of "Research Group for Enterprises in the Southern Area" and received financial support to the tune of 3 million yen (about 240 million yen today) from the IJN and IJA.[196]

The agency placed its stronghold in Bangkok and supported the Burmese nationalist Takin Party led by Takin Baisen, helping leaders of the party escape to Thailand shortly before the war started, where they were trained in guerilla warfare. At the time of the Japanese invasion to Burma, the agency let Burmese nationalists attack the British rearguard and assist in the Japanese attack on Rangoon.

Reviewing the IJA's intelligence activities in Southeast Asia, it seems that the defeat of Britain in Singapore was inevitable. The IJA closely investigated military affairs and topographical data in advance as well as conducted dividing operations toward the British Army. On the other hand, the British Army made little effort to examine the IJA, knowing its invasion was approaching, and remained calm while condemning the IJA as a second-class army. Therefore, it was likely that the British Army would fight with a handicap from the beginning, however superior their forces in the region.

INTELLIGENCE ACTIVITIES IN THE UNITED STATES

As for intelligence gathering against the United States, the IJA's HUMINT remained poor. Although the IJA conducted considerable large-scale HUMINT operations in mainland China and on the Soviet border, they had little concern about the United States, considering it the business of the IJN and the Ministry of Foreign Affairs. In the Army General Staff, they established an American Group in the 2nd Department as a reaction to the restrictive conditions of the Washington Naval Treaty of 1922 and there was a movement for its enlargement from a group to a section. However, with Japanese focus on the Soviet Union, the move to expand intelligence against the United States came to little.[197]

The central figure for HUMINT in North America before the war was Hidenari Terazaki, the First Secretary of the Ministry of Foreign Affairs, and during the war, OSINT was eagerly collected by Masao Tsuda, the chief of Domei's branch in Argentina. The information sources of these activities were mainly analysis of newspapers and journals – except for SIGINT, most of the information collected against the United States was based on such open sources. Military attachés, who were regarded as vital for collecting information, only relayed the talk of private citizens living in New York, leaving practical information gathering to Niseis (second-generation Japanese immigrants in America).[198]

The IJA consequently plunged into the war with little knowledge about the actual strength of the US forces gathering against them. Just before the war, the IJA sent intelligence officers to Mexico, Chile, Brazil, Argentina, Peru, and Colombia. A military attaché in Portugal was also established, with the intention of exchanging information on the United States and Britain with Portugal and the Axis countries. As far as the Philippines were concerned, the Southeast Asia Group sent several officers there before the Pacific War, and the Army Chief of Staff ordered air units in Taiwan to photograph northern parts of Philippines from the air for the campaign.

After the outbreak of war, officers with little experience of intelligence work, and intelligence officers who covered the Soviet Union, were often moved to US-focused intelligence positions. Even in the spring of 1942, the South Area Army abolished its intelligence section, which covered the United States and Britain, because the section could not provide useful information to the operations section. In the same period, the IJA set up a new intelligence apparatus, the 16th Section, but the section was engaged not with the US but in Soviet intelligence, exchanging details with Germany.

The consequences of the information deficit were severe. During the battle of Guadalcanal from August 1942 to February 1943, the IJA fought against the Americans without any intelligence support and they did not grasp the situation on the small island. In fact, most Japanese soldiers died of hunger and malaria. During the battle, Saburo Hayashi visited the island and he was surprised that the situation was much grimmer than he had expected.[199] Only eight staff officers were dedicated to US and UK intelligence within the Army General Staff during the battle. It was only in 1943, after the Japanese defeat in Guadalcanal, that the IJA added the UK and US experts to intelligence officers and began intelligence-relevant education. They finally reversed the priority of Soviet and US intelligence in October 1944, after the Japanese defeat in the battle of Leyte Gulf.[200]

In conclusion, the IJA devoted enormous efforts on intelligence activities against the Soviet Union, in which almost all the SIGINT, HUMINT, and counter-intelligence efforts of the IJA were invested. However, the Soviet Union so aggressively reinforced its counter-intelligence operations against Japan that the IJA struggled to make headway. As for China, the IJA received a number of reports from China specialists and special agencies, as well as information from fighting troops.

Compared to the activities against the Soviet Union and China, intelligence activities against the United States remained sluggish. Even after the outbreak of the Pacific War, the IJA still considered the Soviet Union to be the principal potential enemy for much of the conflict. Though information gathering against the United States began after 1943, intelligence officers could not get qualified quickly enough, as it required long experience to obtain the insight and techniques for intelligence. Thus, after the outbreak of the Pacific War, the IJA could not flexibly shift its emphasis on information collection from the Soviet Union to the United States, nor compensate for its failure by changing policy.

COUNTER-INTELLIGENCE –
KENPEI-TAI (MILITARY POLICE)

The IJA made serious counter-intelligence efforts before the Pacific War. The Military Police organization is well known, but the War Ministry also had an Investigation Department under the direct control of the War Minister, which also conducted counter-intelligence activities covertly. Furthermore, the Interior Ministry possessed the *Tokko*, whose mission was to crack down on thought crimes that were in violation of the Maintenance of Public Order Law.

The fundamental role of Military Police was to enforce strict official discipline. There were two types of the Military Police unit: domestic units that worked on the Japanese mainland and in colonies under the control of the War Ministry; and overseas units that were dispatched abroad and subordinate to a local commander. The main roles of the overseas Military Police were keeping information security regarding fighting troops on the battlefield and counter-intelligence activities.

This section will focus on the IJA's Military Police overseas. The fact that the domestic Military Police had 11,685 staff whereas overseas units had 22,200 in 1945 clearly shows that the IJA allocated more personnel to the latter. The main body of the overseas Military Police was placed between Manchuria and mainland China, in the same manner as the SDA.[201]

It can be said that the SDA of the IJA was the intelligence and espionage apparatus, equivalent to the British Secret Intelligence Service (SIS) or the Special Operations Executive (SOE), while the Military Police was the counter-intelligence apparatus similar to the Security Service (MI5). Therefore, if the SDA was the sword of intelligence gathering, the Military Police was its shield. Without the counter-intelligence activities of the Military Police, the SDA could not work actively. Counter-intelligence is an indispensable function for intelligence activities. It is vital for intelligence to investigate whether the information collected and analyzed leaks out and whether foreign agents penetrate into the organizations.

The primary purpose behind the counter-intelligence activities of the Military Police was to prevent leakage of national secrets, enforcing the legislation of the National Security Act and the Military Secret Act. These acts threatened strict penalties such as "death or life imprisonment" for those who intentionally leaked secrets. The handling of the famous Sorge affair – Richard Sorge had engaged in espionage activities for the Soviets from 1933 – is an example of its application.

The IJA defined counter-intelligence's role as "to protect the country and national forces from foreign espionage and harmful acts against our country."[202] The role of the Military Police was written more concretely in the "Guidelines for Counter-intelligence" of 1933. It says "considering current affairs, [we should] protect national, especially military, secrets from foreign espionage as well as probe their intention covertly in order to promote our national security and operations. For this purpose, [we should] mainly investigate foreign espionage activities by the United States, Soviet Union, and China, and endeavor to prevent them."[203]

As for the Military Secret Act, the one enacted in 1899 as a result of the Sino-Japanese War was limited in scope (it only applied to military officers) and prescribed relatively light penalties such as fines. Therefore the law was revised in 1937, conforming to secrecy and security acts of Britain, the United States, and Germany, and after that the Military Police was allowed to execute full-scale counter-intelligence activities. In addition, the National Security Act was enacted in 1941, which covered not only military but also national secrets. The act was drafted rapidly and the definitions of "national secret" or "national security" were not clear.[204]

At first there were two emphases for counter-intelligence activities: defensive and aggressive. The former focused on genuine counter-intelligence activities, while the latter was concerned with espionage activities. The Military Police dispatched to mainland China focused more on the former.[205]

The Military Police's techniques for intelligence gathering included: 1) spies and agents; 2) direct observation; 3) acquisition of documents; 4) inspection of mail; 5) interrogation of POWs; 6) detection of radio transmissions; 7) interviews; and 8) tailing.[206] This being said, the Military Police did not make much effort to analyze data and the raw information was often simply reported to their superiors. The textbook of the Military Police says "collected information should be quickly reported to the authorities concerned, specifying the means of acquisition."[207]

The principal role of the Military Police sent to Manchuria in the 1930s was to prevent Soviet intelligence activities in the same way as the Intelligence Department of the Kwantung Army mentioned above. The most obvious role was to interrupt Soviet infiltration into Manchuria. The Military Police eagerly fortified the border in a similar manner to the Soviet Border Guard. For instance, the stamp pressed on passports had a fine scratch on its letters to reveal which were fake stamps. Besides, immigration officers changed the angle of the stamps so that genuine passports had stamps with different angles depending on the time of immigration. Even such trifling devices were efficient in exposing fake passports – the Military Police discovered more than 200 in 1940.[208] In Fengtian and other areas, they cut the electricity supply block by block, in cooperation with the with power company, to locate radio transmitters working at night.[209]

In Tsitsihar in September 1940, the Military Police arrested the Soviet spy Wang Yuan who had disguised himself as a Japanese officer. The Soviets had sent these spies equipped with Japanese military uniforms and equipment seized in the Nomonhan incident. Although Wang wore an IJA uniform with the rank indicators for a lieutenant, the scabbard of his sword was not genuine and he confused the equipment of officers and enlisted men. These differences in detail caught the attention of the Military Police, who exposed Wang as a spy.[210]

The Military Police also tried to collect information by not arresting agents they found, but trying to change their allegiance. The Military Police classified suspects into three ranks, *Kou* (A), *Otsu* (B), and *Hei* (C), and made a "black list" that contained 800 names. When the spies were arrested, the Military Police won them over and frequently sent them back to the Soviet Union, mostly to be arrested by the Soviet NKVD. Lieutenant Yutaka Kudo, the chief of the Counter-Intelligence Group in Shinking Military Police, wrote details about agents whom he turned and dispatched to the Soviet Union in his book *Choho Kenpei* (Espionage by the Military Police). The double agents whom Kudo hired were Chinese who originally worked for the Soviets.

His operation had a high probability of success. The key factor of Kudo's activities was that he educated captured Soviet agents thoroughly. For instance, he prepared the agents to fend off NKVD interrogation methods. Soviet intelligence apparatus usually restrained spy suspects for several months and fully investigated those who came into the Soviet Union. First, the authorities asked them about their work before coming to the Soviet Union, then repeated the questioning many times to see whether the answers contained contradictions, and sometimes resorted to force or a honey trap in order to elicit the truth. Without knowledge of the Soviet methods, agents could not have disguised their identity.

Among the training, there was instruction in measuring the length of bridges in the Soviet Union from inside trains. First, the agents counted how many rail joints had passed by the noise of the wheels hitting each joint. Then, knowing the length of a rail on the Siberian Railways and similar lines was 20m (65ft 7in), they multiplied the distance by the number of rails to calculate the length of the bridge. There were other rail-based training programs, such as: 1) counting personnel and estimating the amount of rail freight from train windows when they arrived at stations; 2) distinguishing types of trains and counting the number of cars and the headway when they met other trains; and 3) judging which direction trains were running in by knowing orientation against the stars and environment.

Kudo's agents were trusted by the Soviets, then received training and were sent back to Manchuria as Soviet spies. Thus Kudo could obtain information from the agents who came back to Manchuria. Such positive counter-intelligence by Kudo exposed the lack of counter-intelligence within the

Kwantung Army, demonstrating that secrets concerning the military operations of the Kwantung Army had in fact leaked to the Soviets.

The Military Police also engaged in acquiring documents, especially code books, by penetrating into embassies and consulates. As mentioned previously, the code books obtained by the Military Police were effective in breaking the US Brown Code, but there are other examples of success. In spring of 1939, for example, the Army General Staff ordered Colonel Shuichi Sakai, the chief of the Taiwan Military Police, to obtain a code book kept in the British consulate in Taiwan, which seemed to be inadequately guarded. Since the then British consulate was in Tanshuijie, the operation was named "the Operation of Tanshui Consulate," and was performed by a section of the Military Police in Taipei.

The first problem was how to penetrate into the consulate, which was resolved by a Japanese staff member working there on night duty. The next and more difficult problem was how to open the safe in which the code book lay. The agents continued steady work, probing the dial combination of the safe for several months, then making a master key to open it. During the work, another section opened all the letters to the consulate to read communications from Whitehall, checking whether the consulate staff had noticed the operation. The safe was finally opened after six months' effort, and the code book inside was returned after being photographed. The copy of the code book was sent to the Showa Traffic Station (a branch of the SIGINT Group of the Army General Staff, which conducted traffic interception in Taiwan) in the southern part of Taipei, so that the signals traffic to and from the consulate was decoded.

Later, in 1941, the consulate changed the code book and the combination of the safe, so the Showa Traffic Station was unable to decrypt the coded communications further. In response, the operational group of the Military Police penetrated into the library of the consulate, watched the consul opening the safe, remembered the combination, and seized the code book once the consul went out. During the operation, the operative hiding in the library actually fell unconscious through shortage of air in his hiding place.[211]

The Peking Military Police also penetrated into the Soviet embassy in

Peking to collect documents. Although the detail of this operation has not been confirmed, documents collected at that time are extant. For example, the Soviet intelligence source shows the connection between the Soviet Union and Feng Yu-hsiang, a warlord in China, and the uses of Soviet funds for intelligence operations in Peking.[212] Regarding Feng, the Shanghai branch of the British SIS also gathered information from diplomatic cables between the Soviet embassy and Moscow, intercepted and decoded by the British SIGINT organization, the Government Code and Cypher School (GC&CS). Such information revealed and proved Soviet penetration into China.[213]

The Military Police of the Kwantung Army established a radio direction finding (RDF) group, called "Unit 86," for counter-espionage in Manchuria, and the Military Police of the Expeditionary Army to Central China also established an RDF group called the "6th Section." The name was a play on the "Fifth Column" in China. The formation of the groups illustrated an awareness of the importance of RDF in spy catching.[214]

In July 1942, the 6th Section detected suspicious radio transmissions in the Shanghai area. The section specified the location of the radio source, and arrested a 21-year-old women, Florence Lakota-Martin, who possessed a British passport. The Military Police suspected that Lakota-Martin was a British spy, but she kept silent during interrogation. At that time the other group of the Military Police was watching her flat when a man visited. The Military Police also caught him and revealed that he possessed a Mauser pistol and a Soviet passport. His name was Vladimirov, a 32-year-old Russian. He was interrogated and sold out his accomplices, including the radio operator Marken and Lakota-Martin's lover, Sada, who was running a bar in Shanghai's French settlements.[215]

During interrogation, Sada gave away everything to save his own skin. Finally, Lakota-Martin revealed that she was a member of a Soviet spy ring in Shanghai. The Military Police were shocked by the confessions, and by captured documents showing the IJA's dispositions and details of operational planning and official meetings held in Tokyo – such information had been sent to Moscow. Lakota-Martin was a professional spy who had trained in spy training school in Chita for three years, and she had engaged in espionage missions in Manchuria. She was suspected by the Military Police in Hailar in 1940, but had succeeded in eluding the police, infiltrating into Shanghai. The Military Police tried to find the leader of the spy ring, but failed.[216]

The Military Police also conducted counter-intelligence activities in Japan, a famous example of which involved the arrest of one James Cox, a British man who worked as the chief of the Tokyo branch of Reuters. The case began with a letter for abroad posted in the post office of the Teikoku Hotel in Tokyo. The letter was discovered by the Military Police during investigations following the 2.26 incident in 1936. The letter contained secret information on the refitting plan for the battleship *Nagato*. The name of the sender was written as just "Jimmy." Navy leaders were shocked by the leaking of such secrets, and asked the Military Police to investigate the case, since the IJN had no counter-intelligence or investigation apparatus.

Cox slowly emerged as a suspect. The reasons that the Military Police suspected him were as follows: 1) Cox frequented the Teikoku Hotel; 2) he always used the post office of the hotel; 3) his family nickname was "Jimmy"; (4) he had similar handwriting to that of the letter; 5) he used a similar type of envelope to the one containing the letter.[217]

During the late 1930s, the Military Service Bureau (MSB) in the War Ministry revised the Military Secret Act and in 1937 the revised act, which covered foreigners and civilians, was enacted.[218] The Military Police were now able to act against Cox. In July 1940, the MSB ordered the Military Police to descend on foreign suspects in order to raise the morale of the IJA and IJN. However, the arrest of American suspects was forbidden because of the opposition by the Minister of Foreign Affairs, Yosuke Matsuoka, and Soviet agents could not be found. Cox, therefore, was floated as the top suspect. The Cox case, to which the revised Military Secret Act was applied, advanced the debate on issues of national security, which led to the National Security Act enacted in May 1941.[219]

The Military Police arrested Cox, confiscating secret documents sent by him to Robert Craigie, the British ambassador to Japan. However, three days after the arrest, Cox died by throwing himself out of a room on the fourth floor of the Tokyo Military Police HQ. While there are various views about Cox's end, some say that Cox killed himself because he feared involving Ambassador Craigie. On the other hand, Patrick Dean of the British Foreign Ministry, who investigated this case, implies that Cox was actually tortured and killed.[220] The British Foreign Office document indicated a desire to pay Mrs Cox compensation of £5,000. The possibility cannot be denied that the money bought her silence.[221]

Malcolm Kennedy, the predecessor of Cox in Japan and later an officer of GC&CS, reflected that: "Whether or not he [Cox] and the others are guilty, the fact 10 have been arrested and other arrests are threatened would seem to indicate that Japan is either making, or considering, plans for action against this country and is therefore taking precautionary measures to prevent well-informed Englishmen from passing on information.[222]

Since Kennedy had links with the intelligence community, it is likely that Cox was also engaging in the mission. Though the Military Police could not drag valuable information from Cox, the by-products of the case – the revised Military Secret Act and National Security Act – were applied to the Sorge case later.

THE INVESTIGATION DEPARTMENT OF THE WAR MINISTRY

The War Ministry also possessed intelligence apparatus because they had to control the IJA and its troops, which sometimes ran out of control in China and Manchuria. They did not believe the intelligence data of the IJA and tried to collect foreign information by themselves. The organization was known as the Investigation Department of the War Ministry, and it submitted intelligence to the War Ministry to help in forming military policy. According to ex-Major General Muneharu Kubo, the War Ministry started its systematic intelligence and counter-intelligence duties by leaving the work to the MSB in August 1936.[223] The Police Service Liaison Group was established as the special organization for scientific intelligence. In the same period, again in the MSB, Iwakuro and Akikusa founded the preparatory organization for the establishment of the Nakano School. Thus, the mid- to late 1930s seems to have been a period in which the IJA reorganized its intelligence apparatus.

In 1939, the counter-intelligence section in the MSB turned into the Investigation Department of the War Ministry under the direct control of the War Minister. According to Colonel Mitsuhiko Omori, ex-staff of the Defense Section of the MSB, the Minister of Army Hideki Tojo seemed to receive weekly briefing from the chief of the Investigation Department, Naotomi Mikuni.[224] The Police Service Liaison Group came to work under the chief of the Military Service Section of the MSB, designated as a military top secret organization under the Military Secret Act. Its role was to conduct research into signals intelligence and to collect data for counter-intelligence, and it was reorganized into the Military Source Department (MSD) in August 1939. One year later, it was formed into the Investigation Department, consisting of about 50 staff and requiring 1 million yen (about 8,000 million yen today) per year of funding for intelligence activities.

The focus of the Investigation Department, while trying their best to hide the Japanese intention of waging a war, was mainly foreigners living in Japan. The staff of the department could investigate, but they had no authority to make arrests. When the use of force was needed, they asked the Military Police through the MSB. The roles of the Investigation Department were collection of materials and counter-intelligence, and it also provided educational support for the Military Police and the Nakano School.

The Investigation Department worked field operations as well, via two groups: the Working Group for HUMINT and the Science Group for SIGINT, which engaged in searching for strange radio transmissions and tapping phones – they did not have good relations with the Military Police, which had a similar role. Although the beginning of the famous Sorge case was the result of their radio detection, it was not the Military Police but the SPP who arrested Sorge and his spy ring.

The Investigation Department also watched over Shigeru Yoshida (a future post-war Japanese Prime Minister) during the war. The department tapped politicians' telephones in Japan to collect domestic political information, and they also gathered intelligence through interviews, the agents disguising themselves as journalists. It is said that the counter-intelligence organization called *Yama* (Mountain) was placed under the Investigation Department.[225] Ex-Army Major General Naokata Utsunomiya remembered this organization as follows: "I was in the post of the chief of Counter-Intelligence Group from December 1937 to March 1939. It was only a year and four months of work … but I spent satisfying days, coping with various difficult counter-intelligence matters." The Counter-Intelligence Group was established under Lieutenant Colonel Akikusa, who was regarded as an authority on intelligence against the Soviet Union, and his assistant, Military Police Major Kameji Fukumoto, who was highly estimated as an expert on communist affairs, and it was staffed by some dozen agents and the Military Police officers.

The main work of the group was the covert inspection of international telegrams and letters, phone-tapping in foreign diplomatic establishments, monitoring radio transmissions, as well as other types of information gathering. Reports of international calls were forwarded to the group from the Ministry of Communications. International calls and phone calls between foreign establishments were passed through the Ushigome exchange, then connected to the secret line of the Counter-Intelligence Group to be recorded.

The letters from foreign establishments to their home countries were gathered in the Central Post Office, and some of them were sent to the Counter-Intelligence Group. The group opened and took photos of them, and two hours later sent them back to the Central Post Office. When staff of foreign establishments made a long journey by train, the Japanese operatives also quickly examined their luggage in the baggage car. As for the monitoring of private radio stations, the capability of direction-finding instruments was generally poor in the 1930s, so the results weren't significant.

The greatest catastrophe for the Japanese counter-intelligence community was to overlook the Sorge spy ring for eight years – both the Military Police and SPP failed to prevent his ring from sending reports to Moscow in September and October 1941. Sorge advised the Kremlin that Japan would not strike Russia unless the Germans captured Moscow.[226] The information was based on a Japanese official decision on September 6, 1941, that Japan would wage a war against the United States and Britain, not the Soviet Union, and it was leaked to Sorge through his colleague Hotsumi Ozaki, adviser to Prime Minister Konoe. The information seems to have been vital for Stalin's war planning against Germany.

Although historical sources about the Investigation Department remain scarce, according to the research of Mitsukuni Saito the department had close connections with the Noborito Military Research Institute, the Nakano School, the *Yama* Agency, and the Military Police. The Investigation Department therefore acted as a hub to many other securty apparatuses. The War Ministry also controlled the Army News Service, which obtained information through private press agencies. They were interested in technical information on the air services of Britain, the United States, Germany, France, and the Soviet Union.

3
JAPANESE NAVY INTELLIGENCE

From 1909, the IJN intelligence apparatus targeted its information-gathering efforts on the United States. Yet the Intelligence Department remained in peacetime mode until the outbreak of the Pacific War, and the 5th Section of the 3rd Department in the Navy General Staff, which specialized in intelligence against the United States, consisted of fewer than ten staff until the attack on Pearl Harbor.[227] The organization was far inferior to the IJA intelligence apparatus against the Soviet Union.

Yet the IJN also dispatched 18 officers to the United States, and the military attaché's office in America was quite a large establishment, comprising 30 staff including assistants for the officers. The IJN used these personnel to collect local information. In addition, the Intelligence Department of the IJN also had a Special Intelligence Department that worked on SIGINT; although it didn't have the capacity of the equivalent IJA organization, it nevertheless succeeded in breaking parts of the British and US diplomatic codes.

NAVAL SIGINT

The IJN began its development of SIGINT earlier than the IJA, during the Russo-Japanese War. According to the record of ex-Captain Tsunezo Wachi, one of the leading figures in the IJN's codebreaking activities, when the ships *Russia* and *Kronboi* of the Russian Vladivostok Fleet appeared outside Tokyo Bay, engineer Kimura intercepted radio transmissions sent from the fleet at the IJN's wireless traffic station on Mt. Jizo in Yaizu, Shizuoka prefecture. He reported the movement of the fleet in detail to the Imperial HQ, which proved the importance of traffic interception.[228]

Then in 1929, an annex of the 4th Section was established in the 2nd Group of the Navy General Staff, and seven staff under Lieutenant Colonel Hisajiro Nakasugi began systematic codebreaking activities at a signals traffic interception station in Tachibana village on the riverside of the Tama River, targeting the US (A) and Britain (B).[229] In those days, the British GC&CS consisted of hundreds of staff. By comparison, the IJN SIGINT activities were tiny. As already noted, the IJN and IJA succeeded in breaking the American diplomatic code, Gray Code (AF2) and the US Navy's two-digit code (AN2).[230] The shortage of staff prevented operations against Britain, from which it is inferred that the British diplomatic code was more difficult to break.

The NIDS military archives keeps *Toku-jo* records intercepted and decoded by the IJN from January 29 to September 27, 1932. According to the records, the IJN decrypted about 500 US diplomatic documents during the eight-month period. In addition, the IJN watched the movements of the US naval vessels by intercepting radio transmission. The amount of SIGINT collected by the IJN in those days, therefore, became massive, even just limited to US data.[231]

In 1932, Wachi was placed in the SIGINT annex of the 4th Section, and the organization for traffic interception against China, called the *X Kikan* (X Agency), was established in Shanghai. But enlargement of IJN's SIGINT organization required greater stimulus, and the first Shanghai incident (a short war between China and Japan on January 28–March 3, 1932) became the opportunity.

At that time, the SIGINT annex decrypted the code sent from the American consulate in Shanghai to the Department of State. The message contained the sentence "Nanking government ordered its air force to bombard Japanese Army."[232] While the 4th Section was considering the real meaning of the information, the chief of the X Agency, Lieutenant Tatsuya Yamada, grasped the information from Chinese coded communications about the Chinese Air Force gathering around Hangchou. Thus, in the early morning of February 26, the IJN Air Force raided the airport of Hangchou and annihilated the Chinese Air Force there. The Navy General Staff recorded that "This air raid was carried out by taking advantage of a good opportunity ... The attack had a great influence on the morale of the Nineteenth Army."[233]

The air campaign allowed Japan to command the skies around Shanghai. By this achievement, Lieutenant Yamada of the X Agency was given the *Ko* 5th Class Golden Kite Medal, and the annex of the 4th Section was enlarged to be the 10th Section of the 4th Group in October. At that time, Captain Hisajiro Nakasugi, chief of the section, and Commander Gonichiro Kakimoto joined as a staff. Then in 1933, Lieutenant Imaizumi was dispatched to the X Agency in Shanghai, and the Y Agency and Z Agency were established in Peking and Kanton respectively.[234]

In 1934, Wachi was sent to Shanghai as a civilian to lead the newly established B Operational Group (against Britain) in the X Agency. Although the group aimed to investigate what kind of policy Britain would take in light of the clash between Japan and China around Shanghai, the codebreaking efforts against Britain made only tardy progress. Therefore Wachi and the Shanghai SDA cooperatively made a plan to penetrate into the British consulate and to take several photos of key documents, a plan which failed.[235] At the same time, the Navy General Staff made a decision to steal a code book from the British consulate in Sapporo, when the security was light. In November, a Japanese typist took the opportunity to throw a British diplomatic code book out of the window without the consul's awareness.[236] By means of this code book, the Shanghai X Agency succeeded in breaking the British inter-ministries and government office code (called BF5 in the IJN). The decrypting work demonstrated ties between the RN in the Far East and China, for example the approval of the Commander-in-Chief of the RN Far East Fleet to ship Chinese troops by British vessels.[237] However, Britain changed the codes in 1935, and decryption became difficult again, while the British intelligence efforts continually improved. Commander Motonao Samejima, an expert in naval communications, recollects: "I became aware of the tremendous capability of the UK intelligence" – one of the decrypts demonstrated that the Far Eastern Combined Bureau (FECB), a branch of the British SIGINT section placed in Hong Kong, decrypted IJN coded communications just 24 hours after their dispatch.[238]

In 1936, in addition to Tachibana village receiving station, the IJN established another one in Owada, specializing in communications interception, where the communications from the assistant for American military attachés in Peking to Washington, D.C., were intercepted and decrypted when the Marco Polo Bridge incident (the clash around Peking that led to the onset of the Second Sino-Japanese War) occurred on July 7–9, 1937. The information decrypted on July 10 showed that the Chinese officers were not satisfied with the ceasefire agreement and intended to continue the attack on the Japanese troops.[239]

After the Owada communications station was founded, the IJN's SIGINT activities developed gradually, targeting the United States, Britain, China, and also the Soviet Union. As for the United States, the IJN intercepted the communications from the flagships of the US Asian Fleet and Pacific Fleet to Washington, D.C., and the radio transmissions between Honolulu, San Francisco, and the US capital. The IJN also intercepted the British communications to London from the British China Expeditionary Fleet, Hong Kong, Singapore, Colombo, and Calcutta, and the Soviet communications from the Far East such as Khabarovsk and Vladivostok to Moscow.[240]

As the IJN had broken the US Brown Code in 1938, it was in a position to know the intentions of the US State Department about the war between Japan and China. However, the IJN could not break the US Strip Ciphers, unlike the IJA. Moreover, the IJA did not share its deciphering knowledge with the IJA. During the Pacific War, therefore, a Special Research Section (SRS) was established in the Navy General Staff in order to break the ciphers. Though Rear Admiral Yasunoshin Ito, Rear Admiral Hisajiro Nakasugi, and 20 university students with proficiency in languages or mathematics made serious efforts to break the ciphers, they could not reach the goal.[241] The IJN did not even know that the IJA had already broken the ciphers until 1945.[242]

The IJN had long considered the possibility of a war against Britain or the United States, unlike the IJA. The IJN obtained information that the US Pacific Fleet would continue to stay in Hawaii after the naval maneuvers there in 1937, and so decided to focus SIGINT on the Hawaii area, taking a semi-war footing. Meanwhile, SIGINT often showed that the reports to the US Department of State from its staff in China were steadily becoming anti-Japanese in tone, and the IJN had discussions with the IJA, the Ministry of Foreign Affairs, and other relevant departments every time they received such information.[243] When the American vessel *Paney* was accidentally sunk by Japanese bombing in December 1937, for example, IJN intelligence saw clear resentment from the United States, and used the information in support of diplomatic negotiations.

After 1940, Wachi led the way in intercepting radio transmissions around Hawaii, probing the movements of the Pacific Fleet. He also established the L Agency in Mexico to assist the military attaché in the consulate, watching the American fleet in the Atlantic area from Mexico, with four staff for comunication interception activities.[244]

DIRECTION-FINDING TECHNOLOGY

SIGINT technologies were initially not given too much importance by the Navy General Staff, since they were originally regarded as being for naval communications rather than intelligence. Therefore signal intelligence groups had to work with small staffs and scarce funds. The SIGINT of the IJN focused on interception of communications rather than codebreaking.

However, as conflict with the United States grew more serious, the intelligence side of SIGINT (codebreaking of enemy codes and communications security) received more attention. Thus, in December 1940, the SIGINT apparatus that had been under the 3rd Department of the Navy General Staff became the Special Duty Section (SDS) headed by Captain Gonichiro Kakimoto, under the direct control of the Navy Chief of Staff. The roles of the group were to: 1) establish the SIGINT operational plan; 2) exert command and control over operations; 3) train staff for interception of signals traffic; and 4) collect, compile, and issue SIGINT reports. The section consisted of three groups: the Operational SIGINT Group, Diplomatic SIGINT Group, and Code Research Group. Above all stress was put on the activities of the Operational SIGINT Group.[245] The operational

SIGINT groups against Germany (G) and France (F) were newly established when the apparatus was reorganized in 1940. The "Imperial Wartime Communication Plan of Showa 16 (1941)" defined the remit of the SDS: "the major SIGINT target is Britain and the United States, and the sub targets are the Soviet Union and China. The principal goal of the SIGINT operation is acquisition of tactical intelligence materials."[246]

SDS research examined the possibilities of extracting strategic and tactical information from fragmentary data, relying on deductions from the amount, frequency, and direction of the opponent's communications in cases where codes were unbreakable. In February 1941, the British Group was established in Bangkok as a branch of the Shanghai X Agency, the Dutch Group of the Agency being founded later. The interception of communications by the Americans and British was concentrated in the Shinjo (Sinchang) Section of the Takao (Kaoshun) Communications Unit in Taiwan, because the location was good for receiving radio transmissions.[247] Between them the Takao Branch, Shanghai X Agency, Mexican L Agency, and Owada Communications Station simultaneously intercepted the transmission of the US Navy (USN) statement: "Air raid Pearl Harbor. This is not a drill."[248]

The IJN seemed to have broken part of the Soviet codes. In May 1939, after the outbreak of the battle of Nomonhan, the IJN established its own communications interception stations specializing in Soviet intelligence, these being based in Niigata, Tottori, and the Korean Peninsula.[249] In December 1943, the IJN decrypted a cable from the Soviet attaché to the United States, and obtained information about movement of the US fleets.[250] In the intelligence records of the Navy General Staff of 1944, there were some diplomatic telegrams from the Soviet ambassador in Australia to the Soviet Commissar for Foreign Affairs, called *Ha Toku Cho* (Harbin Special Information) by the IJA.[251]

Integral to the IJN SIGINT efforts was the Allies' Broadcast for Allied Merchant Shipping (BAMS). It became a tool to predict when the USN would begin major assaults – the amount of communications of merchant ships was often linked to the US operations. David Kahn has written:

The *Tokumu Han* (Special Duty Section) cryptanalysts succeeded best with BAMS, the two-part superenciphered Allied merchant ship code. They solved about half of the BAMS intercepts. How were they suddenly able to do so well with so relatively difficult a system? Germany had given them the basic BAMS code book, which had been captured by her raider *Atlantis*. Consequently, the Japanese had only to remove the superencipherment ... By following the bulge in BAMS transmissions from California to Hawaii to, say, Guam, the traffic analysis could predict the general area in which the next American assault would come. Messages from reconnoitering submarines or airplanes reinforced the estimate. The time of the attack was often gauged by non-communications means – such as guesses based on previous movements – but also silence or an increase in the urgency of reconnaissance messages ..."[252]

Colonel Samejima, chief of the Communications Section of the Navy General Staff, explains further the indicators that an attack was coming:

(1) the number of merchants ships in BAMS increased rapidly one month before the next US operation and the location of the radio transmission source defined the operational waters; (2) the amount of traffic data and direction findings increased in one month; (3) the number of US submarines engaged in scouting activities increased in one week; (4) the volume of signals traffic from aircraft and transport ships increased in one month; (5) the frequency of weather broadcasting increased in the week before [the attack]; (6) a new code (usually starting with "Z") appeared over the course of two weeks.[253]

Samejima recollected that the traffic analysis roughly indicated the dates of US advance into the Marshall Islands in January 1944, the Mariana Islands in June 1944, and Iwo Jima in February 1945.[254]

Thus, although the codebreaking work advanced tardily, the IJN could still read intended Allied operations, to a certain extent. They also integrated their SIGINT with other activities such as RDF and observation. For example, IJN watchers alerted ground forces before the US landing operation on Leyte Island.[255]

By 1943, the SDS of the IJN consisted of hundreds of staff, although staff levels among the IJA's SIS, and the branches of the IJN SIGINT apparatus were far fewer than those the in equivalent IJA organizations. Moreover, the IJN fell behind the IJA in training of SIGINT staff. They finally began systematic education in 1945, though it seems to have been too late.[256]

From the inter-war period through the Pacific War, the IJN made a generally poor effort in codebreaking while their own codes were cracked by the Allies, which gave the Allies an advantage in the Washington Naval Conference in 1921 and provided the intelligence to shoot down Admiral Isoroku Yamamoto, commander of the Combined Fleet, in April 1943. However, the IJN did break some US and British codes in the pre-war period and during the war were able to predict the USN's line of advance through RDF and other measures.

NAVAL HUMINT

In the field of HUMINT, the IJN made fewer remarkable achievements than the IJA. Ex-Commander Chikataka Nakajima, head of the Communications Department of the Navy General Staff, recollected: "Regarding intelligence work, the IJN was cautious and even negative."[257] The 3rd Department of the Navy General Staff had its own Special Duty Section, which was the equivalent of the Special Duty Agency of the IJA. The SDS concentrated on information gathering, not embarking upon political plots and covert operations. Compared to the IJA, the scale of the section was small, with an annual fund of about 3 million yen (24 billion yen today) of funding in 1941.[258]

According to the record of the Military Intelligence Section (MIS) of the United States, which investigated Japanese intelligence activities after the war, the SDS started its work under the naval military attachés in Shanghai and Peking and then expanded to all over China and the southern area.[259] A research report of the Office of Strategic Service (OSS) noted that the SDS established branches and collected information in cities on the Chinese coast such as Tsingtao, Shanghai, Canton, Singapore, Surabaya, and Rabaul. Furthermore, in the South China Sea the staff of the SDS seem to have conducted surveillance by disguising themselves as the crew of fishing boats.[260] British intelligence also recorded their suspicions that the Japanese fishing boats were collecting information on the sea near the Andaman-Nikobal Islands in Bengal Bay.[261]

Ex-Captain Naosada Koshiba, who belonged to the North and South China branches of the SDS, kept a comprehensive record of the section. Koshiba was a rarity – a China specialist in the IJN. His role was information gathering in mainland China, especially the area between Shanghai and Bangkok. He worked for the Shanghai landing force at first, then for the Shanghai military attaché's office. The information he obtained, which included SIGINT via intercepting the Chinese Army's communications and HUMINT obtained by personal activities, was called K Information in the Navy General Staff.[262] The K Information contained detailed information about movement of the Chinese Air Force. The IJN also established a private trading company in Shanghai – *Manwa Koshi* – which also collected information.[263]

After his time in Shanghai, Koshiba took training in the codebreaking of Chinese diplomatic codes in the SIS of the Navy General Staff, and trained in the Chinese language at the Navy War College. In 1938, he had worked for the SDS of the North China Navy led by Captain Kazutaka Shiraishi.[264] In the same year, he moved from the North China SDS to the South China SDS to collect information in Hong Kong. Since the IJN had no branches in the area, he entered Hong Kong alone. His ultimate aim was to discover the route by which the British supplied materials to Chiang Kai-shek in China, and he was helped in this task by receiving the cooperation of local Japanese private companies such as Mitsui and Mitsubishi.

In May 1941, Koshiba was in Swatow, a city in South China, searching for the supply route to support Chiang, moving to Bangkok in October. When he left Bangkok, Vice Admiral Seiichi Ito, Vice Chief of Staff, handed him $2,000 (6.5 million yen today) as funds for his operation.[265] At that time, there was almost no naval espionage network in Thailand and the number of local naval staff was only five, including the military attaché. So he was given some people from Shanghai to conduct intelligence operations. The IJA also eagerly conducted intelligence work in the same period and same area, so the IJN may have cooperated with the IJA's Minami Agency, although there is no mention of intelligence cooperation with the IJA in Koshiba's memoir.

Koshiba's main intelligence activity was to penetrate into the local overseas Chinese community and Thai government, and he succeeded in making connection with the overseas Chinese to a certain extent. British intelligence also worked actively in Bangkok, therefore it was debatable which way Thailand would go if UK–Japanese military conflict occurred – would it side with Britain or Japan or keep its neutrality? Deducing this intention became paramount after the Japanese occupation of French Indo-China from 1940. Prime Minister of Thailand Phibun was pro-Japanese, while the conservatives such as Minister of Foreign Affairs Direk were pro-British. Koshiba's conclusion was that Thailand would keep its neutrality during a war. Note that Britain intercepted and decrypted communications between Bangkok and Tokyo through SIGINT; therefore all of these Japanese operations were leaked to the British.

After the outbreak of the Pacific War in late 1941, Koshiba moved south and continued operations against the Chinese people resident in Phuket and Penang. In October 1942, having obtained cooperation from the local Chinese, he founded the *Nantai Koshi* (South Thai Company), which became a stronghold for IJN special duties.[266] Although Koshiba's records stop at this point, it is still quite interesting, since it shows a part of the covert operations by the Special Duty Section of the IJN.

There remain only a few comprehensive records about the HUMINT activities of the IJN. However, details of the IJN's intelligence activities were kept by the British MI5 organization, and the files are accessible in the British National Archives. While the IJA was in an intelligence war with the Soviet NKVD, the IJN fought a battle of wits against MI5.

Although the Navy General Staff actually employed Britons as agents to collect information, MI5's excellent counter-intelligence apparatus meant that IJN operations were compromised to a certain extent. MI5 was very different from the Soviet NKVD. When MI5 found enemy agents, it did not arrest them hastily, but let them move around freely to watch their activities and provide more information.

For example, from 1923 to 1927, Commander Teijiro Toyoda, a naval attaché to Britain, was provided with secret information by British naval officers such as Captain William Sempill and Lieutenant Commander Collin Mayers. Sempill was a specialist aboard the aircraft carrier *Argus*. According to MI5 reports, Toyoda seemed to have received sensitive information from Sempill, but MI5 did not arrest him.[267] Mayers was an expert on submarines. He had retired from the RN in January 1927 and worked for the submarine department of Vickers. According to MI5, Mayers provided Toyoda with a secret about the then newest underwater communication technologies for a price of £300.[268] MI5 and GC&CS intercepted and decoded communications from the Japanese embassy to follow Mayers' moves, and he was finally arrested by the British authorities for violation of the National Security Act in March 1927.[269]

Toyoda wanted information on the latest naval technologies to contribute to Japanese construction of aircraft carriers and submarines. After Toyoda left London, Lieutenant Commander Shiro Takasu, assistant to the naval attaché to Britain, used ex-British officer F. J. Rutland.[270] According to MI5's records, it seems that the IJN changed its object from technologies to international affairs and strategic intelligence after the 1930s.

Rutland had entered in the RN in 1902, and then moved to the newly founded Royal Air Force (RAF) in 1918. In the Great War, he participated in battles such as Jutland and he was awarded the Albert Medal 1st Class and the Distinguished Service Cross (DSC) twice, among other decorations. He was a true British hero of the Great War. In the RAF he rose to the rank of squadron leader. Yet he probably began to feel he had little chance of further promotion because he was from the working class and had entered the RAF late, at the age of 32. Soon after the end of World War I, the Japanese embassy in Britain seemed to approach Rutland, who was then a crew member of the

British aircraft carrier *Eagle* and was regarded as an expert on carrier-based aircraft. Although, of course, the contact between Rutland and Japan proceeded covertly, MI5 obtained secret information on the meeting in December 1922.[271]

According to the later investigations of MI5, the Japanese confided in Rutland that the IJN was covertly recruiting RN officers as advisers, and that his knowledge of carrier-based aircraft was indispensable. The IJN invited Rutland to become an adviser, probably not considering him as an agent. Though he still belonged to the RAF at this point, he readily accepted the Japanese offer without reporting anything to his seniors. He submitted his resignation in the summer of 1923, then in October, MI5 and the Air Ministry accepted his retirement after serious thought.

Thereafter, Rutland stayed in France for a while, then visited Japan in the summer of 1924. He was formally employed by Mitsubishi Shipbuilder, but it is certain that he worked for the IJN. He lived in Kamakura and frequently went to the dockyard in Yokosuka. His task was to teach the IJN details about carrier-based aircraft, which he also tried to design and produce.[272] It is difficult to infer to what extent his instruction contributed to the modernization of the IJN's air force, but his value to the IJN is evident from the size of his reward, probably about several thousand pounds.

In November 1932, the IJN covertly continued contact with Rutland and began to consider using him as an agent, and Lieutenant Commander Takasu met him. Rutland initially offered to engage in intelligence work in Britain, but the Japanese rejected his offer and dispatched him to the United States. The IJN clearly considered the United States as the principal enemy of the future. The conditions of the contract exchanged before his move to the United States included: (1) a reward of £2,000 (50 million yen today); 2) a fund for activities in the United States; 3) an allowance for his family in the case of his death; 4) a minimum five-year stay in the United States.[273] At this point, the IJN estimated the fund for the first year of Rutland's operation at 1 million yen (about 80 million yen today).[274] Of course, MI5 obtained information about this contract through GC&CS.

The major aim of Rutland in the United States was not collecting information itself, but laying the groundwork for Japanese information gathering, such as the foundation of an espionage network and the founding of companies to provide cover status for agents. His job was to build connections and strongholds in the United States, to establish means for the transmission of information to Japan, and, if possible, to report on American intentions toward Japan. Rutland was ordered to collect information actively only when a war between Japan and the US began. In that case, his role was to report on the scale and deployment of the US fleet to Japan, being based in Los Angeles or San Francisco. In other words, he was employed as a sleeper, i.e. a potential agent. A telegram from Japan containing 13 letters was to be the sign of the outbreak of war.[275]

In August 1933, Rutland left Britain to visit the United States, and Commander Arata Oka, who succeeded Takasu, awaited contact, staying in London. According to the British intelligence officer who talked with Rutland on the ship to America while pretending to be an ordinary passenger, Rutland showed considerable interest in the movement of the USN. After that, he traveled across the continent from east to west, then traveled on to Japan where he exchanged contracts. It seems that a person related to the Japanese intelligence had a meeting with him, but their identity is unclear.[276] Then Rutland left Japan, avoiding the RN fleet calling at the port of Yokohama.

In February 1934, Rutland went to the United States again, to settle down this time. He lived under the name of "Manley." He founded Rutland Edwards & Company in Los Angeles with an American acquaintance, and then established the Security Aircraft Company on the site of the Douglas Aircraft Company, the airplane manufacturer in Santa Monica, in April 1938.[277] It seems that the former was a stockbroker firm, accessing the financial circles of the West Coast, while the latter was for information gathering on the Douglas Company, which supplied aircrafts to the US forces. The Security Aircraft Company later changed the name to the Japan Aircraft Company, which was established to give cover status for Japanese military personnel as civilian employees, although it actually sold some training aircraft to Japan.

In those days along the West Coast in America, the Japanese military personnel habitually gathered in the Olympic Hotel in Los Angeles, a fact known to the FBI.[278] Rutland acted the part of a wealthy British entrepreneur and worked his way into prestigious West Coast social circles. He was acquainted with many influential people, both British and American, even an executive of the Douglas Company in the Del Monte Club in Santa Monica.[279] He behaved like a billionaire, living alone in a house with a swimming pool in Beverly Hills, having two cars and employing some servants.[280]

Meanwhile, he went to ports frequently and recorded battleships on film, saying that 16mm filming was his hobby. He often visited a certain shop, apparently to buy films. According to the FBI investigations, however, he went to the shop to deposit his recordings rather than to buy new film.[281] Rutland's films were probably sent to Japan via this shop.

In London in March 1934, Oka suggested that Tokyo employ a German or French agent as well as Rutland.[282] The next year, the Japanese embassy in Berlin hired Bernard Kühn, a member of the Nazi Party, and sent him to Hawaii. It is unclear whether it was as a result of Oka's suggestion or mere coincidence, but in fact the IJN seemed to get down to collecting information in America from around 1935. In this period, the IJN told Oka repeatedly: "The most important thing is information gathering around Hawaii,"[283] which revealed to British intelligence the IJN's main point of interest.

In the same period, Oka also hired a new Briton, Herbert Greene, who was a nephew of William Greene, the highest official in the Admiralty, and a brother of Graham Greene, the famous novelist.[284] Herbert himself had worked as a journalist in South Africa, and then in 1933 became a Japanese agent, recruited by Oka. Coming from a decent family, he was able to move in clubs where only the upper class could enter, so the IJN expected him to collect information there. His code name was *Midorikawa* (Green River) while Rutland's was *Shinkawa* (New River).

From 1934, Greene's focus was on probing British intentions for the Second London Disarmament Conference, scheduled for December 1935. The IJN allocated 10,000 yen (about 8 million yen today) for this mission.[285] Although the IJN also paid £800 to Greene as a reward, he conducted no outstanding intelligence work. On the contrary, he disclosed that he was a Japanese spy to the *Daily Worker* on December 22, 1937, proving himself to be a thoroughly inappropriate Japanese agent.[286]

Meanwhile, Rutland founded an import company, Marston Barrs in London. Of course, it was a dummy company to receive contacts and funds from Japan. However, the communications between the company and Japan leaked out to the British. All of the letters from Rutland to the company and his secretaries were opened and checked by the British security services. Rutland's plan was to establish trading companies in London, Hawaii, and Los Angeles, then to exchange information among Japan, America, and Britain. Information was to be sent from Tokyo to London and from London to Los Angeles, and there was a plan for some new branches in New York, Vancouver, Peking, and other locations. The funds from Japan were usually paid in stocks. For example, £700 sent to Los Angeles and £350 sent to London were invested in 1935. However, the problem was that Rutland's plan was known to MI5 and the FBI, and also the plan was a considerable burden for the IJN, because Rutland's lack of business acumen meant he ran loss-making companies, so Japan had to supply bail-out funds for them.

In May 1935, Rutland sent a report that included opinions such as "The Army and Navy want war and in my view this might be put off for a few years... Everyone I have met in America thinks a war with Japan is inevitable..."[287] Although it was a personal view of Rutland, his report was considered seriously, since he was the only foreign spy the IJN had in those days on the West Coast. Oka had warned Tokyo, "it is too dangerous to rely on Rutland alone in case of war,"[288] and suggested that Rutland engage in collecting information in Hawaii not only as a sleeper, but as an active agent.[289]

According to the GC&CS, the information which the IJN required in 1935 was the US strategy against Japan and the USN policy toward the London

Disarmament Conference to be held at the end of the year.[290] On the other hand, the FBI reported that Rutland was in charge of Japanese intelligence works in America, and was the only agent who understood all of the IJN's codes and had permission to move around the world.[291] This FBI information had no evidence behind it, but the IJN's expectations from him can be seen from the fact that he was supplied with a great deal of funds from Japan.

Rutland frequently moved around London, New York, Los Angeles, Honolulu, and so on. In Hawaii, he possibly had a certain relationship with Ensign Takeo Yoshikawa, who was in charge of the IJN's intelligence operations there, and the above-mentioned German spy Kühn, though there is no definite information about an encounter. Rutland also visited Shanghai in December 1937 and had contact with the IJA there. His visit was known to MI5 through the interception of communications, as well as to the people related to the USN in Shanghai. In August 1938, Rutland visited Japan again, where he received no less than £4,000 and was briefed about a code from an intelligence staff officer named Ito.[292] The code represented vessels such as battleships and cruisers by numbers, and was too simple for sending complicated information, supposedly just for use in the case of war.[293] Only three Japanese made contact with Rutland and exchanged information: Ito, Oka, and Commander Itaru Tachibana, who was running covert operations on the West Coast of the United States.

After his return to the United States, Rutland approached Captain Ellice Zacharias, a Japanese specialist in the USN intelligence, through a British Military Club.[294] Although it is not clear how much Zacharias was interested in Rutland, Rutland himself testified that he had approached Zacharias, saying that he would inhibit Japanese intelligence work. However, if Rutland really made contact, Zacharias must have known Rutland's identity through the FBI; therefore it was possible that it was Zacharias who exploited Rutland instead.

It was Tachibana who kept contact with Rutland in the United States. Though he had not been trained as an intelligence officer, he was so familiar with the USN that he worked in Los Angeles from 1939 and then engaged in intelligence activities in Hawaii. The information obtained by Tachibana and the other agents was to be transferred by Rutland covertly.[295] Rutland himself visited mines around Colorado and Arizona, some of which he seems to have bought. He also went to the US–Mexican border, where it appears that he intended to establish an intelligence network into Mexico. At that time, Japan was trying hard to establish espionage networks and communication lines to take information out of Mexico, choosing cities on the Pacific coast and countries in Central and South America as strongholds. It seems that these plans were led by Hideaki Terasaki, the 2nd Secretary of the Ministry of Foreign Affairs.[296]

In June 1941 the situation changed suddenly. Having worked in Los Angeles to collect information on the US Pacific Fleet, Tachibana was arrested by the FBI on June 6, caught by counter-intelligence operations. Rutland felt he was in danger, and asked the US authorities for protection, only to be rejected. Then he turned to the British authorities, who feared that ex-RAF officer's arrest in the United States would develop into a scandal. They sheltered Rutland and repatriated him to Britain in October.

Rutland had never admitted being a Japanese agent, although under MI5 interrogation he admitted he had connections with the IJN. According to him, he actually worked for the US intelligence, and it was to monitor the Japanese military that he approached the Japanese. Moreover, he even offered himself as a British agent, but his offer was impossible to accept since MI5 had continued its close investigation on his activities. Soon after the outbreak of war against Japan, Rutland was interned as a collaborator under the Defence Regulations 18B and was jailed in Brixton Prison. His case was released formally, but got little attention in the newspapers. Though he was discharged in early 1944, he committed suicide a few years after the end of the war.[297]

While the Japanese side trusted Rutland, he worked for Japan not because of good will or loyalty toward Japan, but just for money and adventure. The IJN made contact with Rutland while he was still in the RAF and succeeded in hiring him. However, it can be said that the IJN relied too much on Rutland alone, a fact that concerned Oka. The IJN failed to watch him, so could not prevent him from being repatriated to the UK. Besides, the IJN invested vast amounts of money in him and his activities on the West Coast of the United States, in Hawaii, and London, but it is questionable whether the investment bore fruit or not. According to Rutland himself, his funding reached at least into the tens of thousands of pounds.[298] The IJN's investment shows its great expectations for Rutland, while he seems not to have reported much genuinely useful information.

From the British perspective, Rutland's activities served as a useful barometer to test the IJN's intentions. In the 1920s, when the IJN worked on expansion of the air force, Rutland was hired as an adviser on carrier-based aircraft. Then in the 1930s when the IJN began to abandon the policy of international cooperation, and considered a war against the British and US navies, Rutland was hired as an agent. Thus, the IJA's use of Rutland roughly matched its strategic intentions.[299] Moreover, Rutland not only revealed the Japanese information gathering by embassies and the Japanese intelligence network and communication lines in the United States, but also suggested that the IJN's interest was concentrated on the US Pacific Fleet and Hawaii through the 1930s. Considering that the greatest concern of the British military in the Far East was the defense of Singapore, there is a possibility that the reports from MI5 affected the British strategy in the Far East to some extent.

Anyway, as Rutland was kept under surveillance by MI5 and the FBI all the time, it was all but impossible for Rutland to succeed in his plans. Kim Philby of the British SIS, who was later revealed as a Soviet agent, was involved in the Rutland case, and the MI5 investigations seem to have been reported to the Soviet Union by Philby. For the Soviets, the revelations about intelligence technique were valuable, and such information fed into the eventual reorganization of the NKVD as the more sophisticated KGB.[300]

IJN COUNTER-INTELLIGENCE

Compared to that of the IJA, the IJN's counter-intelligence was largely ineffective, with the breaking of naval codes leading to serious results, such as the killing of Admiral Yamamoto and compromised security around the battle of Midway in June 1942.[301] In the IJN, although Captain Risaburo Ito presented "a suggestion to the Ministry of Navy regarding codes," pointing out the possibility that IJN codes were being decrypted through their misuse,[302] such cautions were rarely given attention in the IJN. The IJN had admittedly devised its own cipher machines, the Type 91 and 97, through the efforts of Navy engineer Kazuo Tanabe. Even the Ministry of Foreign Affairs used the Type 97, with some improvements. Yet almost all the mechanical codes processed by these machines were broken by the British and Americans.

For example, in the lead-up to the battle of Midway, it was clear that the IJN's operational codes had been compromised, since the Allies had obtained the code books from the *I-go* 124 submarine sunk to the north of Australia in January 1942.[303] Nevertheless, the IJN took no measures against the security failure, and fought the disastrous battles of Coral Sea and Midway. In addition to the code documents of the *I-go* 124 submarine, there were other factors by which the IJN's D code was broken: 1) since the code consisted of finite random numbers, it was theoretically breakable; 2) the IJN could not renew the code book before the Midway operation; 3) the level of communications was increased by the operation, providing the Allies with more opportunities for decryption.[304] In hindsight, the requirements for the breaking of the IJN's D code had been fulfilled well before the battle of Midway.[305]

It is inevitable that secret documents are sometimes intercepted by the enemy and coded communications are decoded, yet the fact remains that the IJN took no counter measures, despite an awareness that secrets were being leaked. Vice Admiral Ryunosuke Kusaka, who joined the Midway operation as the chief staff officer of the 1st Air Fleet, noted: "The major factor of the failure in the operation was the leaking of the Japanese Combined Fleet's plan on the battle of Midway to the US Navy."[306] In the operational diary of the Navy General Staff it was recorded that "the enemy had grasped our intentions beforehand."[307] However, in the minds of the Navy General Staff, the major factors behind the defeat were technical issues, such as a problem in liaison between the fleets and replenishment vessels and the lack of reconnaissance. It is certain that the defeat in the battle of Midway was led not only by the security failures, but by the combination of many factors; nevertheless, the breaking of the codes should at least have been counted as one of them.[308]

The lack of thorough examination regarding code failures resulted in the shooting down of the plane of Admiral Yamamoto on April 18, 1943. The US intercepted and decoded the IJN's coded telegram "NTF Secret, number 131755," then ambushed and shot down the airplane of Yamamoto, who was visiting the Solomon Islands. After the incident, the suspicion that the IJN coded traffic was intercepted and decoded arose among the IJN officers.[309] However, a thorough investigation into the cause of the incident was again unsuccessful, because of the lack of decisive evidence. Captain Motonao Samejima, the Chief of the Communications Section, recollected as follows:

> This incident was so serious for the IJN that a strict investigation was conducted immediately, examining cipher security. However, we could not find the crucial material to infer that the US had known the schedule of Admiral Yamamoto. Rather, the Japanese side came to consider that the case was just accidental. Firstly, we thought our code security was tough enough not to be broken and the table of random numbers was just changed on April 1. Secondly, on 19 April, the US radio in San Francisco simply announced the results of the day, "The US Army's plane shot down two Japanese land assault aircraft and two combat planes in Northern Solomon losing one of our planes." That is to say, they did not state who was on board the aircraft. Therefore, we come to believe that the case was accidental.[310]

It is hardly believable that Samejima, a specialist in cipher security, was this credulous; at least the *possibility* of decoding by the US Army ought to have been pointed out. Moreover, such a soft attitude toward counter-intelligence emerged more clearly in the *Otsu* incident a year later.

The Navy's *Otsu* incident occurred when two IJN flying boats suffered damage during a tropical storm on the way to Davao from Palau on April 1,

1944.[311] On the first aircraft was Admiral Mineichi Koga, the commander-in-chief of the Combined Fleet, who died when the aircraft went down. The second aircraft, containing Vice Admiral Shigeru Fukudome, carried a waterproof attaché case that contained the IJN code book and "Z Plan" document, which explained critical information on future Japanese war strategy, written in plain language, not code. The attaché case was lost when the second boat ditched.[312] Then Fukudome and the others were caught by local guerrillas on Cebu Island.

Meanwhile, the Americans found the Japanese flying-boats off the island of Cebu, and discovered the secret documents, which they carried to the Australian Army's intelligence department by submarine; they then copied them. Then the US floated the attaché case around the emergency landing area to allow the Japanese to find it. Eventually the case was returned to the Japanese side, under the pretence that it had been found by the locals of Cebu.

There was concern as to whether Fukudome and the others had suffered the humiliation of capture; this would be contrary to the principles of the *Senjinkun* (Instructions for the Battlefield), which strictly prohibited surrender on the battlefield. The Navy staff officers discussed at length the possible treatment of Fukudome, rather than focusing on the critical point concerning the temporary loss of the secret documents. Fukudome and the others received no punishment in the end, for the reason that they were caught by the local guerrillas, not by the regular army, therefore they were not official prisoners. The IJN then set about concealing the loss of the secret documents and on his return promoted Fukudome to commander of the 2nd Air Fleet.

This case shows a lack of security mindedness among Navy officers, who did not pay serious attention to lost secret documents, even if that loss was temporary. Ex-Commander Chikataka Nakajima, a communications specialist of the IJN, recollected: "The most serious defect in the code plan of our navy was the lack of consideration about the compromise of code tables and books."[313]

The IJN's conceit that "our codes cannot be broken" severely limited counter-intelligence activities. The Navy had little interest in SIGINT and HUMINT, which resulted in the shortage of funding and personnel for IJN intelligence activities. The number of staff in IJN intelligence work against the United States did not exceed ten until the war started, even though the IJN had regarded the United States as a potential future enemy. The lack of security investment caused not only the loss of secrets, but also poor information exchange with the IJA, which was relatively keen on security.

4

THE ANALYSIS AND EVALUATION OF INTELLIGENCE

THE PROCESS OF ANALYSIS

Regardless of the information collected, it is the process of analysis and evaluation that turns that information into useful intelligence. Albin Coox, an expert on Japanese military history, has explored the inadequacies of the pre-war Japanese analysis system: "The Japanese system of net assessment in the period prior to the attack on Pearl Harbor in 1941 was relatively unsophisticated, parochial, fragmented, adamantine, spasmodic and often vague or waffling to boot."[314] Coox's observation is accurate on Japanese policy making and war planning, but as far as intelligence analysis is concerned, it is not the full picture.

As mentioned above, pre-war information analysis was mainly conducted by the 2nd Department of the Army General Staff in the IJA and the 3rd Department of the Naval General Staff in the IJN. During this period, Japan had no section to synthesize information from the various Intelligence Departments – each intelligence organization collected information and analyzed it unilaterally, then reported the results to the other sections, chiefly to the Operations Department. Saburo Hayashi here comments about the information analysis of the IJA at this time:

When we had judged the reliability of some information, we categorized the accuracy of the information by *Kakudo* (Level of Certainty), which had four levels: *Ko* (certain), *Otsu* (almost certain), *Hei* (a bit uncertain), and *Tei* (uncertain). However, in most cases it was decided by the subjective views of intelligence officers what measure they used to regard information as "certain" and on what basis they evaluated information as "uncertain." The criteria for categorizing the information was as follows: information confirmed by signal intelligence, open source intelligence, and human source intelligence was regarded as *Ko*; information confirmed by two of the three elements was *Otsu*; and information obtained for the first time with analytical context was *Hei* for the time being.[315]

In this description we can see that the work of analyzing and judging information was like assembling puzzles, and the intelligence staff tried to have objective standards for the assembly process.

The Naval General Staff also had its own standard for analysis. When they had to judge whether Japan should occupy northern French Indo-China, their methodology was to compare the merits and demerits of the operation via good intelligence. The process of the analysis will be described below, but generally, the IJN's examination of situations was based on objective standards for collection and analysis of information. So we can argue that the Intelligence Departments of the IJN and IJA did invest in professional analysis; indeed it can be said that the Japanese temperament is very much suited for the steady analysis of information.

Lieutenant Colonel Nobuhiko Imai, who analyzed the US military from the 3rd Department of the Naval General Staff, states on the information analysis of the Naval General Staff: "In those days, our way to derive intelligence could be described as 'intelligence by figures.' We assembled accumulations of every day's detailed news, fully utilizing our skills for mathematical analysis, and analyzing data by arithmetical means."[316] Imai made the following comparison between US and Japanese intelligence analysis techniques:

> They [the US Forces] immediately reported raw news and data that they saw through observation or heard on radio transmissions, unlike our technique: to collect information by various means and to examine the enemy's condition by assembling the information through mathematical means. Although their way of forming intelligence is too simple and direct to be compared with our extremely complicated system, I dare classify the former as "intelligence by power" and the latter as "intelligence by mind."[317]

It would be inappropriate to compare the observation reports of the frontline US units with the information analysis by the Intelligence Department of the IJN General Staff. But at least the IJN had confidence in their information analysis and evaluation techniques. On this point, ex-Captain Yuzuru Sanematsu wrote in more detail. According to him, the IJN intelligence had four steps: 1) collection; 2) evaluation; 3) distillation; 4) judgment. In the second step (evaluation), the intelligence analysts would:

> … examine the value of the materials obtained. In this stage, the "technique" for evaluation was acquired by elaborately analyzing and assembling materials already collected. Moreover, the "eye for intelligence" [in the analyst] would be generated through the repetition of such work. The "technique" and "eye for intelligence" enabled us to select appropriate materials from the mass of information and to evaluate them fairly. The evaluation of materials was basically conducted by senior staff, but even cadets were also able to develop good analytical skills after two years' experience. [318]

The third step, distillation, involved "examining the accuracy of the conclusions by checking them … against the the actual moves of the opponent … As the skill with intelligence work improved by repetition, the errors in the work decreased and we gradually approached the truth." In the last stage, judgment, "the way to approach the truth is the same as the work in the third stage: we examined results by comparing them with the actual operations of the enemy, and checked the cause of any intelligence distortions."

The Navy General Staff made a detailed "Catalog of the Landing Operations of the US Forces" in August 1944 based on information analysis, producing approximate dates for US invasions against Japanese forces. [319] The information and assessents were based on Allied propaganda, the deployments of Allied submarines, SIGINT, open sources describing US operational meetings, the reorganization of the US operational units, major memorial days (there were examples of US operations carried out on some memorial days), weather information, and so on. Where there was no decisive information, the IJN, similar to the IJA, conducted analysis and evaluation of information as elaborate challenges of assembling pieces of information.

THE STATUS OF INTELLIGENCE IN THE ARMY AND NAVY

Security analyst Richard Betts has argued that "a glut of ambiguous data allows intelligence officials linked to operational agencies to indulge a propensity for justifying service performance by issuing optimistic assessments, while analysts in autonomous nonoperational units tend to produce more pessimistic evaluations."[320] This picture is reflected in the reality of Japanese intelligence analysis.

We have already seen how the Army and Navy made efforts to analyze information based on an objective standard. The problem in this effort was a chronic shortage of excellent information analysts and civilian experts. As discussed above, there was a critical need to assemble fragmentary information, so analysts with talent, backed by useful numbers of staff to support their work, were indispensable. Yet Japanese war leaders regarded intelligence as mere information, and considered that intelligence work was a simple matter of passing information from left to right; hence there was no pressing need to allocate many personnel. The problem may have been partly linguistic. The Japanese word *Joho* means both "information" and "intelligence," and the meaning is sometimes vague for Japanese. For operations staff, *Joho* meant "information" and they thought that their job was to gather information or data, such as newspaper clippings. They exaggerated their importance in the IJA and believed that they were capable of analyzing information. On the other hand, for intelligence staff *Joho* meant "intelligence" and they believed that their duty was to analyze information and produce useful intelligence for decision making and war planning. Yet in 1941 there were only 36 staff with a rank above captain in the 2nd Department of the Army General Staff and only 23 in the 3rd Department of the Navy General Staff .[321] Only about 60 staff formed the core of the Japanese intelligence service, which shows the authorities' indifference toward intelligence activities.

Ex-Vice Admiral Minoru Maeda, who served as the chief of the 3rd Department, Navy General Staff, recollected: "Though the 3rd Department formally accounted for a third or fourth of the Navy General Staff, the number of staff was not necessarily enough and not all of the staff were qualified. In fact, it seems that the department was not given much importance in the Navy General Staff."[322] During the war the central intelligence department of the US Army consisted of 168 personnel and the USN 230, and both had almost the same number of civilians; therefore, about 700 people were allocated to intelligence work.[323] Moreover, in Japan few staff settled into work in the field of intelligence, being moved to other departments before they achieved professionalism. Hayashi, the expert in intelligence against the Soviet Union, wrote that:

[During the war] the personnel department officials seemed to have kept the same attitude toward intelligence work as before. Probably, it was because the work seemed easy in the eyes of the layman. Therefore, they allocated second-class officers to the work, many of whom were relieved in two years or so ... In fact, intelligence work may be easy to approach, but it requires at least several years' training to gain a decent level of skill, and has greater depth than operational work. Therefore, the Army General Staff should have allocated more and better officers to the work, vigorously avoided frequent personnel changes, and taken every opportunity to train staff.[324]

Intelligence work is a specialist field with equal importance to, say, the armour and air forces. It requires a special kind of skill together with long experience and professional knowledge. Nevertheless, the logic was not understood in the Army and Navy, and there remained the feeling that intelligence was a temporary post.

This mindset was demonstrated in personnel transfers at the highest levels in the 2nd Department, the Army General Staff. After 1940, the post of chief was occupied variously by French specialist Major General Yuichi Tsuchihashi, German specialists Major General Tadakazu Wakamatsu and Major General Kiyotomi Okamoto, and Italian specialist Major General Seizo Arisue, one after another in only a year, though Arisue stayed in the post for three years to the end of the war. Yet Arisue had served as a staff officer in the Japanese China Army, so that he was not necessarily familiar with British and US affairs. Moreover, though the Army General Staff was preoccupied with the war against the Soviet Union, the last chief of the 2nd Department specializing in the Soviet Union was Major General Toranosuke Hashimoto in 1931.

Looking at this turnover of leadership, it hardly seems that the Army General Staff attached any importance to the 2nd Department. According to Colonel Ichiji Sugita of the 2nd Department: "the post of the chief of the 2nd Department, Army General Staff, was regarded as a sinecure … and was considered as a leisurely post for those who would get important places in the future."[325] In the IJN, too, there were no fewer than five chiefs of the Intelligence Department from 1940 to 1945. After the war, Sugita argued keenly that intelligence officers required professionalism and continuity, stating: "It is necessary to do intelligence work for at least three years."[326]

The IJA and IJN also lacked interest in calling on outside experts for information analysis.[327] Certainly, compromised security is always an issue when using civilian experts in intelligence roles, but the British and Americans depended on civilian knowledge, especially the HUMINT from the universities, to analyze information. For codebreaking and information analysis it is vital to assemble the best brains from various fields such as mathematics and languages. The British intelligence community had its eye on researchers and students of Oxbridge from the earliest days of developed intelligence, and recruited them accordingly.

The fact that British and US intellectuals worked for the military was known to Japan, yet it had no influence on the Army and Navy. They educated their own officers in mathematics and languages, rather than relying on outside talents. Therefore they had little interest in utilizing civilian brains, however talented. For example, while the British respected graduate mathematicians as national assets, Japan sent university students to the frontline as officers.

It wasn't until April 1944 that the IJA finally founded the Military Cryptographic Research Association (also called the Military Mathematical Research Association), asking for cooperation from the mathematicians and linguists of Imperial University of Tokyo. Thus, for most of the war the leading group of the Army and Navy showed little interest in the importance of information analysis, and intelligence personnel were consequently poorly trained. For them, intelligence work meant collecting information such as newspaper or magazine clippings, and they were not familiar with the ideas of analysis and evaluation. It must have been difficult for the military authorities to imagine how keenly intelligence officers collected fragmentary pieces of information and tried to assemble them into a picture. Moreover, the term "intelligence" has a negative meaning for Japanese, even today. This is because the Japanese image of intelligence still remains focused on espionage, within the realm of spies and plots. In Britain and the West in general, "intelligence" literally refers to intellect, providing a level of academic authority.

As seen above, the Intelligence Departments collected considerable amounts of information and tried to process them into useful intelligence. There was no way, however, to compensate for the serious lack of intelligence staff, though there were some intelligence experts in both the Army and Navy General Staff. Besides, the haphazard tendencies to transfer personnel hindered the relevant training of intelligence specialists. In this way, the Intelligence Departments fell into a downward spiral in which an inability to acquire decent intelligence lowered the status of the Intelligence Departments further, so they were supplied with inferior staff.

As a result, the Operations Departments came to distrust reports from the Intelligence Departments, so they turned instead to reports directly from military field operations. Thus, the circulation of information in the Japanese military became more and more distorted. Politicians and war leaders also struggled to obtain timely information, and were sometimes supplied directly with raw information. Therefore, it became impossible for them to make national policy on the basis of precise intelligence.

Nevertheless, pre-war Japan had a kind of central intelligence agency. It was known as the Cabinet Intelligence Department (CID), which originated from the Cabinet Intelligence Committee established in 1936. The Ministry of the Interior, Ministry of Foreign Affairs, and Ministry of Communications, as well as the Ministry of War and the Navy, dispatched staff to the CID, expecting it to work as a central intelligence body. In fact, the CID, headed by Koki Yokomizo, was expected to provide information specifically for the Prime Minister.[328] It was uncomfortable for the IJA and IJN to establish a central intelligence machinery in the Prime Minister's office. They objected to a government plan in August 1940 for the foundation of a new CID by uniting the Intelligence Departments of the Army, Navy, and Ministry of Foreign Affairs.[329] When Chief Yokomizo left the Prime Minister's office in December 1940, the CID was verbally upgraded to the "Intelligence Bureau," but in fact the apparatus was castrated by the military bureaucracy. Eventually, the Intelligence Bureau changed into a mere propaganda organ.

THE ESTRANGEMENT BETWEEN OPERATIONS AND INTELLIGENCE

Within the IJN and IJA, there was a deep-rooted prejudice that the superior staff were chosen for the Operations Departments, while the inferior were placed in the Intelligence Departments – both the Army and Navy placed more importance on operations than intelligence. The 2nd Department first came to deal with intelligence in 1908 after the Russo-Japanese War. Before, the Army General Staff adopted the Prussian system, in which the 1st and 2nd Departments covered both operations and intelligence, working in different areas. Then after 1908, the functions of operations and intelligence were divided into the 1st and 2nd Department respectively.[330]

The "Division of Work for each Department and Section, Army General Staff, December 1908" categorized "collection and examination of internal and external information and military matters attendant on diplomacy" as the duties of the 4th Section of the 2nd Department, and "compilation of inland and outland topography and maps for military use and collection of materials for it" as the responsiblity of the 5th Section. The relationship between the 1st Department as the Operations Department and the 2nd Department as the Intelligence Department still remained unclear.[331]

Although the system was adequate enough for peace time in the Taisho Period, it was significant that the Japanese forces had little experience of the Great War. World War I brought radical changes in many national intelligence systems, and Japan was left behind the international trend.

In the Army General Staff, the Operations Department developed self-righteous operations-centered principles from around 1937, when Major General Kanji Ishiwara became the chief of the 1st Department. He began organizational reform of the General Staff, so that the 1st Department could handle most business of the General Staff, including intelligence matters. Regarding the intelligence work of the 2nd Department as archaic, Ishiwara schemed to weaken the power of the department by reorganizing the structure of the Army General Staff itself.[332]

The workings of intelligence do not work strictly within the military chain of command. The essential point in the intelligence process is the sharing of intelligence up and down the ranks to conduct analysis and evaluation efficiently. However, in the military system, relationships among organizations tend to be vertical relations, therefore there is little room for horizontal coordination between "operations" and "intelligence." For example, in the United States during the 1930s and 1940s, the Army and Navy each had their own Intelligence Departments, but the system hardly worked efficiently. Therefore, they tried to solve the problem by establishing the Director of Central Intelligence (DCI) in 1946, a post with enormous coordinating authority. The British, on the other hand, invested vast energy in creating a laterally cooperative relationship between the intelligence apparatus and others such as policy-making offices and military authorities; that is to say, they emphasized "collegiality."[333] As a result, smooth information sharing was achieved inside the intelligence community and between intelligence organizations and political offices. The British system was based on the idea that "the information must be shared."

In the Japanese case, the structural problem of military-owned intelligence, plus the unenlightened idea of putting more importance on operations, less on intelligence, made it difficult to share information between the Operations and Intelligence Departments with equal status. For instance, in December 1939 the Kwantung Army established "The Committee of Intelligence Experts for the Study of the Nomonhan incident" to review the incident and strengthen the voice of the intelligence community.[334] This attempted to bolster the authority of intelligence not only in the Kwantung Army, but also in the eyes of the Army General Staff and its Operations Department, but such efforts were largely unsuccessful. Rather, the Operation Department's superiority was enlarged in the 1940s. The year 1940 was a time of drastic changes in Japanese policy, including the penetration into French Indo-China and the signing of the Axis alliance, but in the invasion of northern French Indo-China, for example, the Operations Department showed no interest in the judgment of the Intelligence Department. The then Intelligence Department chief was Yuichi Tsuchihashi, the French specialist who had served as a military attaché to France, and he was opposed to the advance into Indo-China. According to his memoir: "We were not allowed to know or try to discover what the 1st Department demanded of Indo-China and what that country replied from July to the end of September."[335] At that time, "The 1st Department of the Army General Staff kept its own intention, which differed from the opinion of the chief and vice chief of the 2nd Department,"[336] and the Operations Department arbitrarily ordered the invasion of Indo-China.

At this time the Army General Staff also held a section study meeting on Southern Operations for the first time, but there was no requirement for information analysis from the Intelligence Department and no request for department staff.[337] Although the Intelligence Department dispatched staff to the Southern Area and also collected information from private companies from the end of 1940, it had no opportunity to be involved in the Operations Department's work in the sector. Moreover, on the outbreak of the Soviet–German War in June 1941, the majority of the Army General Staff expected a rapid German victory. This expectation derived from the subjective view of the Army General Staff, which believed that successive German victories in Europe would be repeated. Yet Hayashi, a specialist in Russian intelligence, argued: "I did not think the Soviet Union would give up soon. The vast distances of the country were a Soviet strength, so that if the Soviets were not beaten by the winter, their forces would revive, I thought." Such a well-judged view attracted no attention from the Operations Department.[338]

Arisue, chief of the 2nd Department during the Pacific War, also recollected: "The 1st Department of the Army General Staff, especially the Operations Section, had a kind of self-righteous atmosphere. They leaked out nothing about operational plans, as well as excluding outside interference with the making of plans, disliking even listening to opinions of others."[339] According to Arisue, it was only once, just before the operation against Imphal in March 1944, that the chief of the Intelligence Department went into the operations room of the Imperial HQ, called by the Operations Department. There, Arisue opposed the operation, only to be ignored.[340]

Ex-Lieutenant General Masatane Kanda, who worked for many SDAs as a specialist in Soviet intelligence and served as the chief of the Military Affairs Department of the Army General Staff, stated:

In the Army General Staff, the relationship between departments of intelligence and operations was traditionally not good. The Operations Department disregarded the opinions of the Intelligence Department. They planned operations based on their own views, sometimes collecting information they needed by themselves. The Operations Department claimed that the work of the Intelligence Department was focused on political information, not supplying the materials required for operations ... But a poor aspect of the Operations Department was that they did not make it clear what information they needed... Therefore, the Intelligence Department gathered information based on guesswork.[341]

Kanda's observations are revealing. Since no intelligence requirement was delivered from the Operations Department to the Intelligence Department, the latter could not know what kind of information they should have supplied, so only rough and irrelevant information was passed over. In consequences, the Operations Department became more doubtful of the abilities of the Intelligence Department.

To break the deadlock, Kanda specially sent Colonel Akio Doi, who used to be the chief of the Operations Department, to the Intelligence Department. Nevertheless, even Doi could not change the relationship between the two departments, as Kanda recollected.[342] Another systemic problem was that the Operations Department could directly obtain information from the field, therefore the relevance of the Intelligence Department declined even more. As a group of the "Best and Brightest" it was enough for the Operations Department to collect information by themselves and elaborate operations based on it. However, the Operations Department tended to select information that suited their strategy and operational aims, producing circular reasoning and decision making. Akio Doi wrote:

The military authorities should have integrated diplomatic, business, and press information and directly reported military information and examined it repeatedly, but this process was not followed often enough. Besides, in the military departments the Operations Department designed the outline of operational planning without exchanging opinions with the departments of intelligence, rear transportation, and communications, insisting on consistency in command and the preservation of secrecy. The Operations Department took only a glance at information supplied by the other departments at best, with selection based on the operations staff's subjective views ... This tendency meant

otting group of the Kwantung Army during the battle of Nomonhan, 1939. (NIDSMA)

crashed Soviet airplane over the Soviet–Manchurian border in December 1937. The Intelligence
ction of the Kwantung Army found letters and documents inside the plane. (NIDSMA)

持情軍極秘

英 1489
外交

昭和15年9月26日　軍令部第十一課 (9455)

佛印側ハ米國ヨリ多量ノ彈藥及飛行機
ヲ購入セント企圖シアルモ之ガ入手ハ
困難ナルベシト

發　英外務大臣　　　　　　9-24-2116 發
宛　駐日英大使　　　　　　　極暗 B12
通報先　上海　重慶　海防　新嘉坡
　　　閔賀　香港　カンベラ
倫敦 (988/22)

1. 兹ニ英大使ガ第2045番電ニテ通報セル所
　ニ依レバ同地佛大使館ト連絡アリト思シキ佛
　印ノ買付密使ハ米政府ニ對シ飛行機約120機
　砲彈1400高彈及宿彈若干ノ賣入方ヲ申入レ
　タリト

2. 米國政府トシテハ佛印總督ガ日本ノ
　侵略ニ抗戰スルヲ支援セント希望シアレド斯
　ル多量ノ彈藥ヲ供給スルコトハ不可能ニシテ
　又飛行機ヲ比德頁ヨリ送附スルコトモ不可能
　ナリ依ッテ15乃至30機ノ老朽英飛行機ヲ

British diplomatic traffic from London to Tokyo decoded by the IJN SIGINT section. The SIGINT helped the Japanese advance into northern Indo-China in September 1940. (NIDSMA).

F 4204/5429/61.

JT FILE 419

DISTRIBUTION "B".

To JAPAN.

Cypher telegram to Sir R. Craigie, (Tokyo).

Foreign Office, 25rd September, 1940.　5 p.m.

No. 988.

In his telegram No. 2045 His Majesty's Ambassador at Washington reported that Indo-China purchasing emissaries with whom French Embassy appear to be conniving had asked United States Government for about 120 aeroplanes, 14,000,00 rounds of S.A.A. and some shells.

2. United States Government wanted to give Governor-General support in resisting Japanese encroachment but could not supply such quantities of ammunition and no aircraft were available from the Phillipine Islands. They have therefore suggested that Australian Government should spare 15 to 20 oldish British machines to be replaced as soon as possible from American stocks. Australian Minister is passing on suggestion to Commonwealth Government but is not hopeful of acceptance.

Repeated to Shanghai No. 995, Chungking No. 117, Haiphong No. 20, Singapore No. 975, Rangoon No. 868, Hong Kong No. 121, His Majesty's High Commissioner, Canberra, No. 311.

The original British diplomatic message from London to Tokyo. (FO 371/24719, National Archives, Kew, UK)

The Koa Agency, which engaged in espionage activities in Southern China and also in Hong Kong, and was stationed at the Hong Kong Hotel. Its central figure was Lieutenant Colonel Yoshimasa Okada, head of the agency. (NIDSMA)

The 2nd Section (Intelligence) of the Kwantung Army.

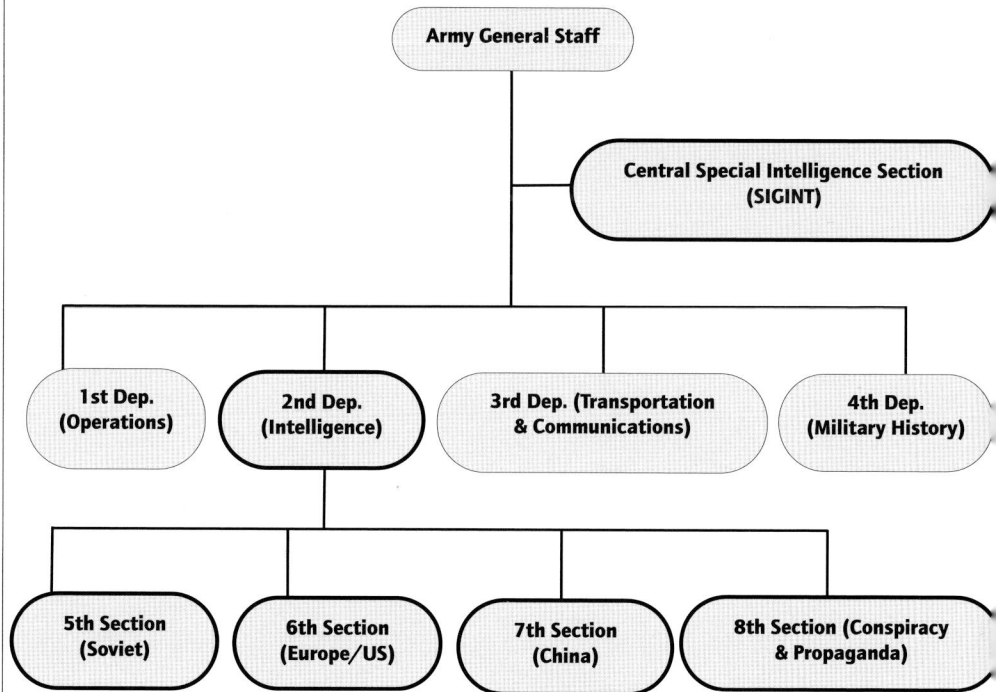

Intelligence organization of the IJA (1941)

Army General Staff

Central Special Intelligence Section (SIGINT)

1st Dep. (Operations)

2nd Dep. (Intelligence)

3rd Dep. (Transportation & Communications)

4th Dep. (Military History)

5th Section (Soviet)

6th Section (Europe/US)

7th Section (China)

8th Section (Conspiracy & Propaganda)

e Army Nakano School. Students are here training in *Kendo* (Japanese fencing).

e 5th Section (Soviet Intelligence) of the Army General Staff.

A US diplomatic message from Washington, D.C., to Tokyo decoded by the IJA SIGINT section. The document was about the *modus vivendi*, but it was decoded on December 1, 1941, after the Japanese Combined Fleet began its sortie to Pearl Harbor.
(JACAR – http://www.jacar.go.jp/english/index.html – Ref. B02030750400)

Jacket cover of the IJA code book. (Rikugun Ango-sho Go Gou, Yasukuni Kaikou Bunko)

A page from the IJA code book. The Army's code was tough to break compared to the Navy's code. (Rikugun Ango-sho Go Gou, Yasukuni Kaikou Bunko)

Officers of the *Tokumu Kikan* (Special Service Agency) in China sometimes engaged in covert operations, disguised as local Chinese. (NIDSMA)

Japanese propaganda placard aimed at Chinese citizens. Japanese soldiers are seen expelling Chiang Kai-shek and the Chinese Communist Party. (NIDSMA)

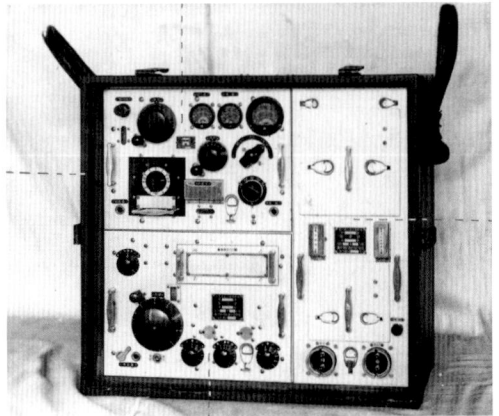

The Army's Type 96 (Version 3) portable radio. (NIDSMA)

Sakada viewing the road to Hong Kong; the road had been destroyed by the British just before the Battle of Hong Kong. (NIDSMA)

Intelligence organization of the IJN (1941)

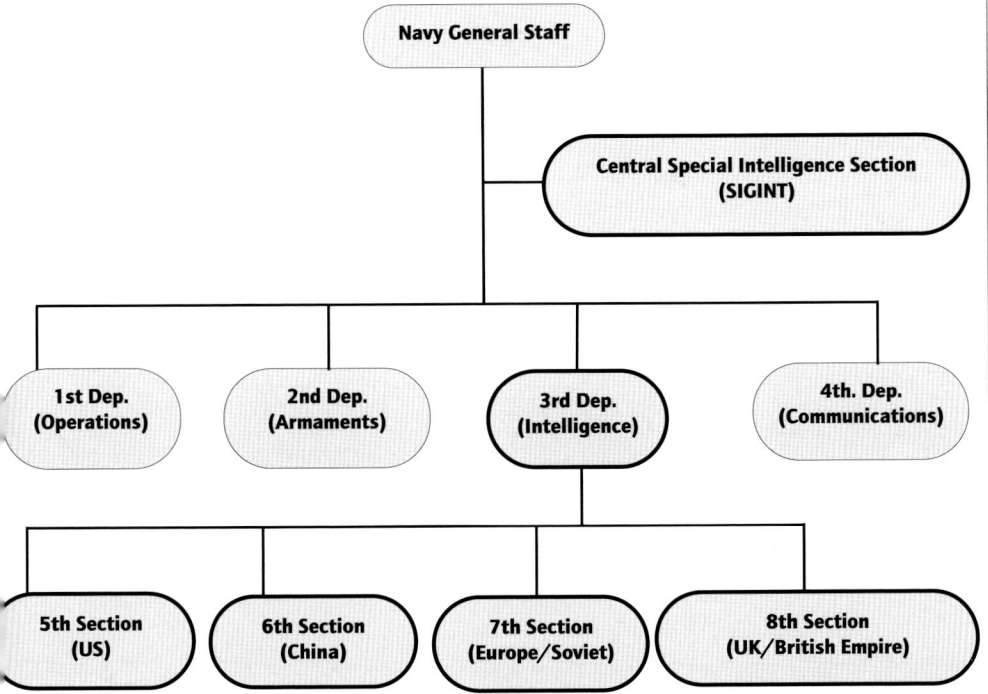

```
                          Navy General Staff

                                    ┌──────────────────────────────────────┐
                                    │  Central Special Intelligence Section  │
                                    │              (SIGINT)                  │
                                    └──────────────────────────────────────┘

  ┌──────────────┬──────────────┬──────────────┬──────────────┐
  1st Dep.        2nd Dep.        3rd Dep.        4th. Dep.
  (Operations)    (Armaments)     (Intelligence)  (Communications)

              ┌──────────────┬──────────────┬──────────────┐
           5th Section     6th Section    7th Section      8th Section
           (US)            (China)        (Europe/Soviet)  (UK/British Empire)
```

Intelligence organization of the Kwantung Army (1941)

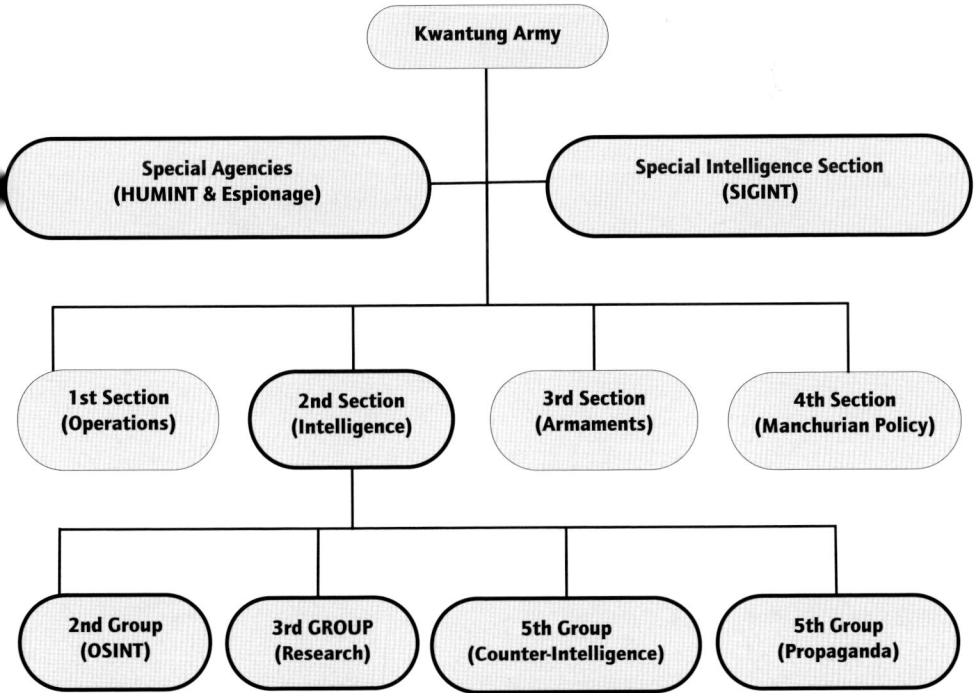

```
                          Kwantung Army

  ┌──────────────────────────────┐      ┌──────────────────────────────┐
  │   Special Agencies            │      │  Special Intelligence Section  │
  │   (HUMINT & Espionage)        │      │            (SIGINT)            │
  └──────────────────────────────┘      └──────────────────────────────┘

  ┌──────────────┬──────────────┬──────────────┬──────────────┐
  1st Section     2nd Section     3rd Section     4th Section
  (Operations)    (Intelligence)  (Armaments)     (Manchurian Policy)

              ┌──────────────┬──────────────┬──────────────┐
           2nd Group       3rd GROUP      5th Group        5th Group
           (OSINT)         (Research)     (Counter-Intelligence)  (Propaganda)
```

1

2

3

4

5

6

7

8

9

1. Officers of the Kempei (Military Police), seen overseas.

2. Lieutenant General Sadaaki Kagesa: Chin specialist of the IJA and the first chief of the Conspiracy Section established in 193 Later he worked as a military adviser to th Wang Chao-ming government.

3. Lieutenant General Hyakutake Haruyoshi: one of the IJA's pioneering codebreakers. He took lessons in codebreaking from experts in Poland.

4. Lieutenant General Akira Muto: chief of the Bureau of Military Affairs, War Ministry, at the beginning of the Pacific conflict. He was sentenced to death after the war.

5. General Motojiro Akashi: famous Army intelligence officer, who was active in Europe during the Russo-Japanese War.

6. General Hideki Tojo: the War Minister and Prime Minister during much of World War II. He was sentenced to death after the war.

7. Admiral Isoroku Yamamoto: commander-in-chief of the IJN Combined Fleet and the mind behind the Pearl Harbor operation. He died when the aircraft he was traveling in was shot down by a US fighter ambush on April 14, 1943.

8. Yosuke Matsuoka: Foreign Minister from (1940–41) and a signatory of the Tripartite pact with Germany and Italy.

9. Major General Akikusa Shun: IJA specialist in Soviet intelligence. He was a head of the Nakano School and Intelligence Chief of the Kuwantong Army. Shun was captured by the Soviets and died in Vladimir prison after the war.

they largely misjudged international affairs and the progress of the war in each period of operational planning ...[343]

During the opening Japanese battles of the Pacific War, known as the Southern Operation, advance information gathering was conducted reasonably efficiently, though without the analytical activities of the Intelligence Department. In December 1940 the IJA established a core intelligence organization for the Southern Operation – the Taiwan Military Research Institution (MRI) in the HQ of Taiwan. The main topics studied there included combat tactics during the Southern Operation, military affairs in Asian countries, topography, and hygiene and the prevention of epidemics.[344] The institution analyzed information gathered from HUMINT across Southeast Asia, and local public and private organs such as the Taiwanese government, Taiwan University, and the Southern Association, which conducted research on the Southern Area for more than ten years. Because the MRI was founded under the direction of the 1st Department, Army General Staff, the relationship with the 2nd Department was not so good.[345]

This kind of problem was seen not only at the central level, but also in units. Koutani criticized the operations planners of the Kwantung Army for ignoring estimations of enemy movements by the Intelligence Department, and developed autonomous operations during the Nomonhan incident.[346] Moreover, in 1942, there arose a situation in which the Southern Army's intelligence section was absorbed into its operations section.

The IJA's indifference toward intelligence was also directed to the most sophisticated intelligence training apparatus, the Army Nakano School. No matter how excellent the performance of the school, it declined gradually in the hostile culture.[347] Fundamentally, in most cases, people not in the field of intelligence cannot analyze and evaluate information correctly. In particular, the most crucial misjudgment seems to have been the conclusion of the Tripartite Treaty (the military alliance between Germany, Japan, and Italy, signed in September 1940). At that time, the Ministry of Foreign

Affairs, the Army, and also the Navy rushed together into the agreement with the attitude of "Don't miss the boat!" Kiichiro Higuchi, chief of the 2nd Department, explained the Army mentality toward intelligence that prevailed at the time: "The major aim of information gathering is 'to investigate the reality of facts objectively.' However, the Japanese like subjective views ... Matters can depend on individuals for personal issues, but as for national affairs, it is most dangerous to employ personal and subjective judgments."[348]

Kanda wrote that only in planning the strategy against Soviet Union did the Operations and Intelligence Departments cooperate with each other.[349] On the one hand, this was because strategy making against the Soviet Union was an urgent issue; on the other, it can be said that the Operations Department trusted the Intelligence Department as far as the Soviets were concerned, since the IJA invested considerable efforts in Soviet intelligence, so they had Soviet specialists and real ability to collect and analyze Soviet information. Generally, however, the Operations Department paid little attention to the Intelligence Department. It is true that the Intelligence Department's reports included a lot of mere enumeration of open sources, which anyone could collect. However, intelligence work is fundamentally about collecting fragmentary information which can initially appear meaningless, and extracting effective intelligence from it. The steady hand required for such work, however, was not appealing to the Operations Department, therefore the department selected raw information likely to fit conveniently with their own activities.

Such situations were seen in the IJN as well. A clear example is the Japanese advance into northern French Indo-China, the details of which will be discussed in the next chapter. In this case, the whole process of the intelligence cycle was concluded in the Operations Department. Operations staff directly collected information from SIGINT, HUMINT, and press sources, analyzed it themselves, and finally drew up a plan for advancing into French Indo-China based on their own analysis.

When war planners or policy makers dealt with intelligence, they tended to make the intelligence fit with their aims. For example, in April 1944, the

Naval Intelligence Department had estimated that the US forces' next target for invasion would be Saipan and the other islands of the Marianas, and that the invasion would be in May to June. The estimation was accurate, but the Operations Department generally felt that the US forces would capture the Philippines and advance to northern New Guinea and the West Caroline Islands, disregarding the estimation of the Intelligence Department, which turned out to be correct. Rear Admiral Tasuku Nakasawa, chief of the Operations Department, recollected: "I thought the United States would come to the Marianas, but not as early as June." Major Chikao Yamamoto, chief of the 1st Section, Operations Department, concurred: "We knew that the the US forces would come to the Marianas, but never thought they would come that early."[350]

Another mishandling of intelligence occurred in the air battle of October 12–16, 1944, off Taiwan, which preceded the battle of Leyte Gulf. Although the Japanese Air Force suffered major losses in this battle, the Imperial HQ (via the Operation Department) swallowed an overestimated report of kills from the frontline and officially announced the claims: 19 US aircraft carriers sunk (in fact, only 17 US air carriers participated in the battle) plus four battleships. The announcement filled the Japanese nation with joy. If the results had been true, the US aircraft carrier force in the west Pacific would have been almost annihilated, yet in fact no aircraft carrier was sunk. The exaggeration was caused by reports from inexperienced pilots and by commanders who neglected the need to confirm such reports. Furthermore, the traffic interception records and war situation reports of the SIS demonstrated that both the aircraft carriers and battleships of the enemy were safe.[351] Staff officers such as Vice Admiral Shigeru Fukudome, commander-in-chief of the 2nd Air Fleet, did not take the reports at face value, and felt that Japanese Air Force had sunk four or five aircraft carriers at most. Such estimations led to the launch of the *Sho Ichi Go* operation, which was regarded as the decisive fleet battle between the US and Japan. Initially buoyed by overconfidence, the IJN suffered devastating losses off Leyte.[352]

It is likely that the gross over-estimation of US losses arose from the need to launch a decisive battle against the USN, the *Sho Ichi Go* operation. Staff officers probably had the impression that the operation could not go ahead if the US aircraft carriers were all safe; in other words, it could proceed only if some carriers were sunk by the Japanese attack.

Compared to the Operations Department's estimation, the Naval Intelligence Department was careful to judge the results of the Taiwan air battle. Captain Yuzuru Sanematsu, senior intelligence staff officer in the IJN, recollected: "At the very least, we had concluded that no aircraft carrier or battleship was sunk."[353] But in the usual way, such judgments of the Intelligence Department received no attention. Ex-Captain Atsushi Oi, staff officer of the Combined Fleet, described the situation at that time:

> The Chief [of the 5th Section, the 3rd Department, Navy General Staff, Captain Kaoru Takeuchi] and a senior staff officer [Sanematsu] talked excitedly and at length. "The staff of the Operations Department are inexcusable. Totally disregarding our opinion, they insist that the US task force was routed. They are insane! It's unbelievable that the insane officers have their own way ..." They took the opportunity to vent their anger against the Operations Department, which always neglected our intelligence.[354]

The disagreement between the Operations and Intelligence Departments reached its peak as the war approached the final stage. The Operations Department calculated the US military strength on the basis of exaggerated frontline reports, as seen in the case of Leyte Gulf. On the other hand, the Intelligence Department produced intelligence based on SIGINT and OSINT in the United States, therefore the department's estimation of the scale of the US Forces was always larger than that of the Operations Department. The Intelligence Department's judgment of situations was not utilized because the negative report would have had a bad influence on the morale of the Army and Navy.[355] When the Intelligence Department reported more realistic estimations of the results of the *kamikaze* suicide attacks, the

Operations Department staff made the following criticism: "Although staff of the Intelligence Department were not in the operation room nor in the battle, they try to refute the estimation of operations staff. That's unforgivable."[356]

By following naval SIGINT, it was not difficult to determine whether an aircraft carrier or battleship had been sunk. If it became clear that the "sunk" vessel was still moving, the mistake would have been obvious. According to the Operations Department's judgments, the US carrier *Lexington* was sunk six times, and the *Saratoga* four times. The judgments were so loose that the Emperor Hirohito complained to Admiral Koshiro Oikawa, the Naval Chief of Staff, that "this is the fourth report of *Saratoga*'s sinking to the best of my memory."[357]

THE ROLE OF THE INTELLIGENCE DEPARTMENT

As the Operations Departments dealt with information directly and unilaterally, not listening to the reports from the Intelligence Departments, what was expected of the Intelligence Departments? Of course, it was the collection of information. That is to say, the task of the Intelligence Departments was to store materials for operational planning by clipping and translating foreign newspapers in order to support the Operations Departments' "information analysis and evaluation." Although the original role of the Intelligence Departments ought to have been collecting and analyzing domestic and foreign information, the realm of analysis slid to the Operations Departments.

During the Japanese advance into northern French Indo-China, the IJA Intelligence Department existed only to pass on the reports from military attachés abroad and SIGINT from the SIS, not being required to analyze information and to report the results. Fundamentally, the Intelligence Department, which should have collected information and processed it into intelligence data, was not expected to perform such a role.

In terms of naval intelligence, Rear Admiral Saburo Horinouchi stated that "The 3rd Department exercised very little influence on other divisions

107

and bureau in the Naval General Staff and the Navy Ministry. Although everybody recognized the importance of military intelligence, quite often the valuable intelligence that we offered was treated in a perfunctory way or even ignored."[358] Captain Yuzuru Sanematsu also recollected: "The IJN in wartime was one of the most indifferent forces toward intelligence. Except for the Pearl Harbor operation at the beginning of the war, the Intelligence Department was of no importance."[359] Both of them complained about the severe snub the Intelligence Department suffered at the hands of the IJN.

Thus, the position of the Intelligence Department in the IJN was not high, and considering its sophisticated information-gathering ability, as seen in *Toku-jo* units, it was a waste of talent. The relations between the naval Operations Department and Intelligence Department became one of estrangement. Commander Nobuhiko Imai wrote: "Except for the chief and Captain Sanematsu, there was no connection with the Operations Department."[360]

In sum, the status of the Intelligence Departments in the IJA and IJN was almost the same. Both of them were treated perfunctorily and discriminated against by the Operations Departments. In addition, there was no communication between the Army and Navy Intelligence Departments, though they were in similar roles. For that reason, although the codebreaking section of the IJA succeeded in breaking the Strip Ciphers, they did not share the method of deciphering with the IJN. Moreover, it is said that the Army General Staff were angry when the Army codebreaking section provided the method of breaking the US mechanical codes to the NID. The story shows the serious sectionalism between the Army and Navy.[361] Under these circumstances, it was difficult for the Intelligence Departments of the Army and Navy to cooperate with each other in their intelligence activities.

Another problem was the uneven flow of raw information and processed information (intelligence). The Intelligence Departments could not control the flow of the two types of the information and sometimes raw information was directly reported to the senior officers. Much raw information was then supplied to policy makers, to whom it made no sense if it was out of their specialty or didn't fit with their intentions. To utilize sensitive information effectively, it should be reported in a timely fashion to the appropriate departments, something neither the IJA nor the IJN were good at.

Toward the end of the war, the Army General Staff came to rely on the *Ha Toku Cho* (Harbin Special Information) from Harbin in North China for information on the southwest Pacific. The source of information was the Soviet consular office in Harbin, although the Soviet Intelligence Section of the Kwantung Army judged that it was contaminated by Soviet counter-intelligence measures. Soviet-intelligence expert Colonel Koutani explained that:

> Around the time of the Nomonhan incident of 1939, we had noticed it [the Harbin Special Information] was sown with false information by the Soviets. Nevertheless, we carefully continued the intelligence operation to unearth the "true information" that was mingled with the false information ... However, once the *Ha Toku Cho* was reported by the Harbin Army SDA, it was classified as "top secret" and tended to attract the attention of other officers. As a result, for those who did not know the details, except for the Russian Section of the Army General Staff, the information was easily misunderstood as signals intelligence.[362]

In this way, though the Harbin Special Information was false information in the eyes of the intelligence experts, it became top secret and "true" when it was passed to the other departments. Such was a terrible misuse of the raw data.

SIGINT is also misleading or partial when it is just intercepted and decoded. However decisive it looks, it is mere raw data. SIGINT turns into genuine intelligence only after being processed through comparison with the HUMINT and document intelligence, but the point was not understood very well by the Army and Navy. During the 1930s and the wartime period, it is likely that only the Intelligence Departments of the IJA and IJN comprehended the true meaning of "intelligence," i.e. analyzed and processed information. For the Operations Departments, by contrast, intelligence was equated with raw data. For them, the Intelligence Departments were just for collecting data, and the operations staff simply cherry-picked data for operational planning. Thus, the origin of the rivalry between the Intelligence and Operations Departments revolved around a core difference in the understanding of "intelligence," and when a conflict occurred between them it was certain that the Operations Departments would push through their viewpoint, utilizing their more authoritative position in Japanese military thinking.

As seen in the *Jokyo Handan Shiryo* (Situation Estimate Document) which remains today, a summary of the vast amount of raw information collected was reported to the Operations Departments almost every day.[363] If the information had been extracted and processed by the Intelligence Department before being reported to the Operations Department, the development of the Pacific War might have changed just a little. For example, if the real outcome of the air battle before Leyte Gulf had been made clear, the *Sho Ichi Go* might not have gone ahead, with all the implications that would have had for the Pacific conflict.

By contrast, Britain established the Joint Intelligence Committee (JIC) as a dam for controlling the intelligence flow. Admittedly, Prime Minister Winston Churchill made the intelligence organizations report raw information to him every day, but Churchill had the personal ability to digest such data. The horizontal cooperative relationship among organizations and the sharing of intelligence are essential for efficient intelligence handling.[364] However, it was difficult to achieve this goal in Japan because of the compartmentalized structure of the forces. The problem was exacerbated by the fact that the IJA and IJN did not conduct systematic information gathering very much. In an environment in which intelligence work was so inconspicuous, with few opportunities for promotion and frequent personnel transfers (even of intelligence specialists), it is natural that there were only a few eager persons who engaged in intelligence work seriously. Both the Army and Navy gave no consideration to intelligence as a long-term career path, and regarded intelligence duty as a temporary post. Eventually, intelligence activities became the work of individuals, to which other departments would pay no attention.

5

PRE-WAR AND EARLY WAR INTELLIGENCE ON ENEMY FORCES

THE ALLIES' IMAGE OF JAPANESE FORCES

From the Japanese point of view, the tactical success at the beginning of the Pacific War largely depended on their skillful operations based on tactical use of intelligence. By contrast, recent intelligence studies in Britain and the United States have revealed that Allied defeats were in large part caused by their neglecting to gather intelligence on the IJA and IJN. Their ethnocentrism also distorted their images of Japan.[365] Major H. P. Thomas, OBE, reflected on the fall of Singapore and made a report in May 1942 as follows:

> As an Asiatic power, maintaining a European standard of efficiency and at the same time operating on Asiatic soil, the Japanese had a great initial advantage, apart from almost complete command in the air, greatly superior numbers on the ground, and tanks. In addition, and unexpectedly, the Japanese gained freedom for their convoys at sea by destroying our two capital ships.
>
> It was soon clear that this campaign had been planned in detail, troops specially trained for it, and best types of equipment provided. The inhabitants in the mass were, at best, a hindrance to us – at the worst, a help to the enemy. Japanese topographical knowledge was exact and up-to-date, and his day to day information of our movements very complete.
>
> Equally disastrous in its consequence and incredible in its inaccuracy was our estimate of the Japanese Army and Air Force. Presumably observers based their opinions on inferior units seen during the early fighting in China, or through a misunderstanding of the real nature of the war in China concluded that failure to subdue the Chinese was due to a low standard of training and efficiency.[366]

Before the Pacific War, the British underestimated the fighting capabilities of the IJA and IJN. MI2c (the British Military Intelligence Section dealing with East Asia) reported: "The Japanese Army is a formidable fighting machine but probably has not reached yet the efficiency of the major western armies. It is however, trained for and will probably only be required to fight in East Asia where it will have inherent advantage over an opponent."[367] The British generally treated the IJA as second-class army, because it was trained to fight against Chinese troops. Lieutenant P. M. Johnson estimated that Japanese artillery had approximately 80 percent and the Japanese infantry 70 percent efficiency when compared to a first-class modern army. He wrote: "They [the Japanese] are still inclined to think gallant infantry can win a modern war ..."[368]

Before the war, the British Naval Intelligence Division (NID) estimated that the IJN possessed ten battleships and ten aircraft carriers in Far Eastern waters, and this estimate was almost accurate. Yet the RN sent only two battleships to the Far East and the NID believed such to be sufficient. In 1935, Colonel J. G. P. Vivian, naval attaché to Japan, wrote a private letter to the NID pronouncing judgment upon the Japanese Navy: "The lack of command experience at sea of the more senior officers must be a serious handicap to fighting efficiency. I cannot believe that the system is capable of producing really efficient ships companies for war purposes, especially for the smaller classes of ships ... I think, that the IJN is of the 2nd class ..."[369] Vivian's report was not based on his observation of the IJN, but his subjective viewpoint. But the NID had no other choice but to accept his report, because the IJN's tight security prevented further British information gathering in Japan. Therefore the RN could not update Vivian's assessment during the run-up to the war. Admiral Sir Henry Moore later wrote: "We grossly underestimated the power and efficiency of the Japanese naval surface and air forces. This may have been due both to lack of intelligence and to a faulty assessment of what we had."[370] The NID also accepted poor appraisals of the IJN, as "the Japanese Navy is believed to be at a lower standard than in our ships ..."[371] A NID report gave numerically inferior RN fleets combat superiority by judging the IJN negatively from a qualitative point of view.

The stereotyped image of the IJN was generally widespread, not only in Britain but also in US naval circles. The US naval attaché to Japan, Lieutenant Commander Smith-Hutton, obtained information through his Japanese friend that the IJN had developed a new type of oxygen-propelled torpedo with a 1,200lb warhead and capable of traveling 10,000 yards at a speed of 45 knots. He sent a report describing the torpedo's performance to the Office of Naval Intelligence (ONI) on April 20, 1940, but his senior and technical experts could not believe such performance data.[372] The torpedo would be later known as Type 93 (Long Lance), which heavily damaged US cruisers in the battle of Tassafaronga in November 1942.

The RN also underestimated Japanese airpower, as "Japanese aircraft show little superiority to our present equipment and are likely to be distinctly inferior to aircraft now in course of production."[373] The Air Intelligence Directorate reported: "Reference has recently been made in this summary to the low operational effectiveness of the Japanese air force as compared with British standards and the probability that it does not exceed that of the Italian air force. This is due not only to the inferiority of performance but also to the probability that among their first line squadrons are some equipped with obsolete aircraft."[374] Japanese pilots were believed not to be able to control their aircraft well because of their hearing problems and squinty eyes. Such ethnic stereotyping was shared between Britain and the United States, causing a dramatic underestimation of Japan.

In 1940, Japan's latest fighter plane, the Mitsubishi A6M "Zero," went into action over China and on September 13, 1940, 13 Zeros shot down 27 Chinese aircraft without a loss. However, information on the Zero did not reach the Air Intelligence Directorate nor the Air Ministry in London, contributing to heavy RAF losses in the battle of Malaya from December 1941. The official history of the RAF explains: "The Japanese had made use of the Navy Zero against the Chinese in the spring of 1940. Some details of its performance had been divulged by American Newspapers ... this information was duly forwarded to the FECB [Far Eastern Combined Bureau] for transmission to the Air HQ. It never arrived there ... The result was a disastrous surprise causing many casualties to pilots who had been informed that the Buffalos they were flying were faster and better than any Japanese fighter ..."[375]

The US forces also had a similar chance to know about Zeros. Claire Chennault, leader of the American Volunteer Group in China known as the "Flying Tigers," delivered information on Zeros to Washington, D.C., but the American military did not learn of the existence of the Zeros until the Japanese Pearl Harbor operation.[376] Even after the attack, there were unfounded rumours that Japanese aircraft were flown by veteran German pilots.

There were several reasons for the Allied underestimation of Japan. As we have seen, tight Japanese security prevented covert activities, and policy makers and war planners in London and Washington largely depended on reports from inadequate diplomatic sources. The lack of Japanologists, and the distance between the West and Japan, also encouraged ethnic stereotypes in political circles in London and Washington. The Allied leaders believed that the IJA and IJN were second-class forces. The British military attaché to Tokyo wrote: "The Japanese are a slow-thinking and naturally cautious people. This applies especially to the Army, in which the officer class is still very largely bound by tradition."[377]

The indifference to Japan and lack of information encouraged ethnic bias. Air Marshal Robert Brooke-Popham, commander-in-chief of the British Forces, Far East, commented on Japanese troops when he visited Hong Kong in December 1940: "I had a good close-up, across the barbed wire, of various sub-human specimens dressed in dirty grey uniform, which I was informed were Japanese soldiers."[378] The British sense of superiority or ethno-centrism militated against the intelligence assessment and strategic planning process in the Far East.

THE IJA'S IMAGE OF THE ALLIED FORCES

Through the inter-war period, the IJA's hypothetical and real opponents had been the Soviet Union and China, and in 1940 they added Britain to the list. For the IJA, the Chinese Army was simply regarded as "clay-brained yokel without any culture" or "as quality iron can never be a box nail, a good man can never be a [Chinese] soldier."[379] The IJA was often indifferent to discovering a true picture of the Chinese Army, especially the Chinese Communist Army (the Eighth Route Army). According to Lieutenant Colonel Shigesaburo Yamazaki, staff officer in the North China Area Army, the China Intelligence Section of the IJA and the Kwantung Army made no attempt to study the CCP during the Sino-Japanese War and on only three occasions did the phrase "Chinese Communist Party" appear in the Army official paper between 1937 and 1945.[380] The IJA's scornful assessment of China was one of the reasons that they were bogged down in eight years of battle there.

As we have seen, the IJA was preoccupied with the Soviet Union, and they concentrated on analyzing the Russian Red Army. The Russian Army was regarded as a great menace for the IJA and the Kwantung Army, and was positively appraised: "The Russians have fought well against overwhelming German forces and it is surprising that they have not lost their fighting spirit. We had thought that the Russian Army was flawed in solidarity and in the efficiency of their organization, but the disadvantage was not seen in the Russo-German war."[381] "Fighting spirit" or "aggressiveness" was an important concept for the IJA's assessment of foreign powers, and from this point of view, the Russians were a formidable opponent for Japan.

Russian industrial power was also evaluated in the IJA. Major Seiichi Niimi, who engaged in information-gathering activities in Germany and the Baltic States, reported: "The Soviet Union is mighty in the military and also the industrial fields. Compared with the age of the Russo-Japanese War (1904–1905), more or less, the power gap between Japan and Russia is widening ..."[382] The IJA had already learnt about the toughness and fighting prowess of the Russian Army in several border conflicts during the 1930s (such as Nomonhan).

In early 1940, the IJA studied that possibility of war against the British in Malaya and started to investigate the British garrisons in Malaya and Singapore. The record of the Army General Staff HQ shows that their general assessment of the garrisons was largely negative because of they were composite British, Australian, Indian, and Malayan forces. Each nationality was rated as follows:

[British:] No matter what they do, they are just colonial garrisons. We have watched their training scenarios; their performance is not good. But their endurance in defensive battle is significant. In case of war with us, most of them will engage in defense of Singapore, and we will not face them in Malayan field battles.

[Australian:] Their quality is bad. The troops are composed chiefly of jobless men and rough individuals. They are not a well-disciplined army. Their valor in battle is famous, but their training and equipment are not adequate.

[Indian and Malayan troops:] Fundamentally they are not hostile to Japan, and many of them are anti-British. Indians are composed of various tribal clans, and it seems difficult for the British rulers to control them. They can fight well in frontal defense battles, but they are weak in mobile warfare. Once we can sneak around back of them, they will be vulnerable to blows from behind.[383]

The IJA also evaluated the RAF: "British pilots are not bad, and some of their aircraft are first class, but their training is inadequate." The IJA concluded that the colonial garrisons were less well trained and their tactical thinking was primarily defensive[384] – for the IJA, the word "defensive" had a negative image. Their image of the Russians, by contrast, was of an offensive army.

The Army General Staff HQ published 400,000 copies of a text entitled *Koredake Yomeba Ikusa wa Kateru* (Surefire Method of Winning the War), distributed to many soldiers at the beginning of the Pacific War. The text again denigrates the British: "Compared with Chinese forces, the Allied forces have weaker solidarity. Their officers are Westerners and the soldiers are native Asians. They are mechanized with aircraft, tanks, and artillery, but their fighting sprit is very poor."[385] The Japanese positively evaluated individual British soldiers, but regarded whole formations as ineffective because of ethnic disunity. The IJA had already sent 11 divisions to Manchuria and 27 divisions to China, and had 13 uncommitted divisions remaining. It was very difficult for the IJA to fight the British, Americans, and Dutch with such limited forces, therefore during the 1920s and much of the 1930s the IJA had the idea of "UK–US separation," which meant that in the case of an Anglo-Japanese war, the US would not declare war on Japan. The IJA worked on the supposition that there would be a war against only the British in Southeast Asia.

The consequence was that the IJA's had only a vague image of US capabilities. They believed that war with the United States was the IJN's remit, and they were not interested in the US garrisons in the Philippines. They believed that "Americans are individualistic and they cannot stand a long-drawn-out war."[386] Their information deficit was filled with subjective imagination, which informed the IJA's operations at the beginning of the Pacific War. The Army General Staff HQ reported on the US forces in the Philippines: "Americans have suffered physically and mentally from the tropical climate. Native soldiers are used to the climate, but their quality is negligible."[387] The IJA rated the US garrisons in the Philippines as second class because they lacked fighting spirit. Even in March 1943, after the battle of Guadalcanal where the IJA was severely defeated by the US forces, Major General Kenryo Sato, Chief of the Bureau of Military Affairs made a speech in the Diet: "As far as the US tactics and strategy are concerned, their technique is amateurish and lacks discipline ... They are good at shooting, but their fighting spirit and morale are very poor ... Most US soldiers do not understand why they are fighting."[388]

One of the main reasons for the Army's long-term indifference to the United States was that they were seriously planning a fight with the Soviets, even after the Pearl Harbor attack. According to the Army's plan, the Pacific War was expected to end by spring 1942, and then they would commence hostilities against the Russians. On January 14, 1942, the Operations Department, Army General Staff HQ, informed the Kwantung Army that they would allocate four more divisions to Manchuria by March 1942 when the Kwantung Army had planned to wage a war against the Soviets.[389]

When Emperor Hirohito visited the Army War College at the end of 1943, he said to the chief aide-de-camp: "I have mixed feelings about the college's educational tendency to attach too much importance to the Soviet Union, although we are fighting with the United States."[390] Now the IJA finally began full-scale studies and information gathering on the United States, but it was too late. Colonel Shinobu Takayama, operations staff, Army General Staff, reflected on his experience: "We should have researched US power and her state of affairs before the war ..."[391] The IJA had been influenced by Sun Tzu's maxim in his *Art of War*, "If you know the enemy and know yourself, you need not fear the result of a hundred battles" – the problem was they simply did not know the enemy.

THE IJN'S IMAGE OF THE ALLIED FORCES

While the IJA focused on the morale of the Allied forces, the IJN tried to assess their enemies from objective and numerical points of view. The IJN's primary on-paper opponents throughout the 1930s were the USN and the RN. In 1941, the IJN fleet was composed of ten battleships, ten aircraft carriers, 28 cruisers, 112 destroyers, and 65 submarines (totaling 980,000 tons) and 3,300 aircraft. The IJN assessed the scale of the USN fleet as 17 battleships, eight aircraft carriers, 37 cruisers, 172 destroyers, and 111 submarines (totaling 1.4 million tons) and 5,500 aircraft. Compared with the USN, the IJN had only 70 percent of the American naval tonnage.[392] After 1941 the gap between the IJN and USN widened on the back of the superior US shipbuilding capability. According to the IJN's estimation, the ratio of Japanese to American ships would decline to 50 percent in 1943 and 30 percent in 1944.[393]

Aircraft production was an even greater issue for the IJN. It was estimated that under war conditions the IJN would possess 12,000 aircraft, while the USN would have more than 100,000. Therefore, the IJN concluded that the best moment for attack on the United States would be 1941. It is a famous story that Prime Minister Fumimaro Konoe asked Admiral Isoroku Yamamoto, the Chief of the Combined Fleet, about the chances of winning a US–Japanese war, and Yamamoto answered: "If I am told to fight ... I shall run wild for the first six months ... but I have absolutely no confidence for the second or third year."[394] Konoe seemed to misunderstand Yamamoto's words as saying that the IJN could beat the USN in a one-year war, but Yamamoto's real meaning was that the IJN would lose after fighting a war lasting several years.

Captain Tasuku Nakazawa, the Operations Department Chief of Navy General Staff, wrote the following about a war with American and Britain: "We have no chance to win the war. War games resulted in heavy losses in shipping and the loss of control of overseas lanes and lines of communication. If we wage a long, drawn-out war, we will not have any means to bring the United States and United Kingdom to terms."[395] The Operations Department, the center of naval war planning, already recognized that they could not beat Allied fleets in war, and many regular Navy officers came to the same conclusion. It was ridiculous for the IJN to declare a war on the United States, but there remained a possibility that the Americans would provoke a war against Japan.

In February 1941, the NID reported: "After 1944, the US Navy would be confident of victory against Japan in case of war. The US can be expected to take a hard-line attitude toward Japan, even threatening military conflict."[396] The IJN's nightmare scenario was as follows: the gap between US and Japanese military and industrial power widens dramatically and Japan's oil stockpile runs dry after 1942; Japan is therefore obliged to bow to American diplomatic demands, such as the Japanese withdrawal from Manchuria and from the Tripartite Pact, the foundations of Japanese foreign policy.

The Japanese oil stockpile was a serious problem. In June 1941, Captain Shingo Ishikawa, Chief of the 2nd Section, Bureau of Naval Affairs in the Navy Ministry, produced a report entitled *Genjo Sekai ni Oite Teikoku Kaigun no Torubeki Taido* (The IJN's Strategy in the Current International Situation). The report estimated that Japan's oil stockpile was about 620 million barrels, which would be consumed in one to two years.[397] More than 80 percent of Japanese oil imports depended on the United States, but these imports were banned in August 1941. Put simply, Japan would run out of oil by the end of 1943.

The IJN's conclusion was as follows – if Japan could not avoid a clash with the United States, an earlier war would be better, especially within 1941. In the event of war with the United States, the IJN should wage a short, fast war.

Admiral Yamamoto found a tactical solution to the strategic problems – a surprise attack on Pearl Harbor. From the strategic point of view, the operation depended on two factors: one was a German victory in Europe and Russia, and the other was the spread of war weariness throughout the United States. Yet Yamamoto's idea lacked strategic perspective. The German Army failed to take Moscow just about the time of the Pearl Harbor operation, and US public opinion was energized by Japan's "sneaky attack on Pearl Harbor." Yamamoto had certainly intended the attack to be a surprise, but also that it should follow a formal declaration of war. However, diplomatic delays resulted in the late delivery of this declaration.[398] Although the IJN betted on German victory and wilting US public opinion, they conducted no research on German military capabilities and made no attempt to execute propaganda campaigns in the United States – the IJN depended on much wishful thinking in their strategy.

In comparison to the USN, the IJN's view of the RN was more optimistic. The scale of the RN Far East Fleet was limited by the war with Germany. According to Japanese estimation, the RN had stationed two battleships, five cruisers, ten destroyers, and 336 aircraft in Far Eastern waters.[399] Originally the RN had been a big brother for the IJN and the IJN's estimation of the RN was very high, especially regarding her traditions and discipline. But in 1941 Captain Kan'ei Chudo, the Chief of the UK Intelligence Section, Navy General Staff, wrote:

> We are confident that the RN's Far East Fleet can be annihilated without much difficulty in the early part of the initial phase of war. If the RN could send a powerful reinforcement to Southeast Asia after that, there would be a problem. However, we believe that the RN would never be able to do this, because the UK has to commit all of her naval power against the German and Italian navies in Europe …"[400]

The IJN also knew the primary armament of their capital ships had a maximum range greater than that of the equivalent British weapons, and also knew that the older capital ships of the RN had not been as fully modernized as their own.[401] The IJN was optimistic about the outcome of war against the

RN alone, yet the United States was always part of the equation. Even if the IJN could wage a separate war on the RN, the IJN's fleet would have to pass through water off the US-controlled Philippines to conduct operations in Southeast Asia, which was a risky maneuver for the IJN fleet. The IJN would have to ensure lines of communication through the South China Sea, and doing so would inevitably bring war with the United States.

6

TACTICAL AND STRATEGIC INTELLIGENCE IN JAPANESE WAR PLANNING

As we have seen, the serious sectionalism between Operations and Intelligence Departments in the Army and Navy was an obstacle to marrying intelligence with Japanese strategy. In the case of the Japanese advance into French Indo-China in September 1940, the IJA made good use of SIGINT. At a tactical level, Japanese troops could utilize intelligence effectively – such as at Pearl Harbor and during the Malaya campaign in late 1941 – but the Japanese use of strategic intelligence was comparatively poor. As Michael Barnhart has written, Japan has a record of "brilliant success and glaring failures in the use of intelligence."[402]

The intelligence cycle required for battlefield use was much clearer than that for strategic decisions, because a field commander usually required very specific intelligence for his operation. The IJA and IJN did understand the importance of intelligence in battle, and they had developed a workable system for using intelligence at tactical levels, whereby the operational commander or staff officer handled both the operation and its intelligence. Hajime Kitaoka, former chief of the Intelligence Bureau of the Ministry of Foreign Affairs, wrote: "A frontline commander understands what kind of intelligence he needs because his goal is clear – beating his opponent in the battle. However, at the strategic and political level, the Army and Navy's goal is sometimes obscure and they spend much time consulting with other governmental organizations and politicians to form a consensus. As a result, their intelligence requirement is unclear from the outset."[403] When we explore the effectiveness of Japanese intelligence, we have to separate tactical and strategic applications. These will be looked at in the separate sections below.

TACTICAL INTELLIGENCE IN THE BATTLE AGAINST RUSSIA

In the summer of 1938, a regional conflict arose between Japan and the Soviets around Lake Khasan, on the border of the Soviet Union, Korea, and Manchuria. The armies fought against each other in a series of intense battles, with the mutual objective of taking a small hill, Changkufeng. During the two-week clash, only 7,000 Japanese soldiers, without any tanks or aircraft, fought against a Russian mechanized force that possessed 15,000 soldiers, 237 artillery guns, 285 tanks, and 250 aircraft. On the night of July 30, the Japanese XIX Corps launched an attack on the Soviet troops, which had held its positions on the border. The Japanese troops succeeded in pushing back the Red Army into its territory, but in response the Soviets began a counter-attack on August 6. The fighting reached a deadlock, with the frontline on the small hill. As a result, the Japanese ambassador to the Soviet Union, Mamoru Shigemitsu, made an armistice with the Soviets on August 11 and both troops withdrew from the border.[404]

During the battle, the Russians suffered 792 dead and 2,752 wounded, and the Japanese lost 526 dead and 914 wounded. The figures show how well the Japanese fought against the overwhelming forces. One key reason for this performance, apart from sheer courage, was that Japanese intelligence broke some Russian signals traffic.

Border clashes between Japan and the Soviet Union occurred over 1,000 times between 1938 and 1945. The biggest incident was the battle of Nomonhan/Khalkhyn Gol in June 1939 and in second place was the Changkufeng/Khasan incident. The Japanese armies in Manchuria and Korea were continually facing the menace of Russian pressure in the 1930s and spent a lot of energy exploring the Soviet military presence in the Far East, mainly through SIGINT.

In May 1936, the Army's codebreaking team obtained one of the Red Army's ciphers, called "OKK5," through the Polish General Staff. Using the code book, the Japanese succeeded in breaking the Soviet Army's four-digit code and the Soviet Border Guard's code "PK1" in July 1936. The success had a significant effect on Soviet–Japanese border conflicts in the late 1930s. On June 19, 1937, Russian Border Guards landed on Kanchatzu Island in the Amur River (the border line between Manchuria and the Soviet Union) and occupied the island. During the incident, the Japanese intelligence team read coded transmissions from the Soviet Border Guard, Red Army, and Soviet Air Force. The team revealed that the Border Guard's reckless landing was not an order from Moscow, but the decision of a local commander, and that Moscow did not want to fight against the Japanese. The Japanese codebreakers also confirmed that the Soviet General Staff did not order a sortie of their air force in the Far East. Based on the SIGINT, the Japanese government started diplomatic negotiations with the Soviets. On June 30, however, three Soviet gunboats suddenly invaded the Manchurian side of the river and fired at the riverbank. But Japanese SIGINT had foreseen the Russian operation and the Japanese and Manchurian Border Guards fired back on the gunboats, sinking one and damaging the others.

One year later, SIGINT again revealed that the Russians had begun construction of field positions on the Changkufeng hill. It was July 6, 1938. SIGINT revealed that Soviet Border Guards were planning to capture the tactically vital hill. The Japanese General Staff in Korea took the SIGINT seriously and ordered XIX Corps to conduct reconnaissance around Changkufeng. As a result, the Soviet development on the border was confirmed and the Japanese troops advanced toward the border. The number of Russians on the border gradually increased from ten to 50 persons. Finally, the Japanese General Staff ordered that a battalion be sent to secure the border. On July 29, 1938, the tension was broken by a Japanese attack on the Soviet troops and the border conflict began. During the battle, SIGINT provided Japanese troops with a critical advantage over the Soviet troops, forewarning them of their enemy's deployments. In particular, the Japanese codebreaking team could follow the movement of Soviet armor from Vladivostock to Changkufeng, and the SIGINT contributed to Japan's final tactical success.[405]

During the battle of Nomonhan in June 1939, the Japanese SIS Section also broke the Border Guard's four-digit code, the Red Army's four-digit code, and the Soviet Air Force's three-digit code. According to the memoir of Colonel Etsuo Koutani, an intelligence staff officer of the Kwantung Army: "The success in breaking the Soviet Border Guard's code contributed to our grasp of the Border Guard's and Air Force's strength and field positions during the battle of Nomonhan."[406] After the battle, the Red Army adopted a new five-digit code, "OK40," which the Japanese found quite difficult to break. However, the five-digit code had been cracked by the Finnish codebreaking team during the Russo-Finnish War, which began in November 1939. The Japanese team obtained the data from the Finnish and proceeded to read the five-digit code. The Japanese also succeeded in breaking the four-digit code of the Soviet Navy and Air Force.

TACTICAL INTELLIGENCE IN THE BATTLE AGAINST CHINA

In China it was an easy task for the IJA to break the KMT's cipher, and they regularly used SIGINT in the battle against Chinese troops. In May and June 1941, six divisions and three brigades of the Japanese Expeditionary Army, North China, fought against 26 divisions of the Chinese Army in an action known as the battle of South Shanxi. In this battle, the Chinese suffered heavy losses (42,000 deaths and 35,000 POWs), while Japanese sacrifices were surprisingly low (672 dead and 2,722 wounded),[407] a fact partly explained by intelligence operations.

Before the battle, Japanese operations staff realized that the Chinese forces held numerical supremacy, so decided to execute deception operations against the Chinese Army. Intelligence staff intentionally sent out false information, stating that overwhelming Japanese forces were approaching the Chinese garrisons. The deception bred confusion and panic in the Chinese ranks and led to careless signals transmissions. The Japanese, therefore, were able to identify Chinese field positions through SIGINT and this insight gave them sufficient advantage to win the clash.[408]

During the battle, Japanese counter-intelligence staff also made good use of SIGINT. On May 15, the Yun Cheng branch of the Military Police traced

Chinese signals to a small farm village, the stronghold of Chinese anti-Japanese activities. After sporadic firefights, the Military Police captured eight Chinese leaders and their radio devices. The group had been sent by the KMT military committee and the Japanese deception operations forced them to make radio transmissions, which were traced by the Military Police. This counter-intelligence severed lines of communications between the Chinese troops and left them in isolated positions. After the battle, the Japanese Expeditionary Army, North China Command, published a report that stated: "It has been difficult to gather information through human sources ... But signal intelligence was useful and operated to our advantage in the battle of South Shanxi."[409]

SIGINT AND THE JAPANESE ADVANCE INTO FRENCH INDO-CHINA, SUMMER 1940

The Japanese advance into French Indo-China and its use of SIGINT can be discussed in detail, because there remain significant diplomatic and intelligence records, despite the fact that the IJA and IJN systematically destroyed many intelligence documents at the end of the Pacific War. Japan's traditional military strategy in East Asia was to advance into Siberia, a northward advance. The roots of the Indo-China problem lay in the Sino-Japanese War of 1937. The Chinese waged an unexpectedly determined defense against the Japanese Army, tying down large numbers of men and great quantities of equipment. Japanese strategists believed that the Chinese continued resisting because of French and British aid transported to China via French Indo-China and the Burma Road. The fall of France to the Germans in June 1940 gave Japan a chance to sever the lines of communication between French Indo-China and Southern China.[410] The Japanese government soon demanded that the French authorities in Indo-China allow Japanese military forces to move into Indo-China and enjoy free use of French airbases there.[411]

Diplomats in Japan and French Indo-China negotiated the issue for a long time.[412] The Japanese government was cautious during the talks for fear of provoking British and American intervention in Indo-China's affairs. In fact, the French had asked for British support during the Singapore Conference in June 1939, which recognized the need for Anglo-French cooperation to retain colonial interests in Asia.[413] However, by 1940 Britain was already engaged in the Battle of Britain, the outcome of which was uncertain. Faced with a life-and-death struggle with Nazi Germany, the British government appeased Japan by announcing the closure of the Burma Road on July 17. The British Chiefs of Staff then conducted a comprehensive examination of British Far Eastern strategy. On July 31, they concluded: "our general policy must be to play for time ... we should not under present conditions go to war with Japan in the event of a Japanese attack on Indo-China."[414]

Japan perceived the discord between Britain and the Vichy government in French Indo-China through SIGINT. A transmission from the American consul in Saigon to the US State Department, for example, stated: "British authorities are reluctant to have an agreement with the French because of their inconsistant foreign policy in Indo-China ... Britain does not want to be involved in Indo-Chinese affairs without American support ..."[415] The American government was also unwilling to intervene in Indo-Chinese affairs with the Presidential election fast approaching. Secretary of State Cordell Hull opposed any alteration in the status quo in Indo-China, but the mere words of the Western powers could not deter Japan.

On July 27, 1940, the Imperial General HQ officially decided that the Japanese national policy would be to pursue a "Southern Advance" by securing French Indo-China, Thailand, the Dutch East Indies, and Malaya within a Japanese economic sphere, even if it meant war against Britain and the United States.[416] (The IJA's overall strategy was to finish the Sino-Japanese War and then wage a war against Russia, called the "Northern Advance," while the IJN planned the war with Britain and the United States, the "Southern Advance".) Although extremists in the IJA wanted to expand by force, the IJN and Ministry of Foreign Affairs pursued diplomatic options in Indo-China. On August 1, Matsuoka asked Arsène Henry, the French ambassador in Tokyo, whether Japanese troops might cross into Tonkin and occupy aerodromes in French Indo-China. The Foreign Minister implied that should the French disagree, Japanese troops would proceed by force. Matsuoka explained that the operation would sever supply lines between French Indo-China and Southern China, and bring the Sino-Japanese War to an end. Matsuoka's demand presented the Vichy government with a disastrous choice. The Vichy Foreign Minister Paul Baudouin wrote: "The position is unhappily very simple; if we refuse Japan, she will attack Indo-China which is incapable of being defended. Indo-China will be a hundred per cent lost. If we negotiate with Japan; if we avoid the worst, that is to say the total loss of the colony; we preserve the chances that the future may perhaps bring us."[417]

Around this time Britain obtained intelligence on Japanese intentions from intercepted Japanese Navy radio traffic on August 5: "Japanese Admiralty informs various Naval Authorities that in order to back up diplomatic talks on Indo-China due to start 1st Aug the Army have ordered a number of air force squadrons and ground personnel from Formosa and North and Central China to be sent to reinforce South China Force. Move to be complete by 5th Aug."[418] The British Foreign Secretary, Lord Halifax, used this intelligence at a War Cabinet meeting of August 7 to direct the British ambassador in Tokyo, Robert Craigie, to make protests to Matsuoka.[419] Halifax's instructions came on the heels of additional protests to Matsuoka by the US ambassador in Tokyo, Joseph Grew, on August 7. Yet fearing that Britain could go no further on its own, Halifax deleted the key phrase in his cable to Craigie: "H.M.G. [His Majesty's Government] could not remain indifferent to any action on the part of the Japanese Government toward Indo-China which would affect the status quo in the Far East."[420] Halifax's attitude toward Japan was too weak to affect Japanese expansion plans. The GC&CS also intercepted a Japanese diplomatic telegram from Matsuoka to the Japanese ambassador in Paris, Renzo Sawada.[421] The telegram detailed the Japanese demands on French Indo-China. The British government leaked this information to the press in hopes of marshaling public opinion against Japan.[422]

Without any active support from Britain or the United States, Henry had to accept Matsuoka's request and in an exchange of letters on August 30, he agreed to Matsuoka's proposal: the Japanese use of air bases and the stationing of 6,000 troops in French Indo-China.[423] As Henry had hoped the agreement was not publicized, and Matsuoka hastened to implement the Japanese move into Indo-China as quickly as possible, since Japanese troops had already been stationed on the border between China and Indo-China for almost two-and-a-half months. By presenting the Western powers with a fait accompli, Matsuoka expected to preclude intervention by third powers, in particular Britain and America.

Throughout August 1940, the Japanese government was able to negotiate with the Vichy government in a favorable position, even against Britain and the United States. Japan exploited the German success in Europe, and chose the right occasion to make her demands on French Indo-China. Perhaps SIGINT contributed to Japanese foreign policy in this period, but an absence of documents dated from August 1940 makes such a possibility impossible to verify. There is a clear link, however, between Japanese foreign policy and the SIGINT gained throughout September 1940.

Based on the agreement in Tokyo on August 30, negotiations to work out the details of the agreement began in Indo-China between the French Governor-General, Jean Decoux, and Major General Issaku Nishihara. During the talks, Decoux procrastinated and played for time in the hope of obtaining Anglo-American support. His approach frustrated the Japanese delegation, especially Nishihara, who was also anxious about British and American intervention. Furthermore, disagreements between the Japanese Army and Navy during the negotiations presented a more serious problem. The IJN wanted a diplomatic solution, while the IJA was willing to use force. Nishihara had to balance the competing Army and Navy demands.

On September 4, the commander-in-chief of the French Army, Indo-China, General Maurice Martin, took over the negotiations from Decoux and signed the Nishihara–Martin Agreement. The same day Martin informed the British consulate-general in Hanoi, Hector Henderson, about the content of the agreement and asked for British support. Whitehall, however, was indifferent to the French position. Prime Minister Winston Churchill told his War Cabinet: "The right course was to go some way in offering inducements to Japan and possibly also to go some way in using threats, but not to commit ourselves irrevocably to forceful action."[424]

On September 5, the situation suddenly changed. Martin was informed that Japanese planes had violated Indo-Chinese airspace and Japanese infantry had crossed the border, invading French territory. Martin immediately suspended the talks with Nishihara, a move that shocked the Imperial Headquarters in Tokyo. On the same day, the 11th Section obtained an intercepted message, sent from the US consular office in Hanoi to the State Department: "The government of French Indo-China informed us that they are trying to put off answering Japanese demands as far as possible. Japan asked to occupy 1 harbor, 3 main roads, 2 railways and 3 air bases ..."[425] This intelligence revealed not only the leak of the Nishihara–Martin Agreement, but also that a link between the French and Americans had been established. The 11th Section also decrypted diplomatic traffic between Henderson and Halifax. In the cable, the French director-general asked Henderson:

> whether His Majesty's Government would assist them in obtaining aeroplanes and munitions if they [the French] resist the Japanese and especially if Indo-China is blockaded. They require shells which could be made in America or India and facilities for transport. French Mission in America is negotiating for early delivery of about 100 aircraft ... In view of British interests in the Far East, French ask whether His Majesty's Government would use influence in America to obtain better terms of payment and quick delivery ..."[426]

The British consul in Haiphong forwarded Decoux's request to London:

> The Governor General [Decoux] has seized the opportunity to break off relations ... The French services and public will be pleased at this decision and

the prestige of the Governor General may be enhanced ... [He] Stated that his action together with American and British diplomatic pressure deterred any Japanese military action in the Far East outside China ... The suggestion has been made today that the American Army aeroplanes in the Philippines may be passed to the French ...[427]

These decrypts suggested that senior authorities in French Indo-China were exchanging information with the British and Americans in an attempt to build up their military arsenal to resist Japanese encroachment. This intelligence caused the Japanese Army General Staff to take a firm line: "We are going to advance our troops based on the agreement on August 30 whether French Indo-China agrees or not."[428] In contrast, the Navy General Staff disagreed with this hard line and insisted that the agreement should be concluded between French Indo-China and the Japanese delegation. The Navy's September 12 proposal stated: "In consideration of foreign powers, especially the United States, we should move into French Indo-China by peaceful means ..."[429]

The divisions between the Army and Navy over a rapid advance into Indo-China were based on the lack of central intelligence coordination in Tokyo. They could obtain SIGINT, but without a central intelligence organization or joint intelligence committee, the Japanese Army and Navy had interpreted the *Toku-jo* differently and they did not coordinate with each other. The SIS also intercepted a conversation between the Chinese ambassador in London, Quo Tai-chi, and R. A. Butler, the Under-Secretary of State for Foreign Affairs. Quo told Butler that he had been asked by the Vichy government to confirm if Britain could assist French resistance in Indo-China in two ways. One was to assure the safe passage of two merchant ships from Djibouti which might bring troops on board. The other was to allow the Vichy regime to transfer 140 aircraft from Martinique, West Indies, to Indo-China.[430] Next day Halifax informed Quo that "we will take all diplomatic and moral support to put pressure on Japan for preventing a Japanese attack against Indo-China, suing to secure US support..."[431] With the Battle of Britain approaching a climax and this intelligence indicating that Britain would be in a position to assist French resistance against Japan in Indo-China, Nishihara reported to Tokyo on September 11: "it is now clear that the French Governor-General is trying to slow the negotiations ..."[432] Nishihara's report and the associated SIGINT irritated Foreign Minister Matsuoka who, notified the Japanese Consul Office in Hanoi: "By analyzing information, we can see that French Indo-China is approaching the United States via the American Consul-General in Hanoi and Chiang Kai-shek is plotting against Japan with the British government ..."[433]

On September 14, Imperial General HQ ordered Japanese troops to move into French Indo-China on the 22nd, regardless of the state of the negotiations. The attitude of the Japanese government shifted to a hard line for three reasons. First, Matsuoka planned to sign the Tripartite Pact with Germany and Italy on September 21 and he thought that the pact would deter the United States and Britain from interfering in Indo-Chinese affairs.[434] Second, in the *Toku-jo* 1423, Halifax wrote to Lothian, the British ambassador in Washington, D.C., that "His Majesty's Government are not in a position themselves to become directly involved or to assist with aircraft or munitions in present circumstances ..."[435] This intelligence indicated that in the case of a Japanese incursion into Indo-China, the British government would not take firm action against Japan. Third, according to SIGINT, the Chinese Army also planned to cross the border between China and Indo-China.[436] The Army General Staff in Tokyo wanted to move troops into Indo-China to preempt the Chinese or Thai seizure of French territory. The SIGINT encouraged the Navy and the Ministry of Foreign Affairs to settle the problem quickly, and Matsuoka cabled the Japanese consul-general in Hanoi, saying that the Japanese government could wait no longer.[437]

Also on September 14, the General Staff ordered Nishihara to resume negotiations with the French in Hanoi. Simultaneously, the Vichy government ordered Martin to haggle with Nishihara. The British FECB at Singapore deciphered the Japanese order and Whitehall discovered that the deadline for the Japanese advance would be September 22.[438] This cipher, transmitted on the 14th, was not broken until the 20th, only two days before the actual deadline. This delay left insufficient time for the British Far Eastern forces to take any counter actions. Anthony Eden wrote: "Our most recent information is that the Japanese have broken off negotiations with the French authorities in Indo-China and we have secret indications that they are preparing for military action on September 22nd."[439]

What Whitehall could do was protest against the Japanese government. On September 16, Craigie called on Matsuoka to ask about Japanese intentions in Indo-China. Matsuoka indignantly rejected Craigie's interference, saying: "the Governor-General of Indo-China was in closest contact with the British, American and Chinese consular representatives, all of whom were encouraging him in his policy of procrastination."[440] Matsuoka knew this because of SIGINT, but Craigie still lacked the decryptions from the area. Thus Craigie's protest was ineffective against the Japanese government and British diplomacy failed to deter the Japanese advance into Indo-China.

The second negotiations between Nishihara and Martin had resumed on September 17. The Japanese delegation's demands were excessive, giving little attention to the Matsuoka–Henry Agreement of August 30. The number of airbases slated for Japanese use in Indo-China was arbitrarily increased from three to five and the number of Japanese troops allowed to enter Indo-China was expanded from 6,000 to 25,000. Martin strongly protested against Japan's new demands, but from Tokyo Ohashi insisted to Henry that "We will advance into French Indo-China forcibly, unless the French accept our demands."[441] Ohashi's words sounded more like a Japanese ultimatum than a negotiation, since the Japanese attitude became increasingly belligerent as the September 22 deadline approached.

At the same time, SIGINT disclosed US intentions regarding Japan. On the 17th, Cordell Hull discussed the Indo-China crisis with Lothian and Australian Minister Richard Casey. Lothian stressed the need for material support to Indo-China, but Hull disagreed stating: "my government had gone almost to the limit in resisting Japanese aggression."[442] Hull seemed indifferent to the fate of Indo-China and Lothian reported the secretary's comments to Halifax as follows:

> The difficulty however was to know what the real policy of France was. If aeroplanes were sent who would they help? Was there a secret agreement between Vichy, the Germans and Japan? He had spoken most strongly to the new French Ambassador in this sense last week saying that if France valued American goodwill it must not become anti-British or in captivity to Hitler or connive at Japanese aggression.[443]

The SIS intercepted this message, which revealed that the US government had no intention to assist further in Indo-China. Hull's policy was presented to the Japanese government on September 20, when Grew handed the secretary's statement to Matsuoka: "the status quo of a third country was seriously affected ... The American Government urges upon all governments the employment of peaceful means only in their relations with all other governments and with all other regions ..."[444] Matsuoka already knew the content of Hull's statement via the intercepts and he ignored the remark.[445]

Without any support from the United States and Britain, Martin in Hanoi had no choice except to obey the Japanese directives. He did get Nishihara to compromise by reducing the number of Japanese to be stationed in Indo-China, but finally signed an agreement with Nishihara on September 22. The next day, Hull publicly denied that the US government had approved the French concessions to Japan,[446] but this too was ineffective in deterring the Japanese encroachment on French Indo-China. *Toku-jo* 1489 revealed that it was almost impossible for the US government to supply aircraft and ammunition to French Indo-China.[447]

On September 23, the 5th Division of the Japanese Expeditionary Army for South China started to move into Indo-China. The commander of the division was unaware that an agreement with the French had been concluded, and sporadic fighting between the Japanese and French troops erupted at Dong Dan and Lang Son, with the French troops finally surrendering to the

Japanese on September 25. Why did the General Staff in Tokyo fail to notify the 5th Division about the agreement? Examining the SIGINT, it could be argued that the hawks among the General Staff did not wish to compromise the source of their intelligence by informing the division. *Toku-jo* numbers 2673 and 2685 show that if the French possessed enough aircraft to resist Japan, they would not have accepted Japanese demands. However, there were only 35 types of aircraft deployed in Indo-China, all obsolete, while the Japanese 5th Division possessed 130 advanced planes.[448]

The Japanese advance into French Indo-China and the signing of the Tripartite Pact on September 27 caused a serious deterioration in Anglo-Japanese relations. On October 2 the British War Cabinet approved the establishment of the Far Eastern Committee to coordinate British Far Eastern strategy and on the 17th they announced the reopening of the Burma Road to allow military supplies from Burma to China to aid Chinese resistance against Japan.

Viewing the affairs of French Indo-China through SIGINT, it is clear that Japan had negotiated with Indo-China on the basis of intelligence about US and British intentions obtained beforehand. SIGINT was one of the reasons Japanese troops could move into French Indo-China without fear of provoking serious Western reaction. Britain also was reading Japanese diplomatic traffic to some extent, but was unable to act on the intelligence because of the demands of the Battle of Britain.

Intelligence was not the primary reason for the Japanese decision to invade French territory – they had sought for the chance since the beginning of 1940. The biggest problem, however, in advancing into Indo-China was the British and American protests against the Japanese. *Toku-Jo* information helped to solve the problem, showing that neither Britain nor the United States was willing to help the French in Indo-China. Traditionally the Japanese Navy was concerned about facing Western powers, but SIGINT finally lifted their apprehension and urged them to advance into Indo-Chinese territory. Therefore, SIGINT was not a trigger but the final push to act.

TACTICAL INTELLIGENCE IN THE PACIFIC WAR

The Pearl Harbor and Palembang (Dutch East Indies) operations were the finest examples of Japanese intelligence use in the Pacific War. Most Japanese operations officers disregarded intelligence in their decision-making process, and they usually tended to decide operations on the basis of personal purpose. Yet at the beginning of the Pacific War even operations staff looked to intelligence assessments for insight.

In January 1941, Admiral Isoroku Yamamoto ordered Rear Admiral Takijiro Onishi, Chief of Staff of the First Fleet, to draft a plan for the Pearl Harbor attack. Onishi was one of the pioneers of naval aviation in the IJN and also famous as a pioneer of suicide bomb attacks – *kamikaze*. Onishi invited Commander Minoru Genda of the Yokosuka Air Group to study Yamamoto's plan.

In August 1940, Ensign Takeo Yoshikawa, an officer of the US and British intelligence section, was appointed as a covert operative in Hawaii. He was sent to Hawaii in March 1941 as a junior diplomat and given the cover name "Tadashi Morimura." From March to December 1941, he made "sight-seeing" trips around Oahu, observing US military installations and airfields. He found spotting locations in Oahu, especially a point on Aiea Heights, which provided an excellent view of Pearl Harbor.[449] He recorded the numbers and positions of the USN ships in the harbor and reported these to Tokyo by diplomatic traffic. In October, Lieutenant Commander Minato Nakajima, Yoshikawa's senior officer, arrived on Honolulu on the Japanese liner ship (Yokohama to San Francisco) *Tatsuta-maru*. Yoshikawa handed a small piece of paper to Nakajima through Nagao Kita, the Japanese consul-general in Honolulu, which reported the size, strength, and location of the US fleet in Pearl Harbor. As we have seen, Bernard Julius Kühn and F. J. Rutland also gathered information for the IJN.

Through the autumn of 1941, the IJN had been trying to decide on a target – Pearl Harbor at Oahu Island, or Lahaina Port at Maui Island, which the USN sometimes used? In October, several Japanese naval officers boarded *Tatsuta-maru* and *Taiyo-maru* (a liner from Yokohama to Honolulu) and investigated the seaway from Japan to Hawaii, plus they gathered information from human sources in Hawaii.[450] This report revealed that the USN was using only Pearl Harbor as a home port. In addition to HUMINT, the IJN's RDF plotted the deployments of the US warships. The Japanese operations staff such as Onishi and Genda planned the Pearl Harbor attack on the basis of the intelligence.

IJN security was almost perfect. The IJA and Ministry of Foreign Affairs were not informed about the target and there were only a few naval officers who knew the specific plan. They never used the word "Pearl Harbor" in their signals traffic so even if the USN could decrypt the traffic, there was no mention of the target. The IJN upgraded the strength of the operational code JN-25b at the beginning of December. Captain Laurance Safford, director of the USN codebreaking team OP-20-G, wrote: "On 1 December 1941, the numbers system became unreadable …"[451]

During the Japanese deployment to attack positions off Pearl Harbor, the Japanese task force kept radio silence. The signals record of the battleship *Kirishima*, which was the only ship permitted to use radio signals in the task force (signal devices of other ships were strictly sealed), tells us that *Kirishima* never made any transmissions just before Pear Harbor attack.[452] On the night of December 2, the task force lost their escort submarine, I-23, but they refused to use radio to search for it. They knew the task force was under the surveillance of the US RDF, and therefore used flag and light signaling when they communicated with each other. Therefore, it was impossible for the US to anticipate the Japanese target; this was not American failure, but the success of Japanese security.

Judicious use of tactical intelligence was also seen in the Palembang operation on February 14, 1942. In this operation, 329 army paratroop soldiers captured vital Dutch oil refineries. In April 1941, Marshal Hajime Sugiyama, Chief of Staff, IJA, had ordered Colonel Masao Ueda, organizer of the Nakano School, to investigate the viability of operations against the Palembang oil refineries. Ueda began his information gathering with Major General Osato Kawamata, head of the Nakano School, and the statistician

Sigeo Okayasu. Their work focused on oil locations, outputs, oil refineries, and oil stocks in Palembang. They obtained aerial photos from private oil companies that had developed oil fields in the area, and conducted test operations against oil refineries in Niigata, Japan. Ueda analyzed the data at the Nakano School and produced operational intelligence.[453] The intelligence was submitted to the Army operations staff and they used it for the airborne assault, with great success.

INTELLIGENCE AND MAJOR WAR STRATEGY

For the Japanese leadership, the role of intelligence was very limited in strategic thinking in the 1940s. Japanese foreign policy and strategy were chiefly directed by the bureaucratic internal relations between the Army, Navy, and the Japanese government (chiefly the Prime Minister and Foreign Minister). This decision-making process needed not foreign intelligence, but close personal and departmental ties for facilitating institutional estrangements.

The Japanese government's grand strategy in the late 1930s was to establish a kind of international economic bloc, called the Great Asian Co-Prosperity Sphere, which was expected to cover East Siberia, India, China, Manchuria, Southeast Asia, and Australia. The Imperial National Defense Plan decided on by the government in 1936 failed to combine the three different strategies of the government, IJA, and IJN. In other words, the plan allowed three political powers to pursue three different goals in the same period. Moreover, the situation became even more complicated by the breakout of World War II in Europe. The government and the IJA tried to approach Germany, while the IJN opposed the tie with Germany and Italy.

There was no departmental or governmental body dedicated to deciding Japanese grand strategy, such as the British CID (or Cabinet Committee). Unlike the American President, the Japanese Prime Minister had limited authority in foreign policy making and grand strategy. By the 1920s, the *Genro* (veteran advisers to the Emperor) had decided the Japanese grand strategy carefully, watching international relations and using foreign intelligence, but the position of the *Genro* was not stipulated in the Japanese constitution and most of them died out in the 1920s. During the inter-war period, the IJA muscled in on *Genro* territory, but the IJA specialized in tactics, not in strategy. In the late 1930s, they began to form military and political strategy in an impromptu manner, which precipitated the Second Sino-Japanese War in 1937 and finally the Pacific War.

In the summer of 1940, the IJA was also studying the possibility of the German domination of Europe and of a pact with Germany. Major General Yuichi Tsuchihashi, Department Chief of Army Intelligence and a specialist in European affairs, had never been invited to a series of study meetings, because he opposed a pact with Germany and Italy.[454] It is amazing that the IJA sought to decide the pact without appropriate intelligence assessments; the Tripartite Pact would be the most serious diplomatic issue between the United States and Japan throughout 1941.

The majority of the Japanese government believed German victory in the Battle of Britain was inevitable, and many IJA officers rushed along with Matsuoka to sign the pact with Germany. By comparison, leading IJN officers, especially Admiral Mitsumasa Yonai, Vice Admiral Isoroku Yamamoto, and Vice Admiral Shigeyoshi Inoue, opposed the pact.

On July 25, the Army Intelligence Department made a report, *Kokusai Josei Geppo* (Monthly Report of International Affairs), referring to the course of the Battle of Britain: "The UK is trying to fight against Germany with great determination. In spite of the Führer's announcement of July 19, British public opinion continues to support their government's hard-line policy."[455] This report also pointed out that delays in the planned German invasion of Britain (Operation *Sealion*) resulted from Germany's lack of rear facilities and logistical capability, plus the failure to achieve air superiority, but the report was ignored in the IJA.

Rear Admiral Eiichi Tatsumi, naval attaché to London, and Colonel Makoto Onodera, military attaché to Stockholm, also sent valuable reports to Tokyo: "It seems very difficult for Germany to beat up Britain."[456] Commander Keisuke Matsunaga, staff officer of the Navy Intelligence Department, also reported that the German losses in the Battle of Britain were much larger than those of the British.[457] Yet the information was labeled as a "pro-British view" by the Army, while the "pro-German view" from the attaché or ambassador to Berlin was more popular among Army officers. Captain Kan'ei Chudo complained that "the information collected and analyzed by the 8th Section [UK section] on the United Kingdom and the Royal Navy was not treated as significant, or even disregarded in some cases by the war planners and policy makers, while the information furnished by our attaché in Germany was treated as more valuable and worthwhile."[458]

War planners of the IJA intentionally treated and politicized intelligence for their own goal – the pact with Germany. Lieutenant Colonel Susumu Nishiura, Bureau of Military Affairs, War Ministry, reflected: "I am impressed that Army officers just discuss their subjective ideas and principles. Now they are just crying out 'Don't miss the bus!' without any specific planning and information."[459] Colonel Shinobu Takayama, on the operations staff of the Army General Staff, wrote: "Of course Army mainstreamers agreed with the Pact. But I doubted that they had studied Anglo-Saxon powers and decided their foreign policy based on such studies. Many of the Army officers were pro-German and anti-Soviet, and they underestimated the United Kingdom and United States. It was stupid that the underestimation was from their blindness..."[460]

Nishiura and Takayama's writings revealed that the IJA depended on their subjective assumptions, not on intelligence assessments of foreign countries. At the point of 1940, the IJA had done no research on German military and industrial powers and vastly overestimated their capabilities, without any certain evidence, until 1943. On the other hand, Foreign Minister Matsuoka planned his foreign policy for the pact on the assumption that Germany would make an alliance with the Soviet Union after beating Britain. Contrary to his expectations, Germany decided to shelve the Operation *Sealion* in September. He believed that there would be a Russo-German rapprochement, on the basis of information from Heinrich Stahmer, the German envoy to Japan.[461]

"Friendly" Russo-German relations, however, had been already worsened by Russia's forceful annexation of Romanian Bessarabia and northern Bukovina in June.[462] The Army Intelligence Department reported the annexation, but the IJA and Matsuoka ignored the report. Ryouei Saito, adviser to the Ministry of Foreign Affairs, testified that the Ministry and the IJA had not conducted any studies on Germany.[463] Matsuoka's image of Germany was the same as that of the general public – overestimating German military and industrial power – and he also truly believed that the Soviet Union would eventually join the Tripartite Pact. Matsuoka finally signed the pact with Germany and Italy on September 27, 1940, but this caused severe protest from the United States.

The IJA now began to lay out a concrete plan to wage wars with the Dutch and British, the aim being to acquire natural resources based on the idea of a British and Dutch separation from the United States, while the IJN believed that in a forthcoming conflict the British and Americans would be allies. In November 1940, Admiral Yamamoto conducted a war game based on a Japanese advance into the Dutch East Indies. He concluded that if Japan advanced into the area, war with the UK and US would be inevitable, and he insisted that the IJN should not go to the south and follow the tide of war in Europe.[464]

The *Automedon* affair subsequently influenced IJN strategy.[465] *Automedon* was a British Blue Funnel cargo liner that was sunk by a German raider, *Atlantis*, in the Indian Ocean on November 11, 1940. *Automedon* possessed a secret copy of the British War Cabinet Minutes for August 1940, which was being sent to Singapore from Liverpool, and the document was captured by the Germans. It consisted of 87 paragraphs and showed a blueprint of the British Far Eastern strategy. This document indicated that Britain would not go to war against Japan, even if the Japanese Army invaded French Indo-China. In the document, British Chiefs of Staff regarded Thailand and Hong Kong as indefensible against Japanese attack.[466]

Bernhard Rogge, captain of the *Atlantis*, recognized the significance of the document and sent it to the German naval attaché in Tokyo, Rear Admiral

Paul Wenneker. In Berlin, the Japanese naval attaché, Captain Tadao Yokoi, sent a summary of the document to the Navy Ministry in Tokyo. On December 12, 1940, Wenneker handed the document to Admiral Nobutake Kondo, the Vice Chief of Staff, and talked about Britain's overstretched empire. At that time, Hitler was urging Japan to attack Singapore to weaken the British Empire.

Admiral Koshiro Oikawa referred to this information in December 1940 and he had a conviction that Britain would not wage a war against Japan over French Indo-China. As mentioned above, Admiral Yamamoto ordered his junior, Vice Admiral Onishi, to plan the Pearl Harbor operation in January 1941, just after the *Automedon* affair.

The next step for Matsuoka was to bring the Soviet Union into the Tripartite Pact. In January 1941, Matsuoka made a report advocating the realization of a Four Powers Pact. However, Russo-German relations had already deteriorated and his plan was make believe. Chihiro Hosoya points out that Matsuoka's failure was from lack of intelligence and access to an espionage network, but fundamentally he ignored intelligence contrary to his view.[467]

Matsuoka paid an official visit to Berlin on March 27, 1941, and talked with Hitler and his generals. Winston Churchill was made uncomfortable by the news of Matsuoka's visit and wrote to him a few days later:

I venture to suggest a few questions which it seems to me deserve the attention of the Imperial Japanese Government and people.

1. Will Germany, without the command of the sea or the command of the British daylight air, be able to invade and conquer Great Britain in the spring, summer or autumn of 1941? Will Germany try to do so? Would it not be in the interests of Japan to wait until these questions have answered themselves?

2. Will the German attack on British shipping be strong enough to prevent American aid from reaching British shores, with Great Britain and the United States transforming their whole industry to war purposes?

3. Did Japan's accession to the Triple Pact make it more likely or less likely that the United States would come into the present war?

4. If the United States entered the war at the side of Great Britain, and Japan ranged herself with the Axis Powers, would not the naval superiority of the two English-speaking nations enable them to dispose of the Axis Powers in Europe before turning their united strength upon Japan?

5. Is Italy a strength or a burden to Germany? Is the Italian Fleet as good at sea as on paper? Is it as good as it used to be?

6. Will the British Air Force be stronger than the German Air Force before the end of 1941, and far stronger before the end of 1942?

7. Will the many countries which are being held down by the German army and Gestapo learn to like the Germans more or will they like them less as the years pass by?

8. Is it true that the production of steel in the United States during 1941 will be 75 millions tons and in Great Britain about 12½, making a total of nearly 90 million tons? If Germany should happen to be defeated, as she was last time, would not the 7 million tons' steel production of Japan be inadequate for a single-handed war?

From the answers to these questions may spring the avoidance by Japan of a serious catastrophe, and a marked improvement in the relations between Japan and the two great Sea-Powers of the West.[468]

Of course, Churchill sent his message to Matsuoka not out of of kindness, but because he hoped Japan would drop out of the pact. He also wanted to avoid war against Japan without definite American back-up in the Far East. But Matsuoka seemed to be dismissive of Churchill's warning. He replied in a noncommittal fashion to Churchill: "the foreign policy of Japan is determined upon and after an unbiased examination of all the facts and a very careful weighing of all the elements of the situation she confronts."[469] Matsuoka's grand strategy had been already wrecked at the end of 1940, but he finally signed the Soviet–Japanese Neutrality Pact with Soviet Foreign Minister Molotov on April 13, 1941.

It was in 1943 that the IJA saw the reality of German power. In February 1943, after the battle of Guadalcanal, the IJA dispatched a delegation to Berlin, headed by Major General Kiyotomi Okamoto, former Department Chief of Army Intelligence. Their report stated that "German national power was lower than we had expected before the Pacific War. It seems difficult to expect German victory in the war unless she can overcome many challenges."[470] Except for those working in intelligence, most Army officers were shocked by the report, but it was too late.

The Tripartite Pact was based on policy makers' subjective speculation, not on objective intelligence assessments. They had pursued the "Don't miss the bus!" policy, and the unrealistic war planning would be repeated throughout the Pacific War as "Best Case Analysis."[471]

THE OSHIMA REPORT AND THE SOVIET–GERMAN WAR

The wartime Japanese government was not good at flexible and prompt decision making. In the process, decision makers and war planners also needed to build consensus among different ministries. Therefore, even in urgent situations, the government could not decide a policy, even if they had received vital intelligence. For example, Japan and Britain obtained the same information about the future outbreak of the Soviet–German war, but their responses were different.

In 1940 the IJA reconsidered its plans for war with the Soviet Union. This was on account of the Japanese defeat at the battle of Nomonhan in 1939, and also because the strength of the Far Eastern Red Army did not decrease in spite of the war in Europe. The IJA estimated that this army had 30 divisions, while there were only 11 divisions of IJA troops stationed in Manchuria. At most the IJA could send another 15 divisions, but the total of 26 divisions was still insufficient to wage a war against the Soviets.[472] The first priority for the IJA was to conclude the war with China, and to this end, severing supply lines from Southeast Asia to China and gaining access to natural resources in the Dutch East Indies were imperative. Therefore, the IJA temporally shelved the plan for the Northern Advance and veered to the south.

Matsuoka's signing of the neutrality pact with the Soviet Union was welcomed by the IJA. Lieutenant General Akira Muto, chief of the Bureau of Military Affairs of the War Ministry, wrote: "It was a tremendous success that Matsuoka signed the pact."[473] However, the IJN still opposed the Southern Advance, which would lead to a war with Britain and the United States. The IJA had to persuade the IJN to agree with the Army's planning. There were several joint meetings between the IJA and IJN held from the beginning of 1941, and they finally reached an agreement to write up the *Tai Nanpo Shisaku Yoko* (The Army and Navy Plan for the Southeast Asian Policy) in June. According to the plan, the Army and Navy decided to advance into southern French Indo-China, severing supply lines to China and containing the British Far Eastern empire. If the Japanese advance should provoke British and US trade sanctions, Japan would be constrained to fight with the British, Dutch, and Americans. In fact, they did not expect Allied economic sanctions in the event of the invasion of French Indo-China.

On April 18, 1941, Major General Hiroshi Oshima, ambassador to Berlin, reported the possibility of the Soviet–German war, but the Japanese government was indifferent to the report, because they were devoting their efforts to improving relations with the United States at that time. The Prime Minister's secretary, Kenji Tomita, wrote: "Prime Minister Konoe seemed to be worried about the report from Oshima, but Matsuoka denied the possibility of the war. The Army and Navy also followed Matsuoka's opinion and the report was passed over."[474] Oshima interviewed the Führer and sent another report to Tokyo on June 4: "Hitler felt that the Soviet attitude, though outwardly friendly, was habitually obstructive and he had decided that Communist Russia must be eliminated ... If Japan lagged behind when Germany declared a state of war against Russia, it was quite open to her to do so ... neither Hitler nor Ribbentrop mentioned a date, but the atmosphere of urgency suggested that it was close at hand."[475]

The British GC&CS shrewdly intercepted Oshima's diplomatic message to Tokyo, and the SIGINT was urgently considered by the JIC.[476] The JIC was convinced about the breakout of a Soviet–German war, and concluded: "fresh evidence is now to hand that Hitler has made up his mind to have done with Soviet obstruction and intends to attack her."[477] Churchill immediately understood the importance of the JIC's conclusion and wrote to US President Franklin Roosevelt: "From every source at my disposal, including some most trustworthy, it looks as if a vast German onslaught on Russia is imminent ... Should this new war break out, we shall, of course, give all encouragement and any help we can spare to the Russians, following the principle that Hitler is the foe we have to beat."[478] The information was passed to Alexander Cadogan, Permanent Under-Secretary for Foreign Affairs, who wrote on June 17: "Meeting at 11:30 to discuss what we do about propaganda in case of German–Soviet conflict ..."[479]

By contrast, Japan's response to the information was very slow. They had been given a preliminary warning about the impending Soviet–German war from Onodera.[480] The IJA and the IJN had already built a consensus that they would advance into southern French Indo-China following the advance into northern French Indo-China of September 1940, but the information from Oshima and Onodera urged them to reconsider their Southern Advance strategy. Oshima's report was distributed to every department of the IJA, and each department had an opportunity to interpret the information. Those who hoped for the Northern Advance promoted a war with the Soviet Union, and those who hoped for the Southern Advance encouraged Japan to invade southern French Indo-China, because Britain and the United States were expected to focus on the Soviet–German war. On June 6, an Army section chiefs' meeting was held to discuss Oshima's report, but the meeting was messed up by confrontation between advocates of the Northern and Southern Advances.[481]

Even at cabinet level, it was difficult to build a consensus on Oshima's report. Although Major General Kiyotomi Okamoto, the Army Intelligence Department Chief, said: "Germany would probably wage a war against the Soviet Union, since the Führer had said so," Foreign Minister Matsuoka objected: "In spite of Oshima's report, I think that the possibility of war would be 40 percent, of Russo-German rapprochement, 60 percent." War Minister

Hideki Tojo simply commented: "I do not think it is an urgent matter."[482] Prime Minister Konoe made it known to Koichi Kido, Ministerial Adviser to the Emperor, that he believed in the outbreak of a Soviet–German war.[483]

It was difficult for the Japanese government to devise a new strategy following Oshima's report, and war planners within the IJA politicized the report to support the preferred policy. Sin'ichi Kamata has described the inadequacies of the Japanese decision-making process.[484] In Kamata's model, policy makers and war planners refrained from making conclusions and felt uncomfortable if they had to decide something. Issues were held over to the next meeting and after several meetings they with luck found a point of compromise. This decision-making model was good for building consensus among departments without causing serious confrontation, but it was time-consuming. Moreover, nobody took definite leadership in decision making.

As far as Oshima's report was concerned, the Japanese government could not come to a conclusion, and sedately rescheduled discussion to the next meeting. They did not engage with the fact that the future Soviet–German war would change the balance between the Allied and Axis powers, but just thought they were betting on the right horse. Actually, the IJA and IJN were only interested in executing their prescribed policy decided in June, the Southern Advance. The IJA connived with the Navy to ignore Oshima's report and did not tackle the problem until the German invasion of the Soviet Union on June 22.[485]

Yet the IJA's Russian Intelligence Section began tackling the issue of the new Soviet–German war at the beginning of June. Lieutenant Colonel Isamu Asai, an officer within the section, had obtained information from the Kwantung Army and was following the movements of the Soviet Army in Siberia.[486] Asai also tried to gain information from the Ministry of Foreign Affairs and the Manchurian Railway Service, and researched into the following topics: 1) Stalin's power base; 2) solidarity within the Soviet government; 3) the Soviet character; 4) the strategic value of Russia's vast territory; 5) Soviet manpower; 6) Soviet national power; 7) Soviet military power; 8) Soviet deployments in the Far East; 9) a comparison of the Soviet Army with the

German Army; 10) German war capability; 11) relations between the Soviet Union, Britain, and the United States; and 12) the influence of the war on world affairs.[487]

Asai wrote that the plan of the Trans-Siberian Railway, which the Russian Section had secretly drawn up, was useful for calculating the transport and logistics capability of the Soviets.[488] Consequently, it became clear that the Soviet Union had not initially diverted its Far Eastern troops to Europe; they still kept at least 30 divisions in East Asia. On July 7, the IJA Operations Department judged that the Soviet–German war was a favorable opportunity for the IJA, and sent 14 divisions to the Kwantung Army in Manchuria to execute the *Kantokuen* (Kwantung Army Special Exercise). The exercise focused on a coming war against the Soviets, but the Intelligence Department warned against such an option, estimating that the Kwantung Army still lacked the manpower to take on 30 Soviet divisions.[489]

Saburo Hayashi concluded: "It is expected that the Germans will occupy Moscow, but have no more success within 1941. During winter time, the Soviet Army can take a breath and they will never surrender. The Communist Party has very strong solidarity. After the fall of Moscow, the Germans will be obliged to continue the war, holding vast captured territory. In summary, the war will not end in the short term." Asai agreed with Hayashi, saying: "the Russians are also expecting UK–US support and they will resist whatever happens, retiring to the Ural Mountains."[490] Contrary to the opinions of many in the Russian Section, mainstream Army officers expected German victory during 1941. The Operations Department predicted that Stalin's government would be overturned through a rebellion after September 1941.[491] Policy makers and war planners of the IJA intentionally ignored those intelligence assessments of the Russian Section that went against their calculations.

On August 7, 1941, Colonel Takeaki Isomura, chief of the Russian Intelligence Section, told Lieutenant Colonel Akiho Ishii of the Military Affairs Bureau, War Ministry that the Soviet–German war would continue beyond 1941.[492] Isomura also reported to the Minister of War, Hideki

Tojo, and the report satisfied Tojo, who was not willing to fight with the Soviet Union.[493]

Major General Shin'ichi Tanaka, Department Chief of Operations, Army General Staff, who was a strong supporter of the Northern Advance, wrote on August 9: "According to the intelligence assessment, a Russian surrender is not expected within 1941. That means we have no chance to wage a war against her in the short term …"[494] In this period the IJA officially decided on the Southern Advance strategy, which meant war with Britain, Holland, and the United States. The IJA ignored reports from Oshima and Onodera through June 1941, and even after the outbreak of war they simply went ahead with their Indo-China strategy. After the advance, some Army officers still expected to wage a war against the Soviet Union, but they gave up the idea when they used the intelligence assessments from the Russian Intelligence Section.

The Oshima case shows us that the Japanese bureaucracy had no flexibility when it had decided on a prescribed plan, even if they had received timely and crucial intelligence. According to Atsushi Moriyama's study, the IJA's policy-making process was fundamentally bottom-up. First, a section chief made a draft policy and the draft was checked and sealed by the Department Chief, Assistant Chief of General Staff, Chief of General Staff, Chief of the Bureau of Military Affairs of War Ministry, Vice Minister of War Ministry, and War Minister. During this bureaucratic procedure, the IJA would submit the Army's draft to the Navy and to the Ministry of Foreign Affairs, and then they tried to build consensus through inter-ministerial discussion.[495] The best prescription for the consensus was actually an ambiguous policy paper. Furthermore, war planners were often preoccupied with the opinions of other sections or departments, and spent valuable time investigating their own people, rather than the enemy.

Such a process was confusing when compared with the policy cycle of the British. As already explained, in the British process the Oshima information was passed from the GC&CS to the JIC and finally reached Churchill's hand within ten days. Churchill had enough time to write to

Roosevelt, and make ready for the coming war. In the Japanese process, the section chief needed intelligence at the first stage of writing a new draft, but he did not require intelligence after sealing his draft. After that, even if he received vital foreign intelligence he could rarely change the original draft, or if he could, it took too much time to start everything over again. This convoluted management was a major reason why the Japanese bureaucracy failed to exploit intelligence efficiently and wasted 18 days of time in the handling of Oshima's report. Major Shiro Hara of the 20th Section of the Army General Staff reflected on this failure: "Ohsima's information was vital for the Japanese government. We should have studied our plan before the outbreak of war."[496] But the fundamental problem was the Japanese decision-making system itself, which could not handle intelligence for war planning or for strategic policy.

A constant theme in Japanese intelligence is of good work being ignored by higher authorities. Back in September 1940, the Japanese government had established the *Soryokusen Kenkyujo* (National Institute for Total War Studies), gathering 30–40 research officers from the IJA, the IJN, and the other government ministries. They conducted war games based on the model of Japan's advance into Southeast Asia. They studied the following: 1) Japanese grand strategy in total war; 2) the war plans of the IJA and IJN; 3) Japanese future foreign policy; 4) propaganda plans; and 5) economic and industrial plans. Their conclusion was that Japan's national power would allow her to fight against the Allied powers for at most two years, and that the Soviet entry into the war would deliver a final blow to Japan. The preliminary survey was quite accurate in terms of mapping future events, except for the US development of the atomic bomb. The institute reported the conclusion to Prime Minister Konoe and War Minister Tojo on August 27 and 28. Tojo commented as follows: "You did a good job, but your report is based on a kind of armchair theory, not a real war. As you can imagine, we had never expected to beat Russia before the Russo-Japanese war, but we won. War is not always carried out as planned. We will face unpredicted elements in war …[497]

The Economic War Planning Section of the War Ministry also reported to the Army General Staff in September 1941: "The Japanese industrial capacity will peak in the near future, while Allied capacity will continue to increase. We cannot fight a long drawn-out war with the Allies." Marshal Hajime Sugiyama, the Chief of Staff for the IJA, said: "The report is perfect and there is no room to argue. But the report is against our national policy [war with the Allies]." He ordered that the report be burnt.[498]

In Japanese war making, we see that once a prescribed plan was officially decided by political leaders, it was almost impossible to change course by rational ideas and intelligence, even if the strategy had been decided on the basis of unsupported and subjective data. In other words, building a consensus among ministries took priority over understanding international relations and world affairs. Making a hard-line foreign policy was generally the easiest form of compromise between the IJA and IJN. The moderate IJN fully understood that they would never beat the United States in a war, but supporting the war was the best way to reach agreement with the IJA.[499] The IJN's goal was also to acquire more funding and expand their ship numbers, and the Pacific War gave them the means to attain both these goals.

THE ADVANCE INTO SOUTHERN INDO-CHINA

As mentioned above, in the case of the Japanese advance into northern French Indo-China in September 1940, Japan monitored British and American diplomatic intentions through SIGINT, and succeeded in advancing into the area without their serious protest. However, in the case of southern Indo-China, Japan made a blunder in its use of signals traffic.

The British GC&CS could not break the Japanese diplomatic cipher "Purple" in early 1941. As a result, at the end of January 1941 the lack of SIGINT combined with Japanese naval maneuvers in Southeast Asian waters caused the "February Crisis" for the British, who feared that their Far Eastern empire was now in real jeopardy.[500] The British government had no way of knowing Japanese intentions, and the JIC concluded: "We have considered in the light of the most recent intelligence, the likelihood of the

Japanese making a hostile move in the near future which would lead to war between ourselves and the Japanese Empire"[501] *The Times* referred to Foreign Minister Matsuoka's provocative speech in the Diet and denounced his words in the press as a threat to peace.[502] Yet at this stage Japan actually did not intend to advance into the British Empire and the feverish British response was caused by lack of solid information. At this point the GC&CS finally succeeded in breaking the cipher with the help of a visiting US codebreaking team.[503] The interception gratified Churchill, who had been worried about the situation in the Far East. He wrote to Cadogan: "These conversations and the delayed telegram have the air of being true, and make one feel the earlier conversations were real ... the danger for the moment seems to have passed."[504]

The outbreak of the Soviet–German war did not change the course of Japanese foreign policy – Japan tried to execute their Southern Advance plan decided in June. On June 16, Matsuoka sent a telegram to Oshima in Berlin: "The Japanese government considers it necessary in view of the existing circumstances, to secure without any delay guarantees for the establishment of air bases in southern Indo-China, and freedom for warships and merchant vessels to come in and out, to anchor, etc. in that area."[505] The telegram was decrypted by the GC&CS on June 21, but the outbreak of the Soviet–German war made the situation uncertain for the British government.

The Japanese government held the *Gozenkaigi* (the supreme decision-making meeting with the Emperor) on July 2 and officially reconfirmed the Southern Advance policy. Matsuoka forwarded the Japanese intentions to Berlin: "the Japanese government has decided to secure *point d'appui* in French Indo-China which will enable Japan to strengthen her pressure further upon Great Britain and the United States."[506] The telegram was also decrypted by the GS&CS and the British government took the interception seriously.

At this point, the British Foreign Minister, Anthony Eden, tried diplomatic means to deter Japan from advancing to the south. He proposed to John Winant, US ambassador to London, that Britain and the United States issue a joint warning to Japan that would quash Japanese ambitions, but the US government did not take the situation seriously.[507] This was primarily because the US government expected that Japan would wage a war against the Soviet Union. Eden hastily leaked the information to the *Daily Telegraph* and ordered Robert Craigie, the British ambassador to Tokyo, to issue warnings to the Japanese government.[508] On July 5, Craigie called on Chuichi Ohashi, the Vice Foreign Minister, to put a brake on Japanese plans. Oshima was stunned by Craigie's visit, writing: "I was really shocked! I do not know how the Britain got our top secret, but it was leaked … When we were about to advance into French Indo-China, Craigie warned us against it … I abruptly said to him, 'it has no basis in fact …'"[509] Craigie's warning did have some influence on Japanese planning, however. The Japanese government did not give up the advance, but became concerned about their intelligence security and decided to delay the operation.[510]

Without any concrete US assistance in the Far East, there was little that Britain could do, however, to control Japanese long-term ambitions. Churchill and Eden did not want a clash with Japan over French Indo-China. John Sterndale Bennett, Chief of the Far Eastern Department, the Foreign Office, wrote:

> In the case of Indo-China, we were not in a position to give an advance warning to Japan for various reasons. Firstly, we were not able to compromise the source of our information. Secondly the measures we were at first preparing were not in our view sufficiently serious to cause the Japanese to cancel their plans in Indo-China. Thirdly, when the US decided on more drastic action the Japanese had already committed themselves and the US were still opposed to anything of a minatory character … we will approach the US government with a view to extracting some assurance of support if we become involved in war with Japan.[511]

The British had gained a breathing space and discussed with the US government courses of action should Japan expand itself into Indo-China. The Japanese government, meanwhile, had decided the date of the operation and Matsuoka sent a message to the Japanese ambassador in Paris. The GC&CS again read this message, and Cadogan wrote: "About 7 we got Japanese intercepts showing the monkeys have decided to seize bases in Indo-China by the 20th."[512] In Washington, D.C., discussions were continuing between the British ambassador, Lord Halifax, and Dean Acheson, the US Assistant Secretary of State, throughout July, and around July 21 they reached an agreement over the British–US joint economic sanctions against Japan. Halifax was convinced that trade sanctions against Japan were approved by President Roosevelt.[513] The IJA and IJN did not know of the talks in Washington, nor expect trade sanctions. In the same month, however, Prime Minister Konoe decided to eject Matsuoka from the cabinet. Konoe set up his new cabinet on July 17 and ordered that Japanese troops move into southern French Indo-China on the 22nd. The United States imposed trade sanctions against Japan on July 25, resulting in a dramatic deterioration in US–Japanese relations.

From the Japanese perspective, the Southern Advance was a well-executed mission, as in the IJA's words: "The advance was a diplomatic success backed by our deliberate preparations and strong military power."[514] However, the British and Americans secretly read Japanese diplomatic traffic and developed measures to increase the impact of the economic sanctions throughout July.

Clearly there was a lack of security awareness among the Japanese government. According to the pre-established Japanese policy, in the event of hostile trade sanctions war with Britain and the United States would be inevitable; hence they were now obliged to think about war. The sanctions threatened the IJN with utter ruin, because it depended heavily on imported oil from the United States. Without any oil, they began to think that a war against the United States was never too early. In addition, on August 14 Churchill and Roosevelt jointly issued the Atlantic Charter, a series of foreign policy statements that made the IJA realize that Britain and the United States could not be separated.

The Japanese government held the *Gozenkaigi* on September 6 and officially decided to wage a war against Britain and the United States in the event of US–Japanese diplomatic talks ending in failure. The IJA and IJN also examined how to win such a war. They concluded that the best-case scenario ran as follows: after securing British, Dutch, and American colonies in the western Pacific, and concluding the Sino-Japanese War, Japan would build up the Great East Asian Co-Prosperity Sphere, providing them with the means for fighting a long, drawn-out war against the Allies. They did not, however, have any concrete plans about how to drive the Americans into surrender, and just assumed a German victory in Europe. Colonel Akiho Ishii, who planned the course of the war for the IJA, admitted with reluctance: "Actually we do not have any ideas …"[515] Captain Tasuku Nakazawa, Chief of the Operations Department of the IJN, also wrote: "We have a weakness in that we do not possess a decisive blow to knock down the UK and US."[516] Neither the IJA nor IJN had studied how to finish the war, but they decided to wage it nevertheless – they had already spent a lot of energy in war planning through 1941. The point of no return was passed in the autumn of 1941.

The IJA leaders had a rather optimistic view of the coming war. They expected that the occupation of Southeast Asia would go smoothly, while a Soviet surrender to Germany and the conclusion of the Sino-Japanese War would free up IJA resources. By contrast, the IJN estimated that they could not fight beyond 1943, while they were concerned that a British and American counter-offensive would emerge. The IJN perspective was more realistic.

The issue was discussed again at the governmental meeting on November 1, which lasted more than 16 hours, but the meeting could not change the commitment to war. War against Britain and the United States became confirmed policy, which was finally submitted to Emperor Hirohito on November 5. Ten days later, the IJA ordered General Hisaichi Terauchi, commander of the IJA South Area Army, to carry out the Southern Advance on the agreed date. On November 26, the IJN's task force began its maneuvers toward Pearl Harbor, the day on which the US government handed the Hull Note to Japan.

THE HULL NOTE AND THE *MODUS VIVENDI*

In the case of the Tripartite Pact and Oshima's report, Japanese strategic thinkers paid no attention to intelligence when they made foreign policy or strategy. Yet at the end of the November 1941, the Japanese government admitted that it required intelligence regarding US intentions.

On November 6, the Japanese government presented *Kou-An* (Proposal A) to the US government through Admiral Kichisaburo Nomura, ambassador to the United States, which proposed a final settlement of the Sino-Japanese War with a partial withdrawal of Japanese troops. However the US government had known through SIGINT (Magic) that there was a follow-up proposal in case Proposal A failed. The US government rejected Proposal A on November 14, and six days later Nomura presented *Otsu-An* (Proposal B) as the Americans had predicted, which proposed that Japan would stop further military action in return for aviation fuel from the United States.[517]

Cordell Hull told the British, Dutch, Australian, and Chinese ambassadors about Proposal B and his outlined counter-proposal, in which the removal of the Japanese troops from southern Indo-China would cause a slight relaxation of the US embargo, including on the oil supply. Hull had also been alerted by Magic intelligence that a breakdown in the negotiations would lead to a war with Japan, and to gain time he was developing a compromise proposal with Japan, known as the *modus vivendi*, which was effectively a short truce along similar lines to Proposal B. He secretly revealed the plan to British, Dutch, Australian, and Chinese representatives on November 22, in Washington, D.C. The Japanese needed to know what was being said.

For the UK, Holland, and Australia, the *modus vivendi* was ideal because they would gain an additional three months for their defensive preparations in Southeast Asia, but it was not acceptable to China. If a compromise were struck between the United States and Japan, China could not expect material support from the Americans in the Sino-Japanese War, which had been running since 1937. In other words, a US–Japanese compromise could mean the US abandonment of China, and the Chinese government insisted that they would never accept the proposal.

The Japanese government keenly awaited a final American decision. On November 25, Lieutenant General Akira Muto said in a meeting:

> US–Japanese negotiations are now in process. Based on information received on the 22nd, the US government did not understand the nature of the Japanese proposal. They are now in discussion with Allied nations in Washington, D.C. I am not sure what they are discussing, but I suppose that they are making a counter-proposal to Japan, a co-sponsored plan for the Pacific region. Our government expected that their proposal would be submitted to us by the 24th, but it has not yet arrived.[518]

Muto, who was the center of power in the IJA, could not obtain information on the *modus vivendi*. Two days later, Muto's junior, Major General Kenryo Sato, Section Chief of the Bureau of Military Affairs, said:

> The US–Japanese negotiations were rescheduled on the 24th and the United States intended to give us a counter-proposal on the 26th, but nothing has transpired. I suppose the delay was caused by disagreement between the United States and United Kingdom about our proposal. I expect that the US–Japanese negotiations will be held on the 27th, and the result will be sent to us soon. I assume that the US proposal will require that Japan stop further military action in return for a relaxation of the US embargo[519]

The words of Sato show that he also was blind to US intentions. This passage suggests that he thought the United States would compromise with Japan, but his speculation was based on headlines from the *Tokyo Nichi Nichi Shinbun* (Tokyo Daily News) on the 27th: "US are ready for trade-off." The article was originally from the *New York Times* of the 25th. As for the article, historian Waldo Heinrichs wrote: "Supplementing official objections were leaks to the press, one, for example, to a *United Press* correspondent by the Chinese embassy in London. Readers of the November 25 *New York Times*, for example, learned the essential provisions of the *modus vivendi*."[520] Foreign Minister

Shigenori Togo, who was responsible for the negotiations with the United States, read this article and also expected the US appeasement of Japan. He sent a message to Ambassador Nomura in Washington: "According to the US press, the United States will request our withdrawal from Indo-China in exchange for the removal of economic pressure."[521]

Policy makers of the IJA and Ministry of Foreign Affairs did buy into the newspaper article, which China had leaked. The IJA and the Foreign Ministry had intelligence branches in Washington, D.C., but none of them were required to produce intelligence assessments on US policy, or execute any espionage or information gathering in the US capital.

Chiang Kai-shek strongly objected to the US appeasement policy through the Chinese ambassadors Hu Shi and Song Zi-wen, and also Owen Lattimore, Chiang's personal American adviser. Heinrichs states that "The Chinese response lacked all subtlety."[522] Hull was fed up with fielding Chinese protests and dropped his complaints to British ambassador Lord Halifax on the Chinese leak to the *New York Times*.[523] In addition, Hull received news that there were signs of an imminent Japanese operation in Southeast Asia. Hull delivered the final Allied proposal, known as the "Hull Note," to Ambassador Nomura on November 26.

The conditions of the Hull Note were severe, demanding the complete withdrawal of all Japanese troops from French Indo-China and also from China. Sato was informed of the note and commented on the 29th: "Reading the proposal, it was far more belligerent than we had expected. Now we decide to wage a war against the United States."[524] Togo was shocked by the proposal because of the gap between his expectation of US appeasement and the harsh terms of the Hull Note, and gave up his diplomatic talks with the United States.[525]

Togo's abandonment of the negotiations paved the way for the outbreak of the Pacific War. On December 2, the Navy General Staff sent a coded message to the IJN Combined Fleet: "Nii Taka Yama Nobore 1208", which means "Execute the Hawaii Operation on December 8 [Japan time]."

CONCLUSION

In the first phase of the Pacific War, Japan was good at using tactical intelligence, as we have seen in the case of the Pearl Harbor and Palembang operations. However, at the strategic level, Japanese policy makers and war planners were not interested in intelligence assessments, despite the fact that they had competent intelligence services. Japanese policy making and the war-planning process were heavily influenced by the IJA, which was not able to handle the full spectrum of political, economic, and international affairs. Success at the beginning of the war, furthermore, encouraged the IJA's spiritualism and IJN's optimism. On the other hand, the British and Americans learned lessons from their defeats and steadily increased their research on Japan. Their intelligence effort would finally lead to their victory in the Far East.

There were several structural problems in Japanese strategic use of intelligence in the war: 1) the vulnerable position of the Intelligence Departments; 2) the lack of central intelligence machinery; and 3) the war planners' indifference to intelligence.

As we have explored throughout this book, IJA and the IJN information gathering was not poor, but structural flaws meant that the efforts were often wasted. In principle, it was Intelligence Departments (the 2nd Department of the Army General Staff and the 3rd Department of the Navy General Staff) that analyzed and assessed foreign intelligence, but in fact it was Operations Departments (the 1st Department of the Army General Staff and the 1st Department of the Navy General Staff) that conducted their own investigations. The best and brightest of the IJA and IJN were usually deployed to the Operations Departments, and the second best were deployed to intelligence. Moreover, both departments had the same information sources, and the operations staff believed that their assessment was superior to that of the intelligence staff. Consequently the operations staff, who were laymen in intelligence analysis, handled both operations and intelligence and tended to look down on the intelligence staff.

The gap between the operations and intelligence staff was so serious that the Chief of the Army's Intelligence Department was alienated from IJA war planning throughout the Pacific War. During the battle of Guadalcanal, Major General Seizo Arisue, Department Chief of Army Intelligence, realized that their intelligence assessment had been neglected by the operations staff and finally he resented integrating the Operations and Intelligence Departments.[526] As an exception, intelligence work on Soviet themes was accepted by the IJA Operations Department, because the Army Russian Intelligence Section had to justify its performance to the Army leaders. Intelligence staff discouraged the Operations Department chief from attacking the Soviets in July and August 1941, and their intelligence report *Taiso Sakusen Shiryo* (Operational Report on the Soviets) was broadly read in IJA circles.

The operations staff usually politicized their intelligence assessment to match their strategic goals. They confused expectations with logical analysis – for example, they believed in a German victory during the Battle of Britain, ignoring information about British performance, and they accepted the idea of a Soviet–German rapprochement just before the German invasion of the Soviet Union. The Army and Navy Intelligence Departments were opposed to such wishful thinking, but they were ignored.

Considering this problem, we can understand why the IJA and IJN were better at tactical intelligence. At a tactical level, intelligence was used for operations before it was politicized or distorted. Yet at broader levels the IJA and IJN failed to construct smooth relations between operations and intelligence. Percy Cradock, who served as chairman of the British JIC, explained that "The best arrangement is intelligence and policy in separate but adjoining rooms, with communication doors and thin partition walls, as in cheap hotels."[527] Japanese intelligence was more specialized at a tactical level, which meant that its use tended to be shortsighted. The IJA's war planning was based on the idea of a short war, such as the First Sino-Japanese and Russo-Japanese Wars. In such conflicts, Japan smashed the opponents on the battlefield, and concluded peace treaties immediately.

The IJN planned the Pearl Harbor operation based on shortsighted tactical information, such as total tonnage of the IJN or weather conditions in the North Pacific, not based on US–Japan relations or the Soviet–German War. According to Admiral Yamamoto, he just hoped for a decline in US morale by attacking Pearl Harbor – there was no exact plan of what to do after the attack.

The Prussian-style war of annihilation needed operational intelligence rather than economic and political intelligence, but the outbreak of World War I had changed war itself, from limited war to total war. The IJA did not seriously join World War I, apart from limited fighting against German garrisons in the Far East. It subsequently researched the war mainly from operational and weapon-based perspectives. Historian John Ferris has written: "In 1914 the IJA was regarded as a formidable and modern army. Since it missed the military revolution forced by the First World War, its reputation declined."[528]

In general an intelligence community needs central intelligence machinery (such as the JIC in Britain and the DNI in the United States) to organize or share the flood of information or intelligence, and such machinery also has a duty to deliver intelligence to policy makers and war planners. In 1940, the Japanese government tried to establish the Cabinet Intelligence Bureau for sharing national intelligence, but the Army and Navy undermined the plan. Finally, the Bureau was assigned only propaganda work.

The lack of a central intelligence organization caused significant troubles during the Pacific War. For example, in the battle of Leyte Gulf in October 1944, the IJN suffered heavy losses, but they falsely announced to the public that the IJN had sunk 11 aircraft carriers, two battleships, and three cruisers – if true, that would mean the USN was effectively defeated. The IJA, which was not informed of the result of the battle by the Navy, believed the false figures of the announcement and changed its strategy accordingly. The IJA had planned to wage a decisive battle against the US troops on Luzon Island, but the news of annihilation of the USN made it provoke a battle on Leyte Island, located hundreds of miles south of Luzon. For the operation the IJA sent its main corps from Luzon to Leyte, but most of them were annihilated by US air raids during transit.

In codebreaking fields there was also a serious split between the IJA and IJN. Although the Army SIS could break some of the US military ciphers made by the M-94 and M-209 ciphering machines, the Navy SIS failed to break them. The Army was superior to the Navy in codebreaking, and the codebreakers of the IJA knew the vulnerability of the Navy's code. However they did not share their knowledge of codebreaking, and the Navy was not informed of their vulnerability. The security of the IJA's operational cipher was comparatively tough, but the IJN's operational cipher was broken by US codebreakers just before the battle of Midway in June 1942. It was not until mid-1943 that an intelligence meeting was held between the Army and Navy intelligence section chiefs on a regular and systematic basis. Finally in January 1945, Major Kazuo Kamaga, specialist in breaking US codes, gave lessons to Navy codebreakers, but the lesson was not an official one. The Army General Staff appeared displeased with the tutoring because their method of codebreaking was a top secret matter known only within the IJA.[529] At any rate, it was too late for the Navy to learn the requisite skills.

As already mentioned, war planners and decision makers were often only interested in gathering internal information to give them an advantage in negotiating with other branches of the government or military, and spent much energy building a consensus and a career among ministries. This situation was dangerous for the IJA and IJN, and led to many mistakes in judging situations in the Pacific War.

Japanese politicians were even less interested in foreign intelligence. Foreign Minister Matsuoka strongly pushed his design of a Four-Powers treaty with the Soviets, Italy, and Germany, but his foreign policy was not based on strategic intelligence estimations. There was no intelligence consumer in the Japanese government, and this void caused an incomplete intelligence cycle. Mark Lowenthal has written that "once the intelligence has been given to the policy client, the intelligence process is complete."[530] Such was far from the case in both pre-war and wartime Japan.

It is true that the IJA and IJN were defeated in the "intelligence war" by the Allied forces in World War II. The defeat was partly fueled by their "best case analysis" mindset, which caused lack of foresight at a strategic level. Yet it was not Intelligence Departments, but war planners in Operations Departments who decided strategy. The war planners usually chose intelligence reports in an arbitrary and impromptu manner for their own strategic goals. Clearly, they failed to use intelligence with a strategic point of view.

Intelligence Departments in the IJA and IJN did, however, perform well despite limited budgets and staff. They demonstrated skill in several tactical settings, such as the conflicts with China and Russia and the early stages of the Pacific War. Surviving official documents of the Army and Navy have preserved a vestige of their efforts at collecting and analyzing information for tactical operations.

It is well known that the Army's *Tokumu Kikan* groups, such as *F Kikan* and *Koua Kikan*, undertook intelligence operations in Manchuria, China, and Southeast Asia, as shown in many books published on such subjects after the war. We can also read several books on the Sorge affair, and newly released documents in Britain have revealed the espionage activities of individuals such as Rutland and Mayers. As far as SIGINT is concerned, there was a rumor spread after the war that officers who engaged in SIGINT would be sentenced to life imprisonment. Due to the rumor, intelligence officers destroyed most of their secret documents and have kept silence since the war. Some ex-officers whom I interviewed are still afraid of the United States conducting investigations into their SIGINT activities during the war.

Studies on Japanese intelligence are in their infancy in Japan, especially regarding SIGINT. Further studies on Japanese SIGINT capability will throw a new spotlight on diplomatic and military history in the 1930s and 1940s. For example, Japanese SIGINT revealed Allied weakness and vacillation, which was one of the reasons behind the Japanese decision to advance into northern French Indo-China in September 1940. On the other hand, it is becoming clear that the IJA's codebreaking negatively influenced Japanese diplomacy in the 1940s. Japanese political leaders were afraid of the Army's eavesdropping, and they realized that they were not allowed to reach compromises with foreign diplomats without the Army's consent. The internal codebreaking activities made Japanese diplomatic policy rigid in the 1940s.

If the former Allied and Axis countries could read their opponents' diplomatic and military traffic, "Reading Each Other's Mail"[531] in Edward Drea's words, we might have to reconsider the history of World War II. Archives in several countries still hold onto intelligence documents, and without seeing those documents we cannot entirely understand the whole process of history up to and during the war.

NOTES

Introduction

1   Tsutao Ariga, *Nihon Riku Kai Gun no Joho Kiko to Sono Katsudo* (The Organization and Activities of the IJA and IJN) (Kindai Bungeisha, 1994).

2   Takeo Imai, *Showa no Boryaku* (Conspiracies in the Showa Era) (Hara Shobo, 1967); Saburo Hayashi, *Kantogun to Kyokuto Sorengun* (The Kwantung Army and the Soviet Far Eastern Army) (Fuyo Shobo, 1974); Yukio Nishihara, *Zen Kiroku Harbin Tokumu Kikan* (Complete Record of the Harbin Special Agency) (Mainichi Shinbunsha, 1980); Iwaichi Fujiwara, *F Kikan* (F Agency) (Hara Shobo, 1966).

3   Nakano Koyukai, *Rikugun Nakano Gakko* (Army Nakano School) (Hara Shobo, 1978).

4   Ichiji Sugita, *Joho Naki Senso Shido* (Conducting War Without Intelligence) (Hara Shobo, 1987); Eizo Hori, *Nichibei Joho Senki* (Record of the US–Japanese Intelligence War) (Bungei Shunju, 1994).

5   Ishiki Yamamoto, *Nihon Bocho shi* (History of Japanese Counter-Intelligence) (Jinbunkaku, 1942); Kenpci-tai (Military Police) HQ, *Nihon Kenpei Showa Shi* (History of the Japanese Military Police in the Showa Era) (original text was reprinted by Kyokuto Shuppan Kenkyukai in 1969); Zenkoku Kenyukai Rengokai, *Nihon Kenpei Seishi* (Orthodox History of the Japanese Military Police) (Kenbun Shoin, 1975); Zenkoku Kenyukai Rengokai, *Nihon Kenpei Gaishi* (Another History of the Military Police) (Kenbun Shoin, 1983); Keijiro Otani, *Showa Kenpei shi* (History of the Military Police in the Showa Era) (Misuzu Shobo, 1966); Yutaka Kudo, *Cho-ho Kenpei* (Espionage by the Military Police) (Tosho Shuppansha, 1984).

6   Toshiyuki Yokoi, *Nihon no Kimitsu shitsu* (Japanese Black Chamber) (Rokumeisha, 1951); Yuzuru Sanematsu, *Joho Senso* (Intelligence War) (Tosho Shuppansha, 1972); Kenichi Nakamuta, *Joho Shikan no Kaiso* (Memoir of an Intelligence Officer) (Daiyamondosha, 1974); Motonao Samejima, *Moto Gunreibu Tsushin Kacho no Kaiso* (Memoir of an Ex-Chief of Communications, Navy General Staff) (not for sale, 1981).

7   Hisashi Takahashi, "Nihon Rikugun to Taichu Joho" (The IJA and its Intelligence in China), *Gunji Shigaku* (The Journal of Military History) WWII (2) 1996.

8   Ryouichi Tobe, *Nihon Rikugun to Chugoku:"Shina-tsu"ni Miru Yume to Satetsu* (The Japanese Imperial Army and China: Dream and Failure of China-hands) (Kodansha Sensho Metier, 1999).

9   David Barrett and Larry Shyu, *Chinese Collaboration with Japan 1932–1945; The Limits of Accommodation* (Stanford UP, 2001); Timothy Brook, *Collaboration: Japanese Agents and Local Elites in Wartime China* (Harvard UP, 2007).

10   David Kahn, *The Codebreakers: The Story of Secret Writing* (Macmillan, 1967) pp. 579–610.

11   Arthur Marder, *Old Friends, New Enemies: The Royal Navy and the Imperial Japanese Navy* (Oxford UP, 1981).

12   F. W. Deakin and G. R. Storry, *The Case of Richard Sorge* (Chatto & Windus, 1966); Gordon Prange, *Target Tokyo: The Story of the Sorge Spy Ring* (McGraw-Hill, 1984).

13   Joyce Lebra, *Japanese Trained Armies in South-East Asia* (Columbia UP, 1971); Peter Fay, *The Forgotten Army: India's Armed Struggle for Independence, 1942–1945* (University of Michigan Press, 1993).

14   Ian Nish, "Japanese Intelligence and the Approach of the Russo-Japanese War," in Christopher Andrew and David Dilks (eds.), *The Missing Dimension* (University of Illinois Press, 1984); J. W. M..Chapman, "Japanese Intelligence 1918–1945: A Suitable Case for Treatment," in Christopher Andrew and Jeremy Noakes, *Intelligence and International Relations 1900–1945* (Exeter UP, 1987); Michael Barnhart, "Japanese Intelligence before the Second World War: 'Best Case' Analysis'," in Ernest May, *Knowing One's Enemy* (Princeton UP, 1986); Louis Allen, "Japanese Intelligence Systems," *Journal of Contemporary History*, Vol. 22 (1987).

15   Tony Matthews, *Shadow Dancing: Japanese Espionage against the West, 1939–1945* (St. Martin's Press, 1993); Stephen Mercado, *The Shadow Warriors of Nakano: A History of the Imperial Japanese Army's Elite Intelligence School* (Brassey's, 2002).

16   Kahn, op. cit.; Edward Drea, "Reading Each Other's Mail: Japanese Communications Intelligence, 1920–1941," *Journal of Military History*, Vol. 55, No. 2 (April 1991); Edward Drea, "New Evidence on Breaking the Japanese Army Codes," *Intelligence and National Security*, Vol. 14, No. 1 (Spring 1999); John Prados, *Combined Fleet Decoded: The Secret History of American Intelligence and the Japanese Navy in World War II* (Annapolis, 1995); Elmer Potter, "The Crypt of Cryptanalysts," *US Naval Institute Proceedings*, Vol. 109, No. 8 (August 1983).

17   J. W. Bennett, W. A. Hobart, and J. B. Spitzer, *Intelligence and Cryptanalytic Activities of the Japanese during World War II* (Aegean Park Press, 1986) p. 6.

18   Recently released documents in the British National Archives are useful in studying Japanese Intelligence in WWII. "Security of British and Allied Communications," HW 40/8, PRO; "Japanese Security Services: Home Organization," KV 3/295–297, PRO.

19   Ariga comprehensively organized the historical transitions of the Army and Navy's intelligence apparatus from the 1870s to 1945. Tsutao Ariga, *Nihon Riku*

Kai Gun no Joho Kiko to Sono Katsudo (The Organizations and Activities of the IJA and IJN) (Kindai Bungeisha, 1994). Moriyama shows how the IJA broke the US diplomatic traffic, comparing US documents decoded by the IJA with original US diplomatic drafts in the 1940s. He also mathematically broke the US Strip Ciphers by himself. Atsushi Moriyama, "Senkanki ni okeru Nihon no Ango Nouryoku ni Kansuru Kiso Kenkyu" (Basic Research on Japanese Codebreaking Capability in the Inter-War Period)," *Kokusai Kankei Hikaku Bunka Kenkyu*, Vol. 3, No. 1 (September 2004). Teruji Kondo, who was the youngest codebreaker of the IJA at the end of the Pacific War and engaged in codebreaking after the war, occasionally wrote essays for *Kaiko*. His essay "Ango Sen" (Codebreaking War) appeared in December 1999. Hiroyasu Miyasugi also wrote an impressive essay about Japanese codebreaking and the diplomatic decision-making process in the 1930s: Hiroyasu Miyasugi, "Senzen Nihon no Ango Kaidoku Joho no Dentatsu Ruto" (Communication Routes of Japanese Signal Intelligence before the Pacific War), *Nihon Rekishi* (December 2006). Ken Kotani shows that the Japanese Navy was able to read the British, US, French, and Chinese diplomatic traffic in 1940. Ken Kotani, "Could Japan Read Allied Signal Traffic?: Japanese Codebreaking and the Advance into French Indo-China, September 1940," *Intelligence and National Security*, Vol. 20, No. 2 (June 2005).

20   Chapman, op. cit.; Edward Drea, "Reading Each Other's Mail."

1. Japanese Intelligence: A Brief History

21   Kenji Sato, *Sonshi no Shisoteki Kenkyu* (Studies of Sun Tzu's Thought) (Hara Shobo, 1980).

22   Soko Yamaga, *Sonshi Kogi* (Lecture of Sun Tzu) (1911) p.10.

23   Nish, op. cit., Chapman, op. cit.

24   Nakano Koyukai, *Rikugun Nakano Gakko* (Army Nakano School) (Hara Shobo, 1978) p.7.

25   Kenichiro Igarashi, "Nisshin Senso Kaisen Zengo no Teikoku Riku Kai Gun no Josei Handan to Joho Katsudo (IJA and IJN Intelligence Activities and their Estimations before the Sino-Japanese War), in Boei-cho Boei Kenkyu-jo (The National Institute for Defense Studies), *Senshi Kenkyu Nenpo* (Military History Studies Annual), Vol. 4 (2001).

26   Kenichiro Igarashi, "Teikoku Riku Kaigun no Joho to Josei Handan: Hokushinjihen kara Nichiro Senso e" (Intelligence and Analysis of the IJA and IJN: From the Boxer Rebellion to the Russo-Japanese War), *NIDS Security Report*, Vol. 5, No. 2 (March 2003) p.176.

27   Morio Sato, "Joho Senso to shite no Nichiro Senso (3)" (Russo-Japanese War as an Intelligence War, Vol. 3), *Hokudai Hogaku Ronshu* (Hokkaido University

Collection of Scholarly and Academic Papers, Graduate School of Law), Vol. 51, No. 2 (2000) p.570.

28 Shigeyoshi Shimanuki, *Senryaku Nichiro Senso, Jo* (Strategy in the Russo-Japanese War, Vol. 1) (Hara Shobo, 1980) p.196.

29 Motojiro Akashi, *Rakka Ryusui: Colonel Akashi's Report on His Secret Cooperation with the Russian Revolutionary Parties during the Russo-Japanese War*, O. Fält and A. Kujala (eds), *Studia Historica 31* (Helsinki, 1988).

30 Michael Herman, *Intelligence Power in Peace and War* (Cambridge UP, 1996), p.25.

31 *Joho Kinmu no Sanko* (Textbook for the Intelligence Service), NIDS Military Archives (NIDSMA).

32 *Nai Gai Josei no Gaiyo Hyo* (Summary of Domestic and Foreign Affairs) (NIDSMA).

33 *Jokyo Handan Shiryo* (Situation Estimate Document) (NIDSMA)

34 Yuzuru Sanematsu, "Joho Sakusen ni Tsuite" (On Intelligence in Operations) (NIDSMA).

35 Nobuhiko Imai, "Gunrei-bu Tai-bei Joho Buin Imai Nobuhiko Shuki" (Memoir of Nobuhiko Imai, Staff Officer of US Intelligence Section, the Navy General Staff) (NIDSMA).

36 Ibid.

37 Ibid.

38 *Tekisei Joho Shusen Zenya* (Information on Enemies at the Last Stage of the War), (NIDSMA).

39 There are FBI reports on Masao Tsuda in Argentina: RG 38 ONI Records, Counter Intelligence Branch; Sabotage, Espionage and Counterespionage Section, Records of the Oriental Desk, 1936–1946 Box 18, NARA.

40 Marder, op. cit., p.337.

2. Japanese Army Intelligence

41 Ryohei Osawa (ed.), *Sakae Butai-shi* (The History of the 'Sakae' Troop) (not for sale, 1995) p.56.

42 Yukio Yokoyama, "Tokushu Joho Kaiso-ki" (Memories of Special Intelligence) (NIDSMA).

43 Toshijiro Okubo, "Tai-ro Ango Kaidoku ni Kansuru Soushi Narabi ni Senkun-to ni Kansuru Shiryo (Materials on the Origins of Codebreaking against the Soviet Union and on the Guidelines for the War etc.) (NIDSMA).

44 Ibid.

45 Yokoyama, op. cit.

Notes

46   Teruji Kondo, "Ango-sen 3: Bei Kokumu-sho Gure Kodo no Kaidoku" (Codebreaking War, Vol. 3: Decrypt of the Gray Code of the US Department of State), *Kaiko* (March 2000) p.40.

47   Yokoyama, op. cit.

48   Ariga, op. cit., p.72.

49   Okubo, op. cit.

50   Ariga, op. cit., p.58.

51   Yokoi, op. cit.

52   Denpa Kankei Bukkosha Kensho Ireikai, *Kaigun Denpa Tsuioku-shu Dai 1 go* (Memories of Naval Signal Traffic Vol. 1) (not for sale, 1955) p.252.

53   Moriyama, op. cit.

54   "Enemy Success with US Strip Ciphers" (10 April 1943) HW 40/258, PRO.

55   The Finnish codebreaking organization also broke the Strip Ciphers.

56   Ariga, op. cit., p.315.

57   Kanehara Setsuzo, *Daitoa Senso Rikugun Eiseishi* (The Army Medical History of the Pacific War) (not for sale, 1971) p.281.

58   Eiichi Hirose, "Finrando ni Okeru Tsushin Choho" (Signals Intelligence in Finland), in Dodai Kurabu Keizai Konwakai, *Showa Gunji Hiwa (Jo)* (Secret Military Stories of the Showa Era, Vol. 1) (Doudai Keizai Konwakai, 1989) p.60.

59   This kind of source has been open since 2003. According to the archives, Japan broke four types of British code: Cipher M, the Admiralty Reporting Code, the Interdepartmental Cipher, and R Code. "Copies of British Cipher Documents Captured by the Japanese and Found in German OKW/CHI Archives," HW 40/211, PRO.

60   Muneharu Kubo, "Bocho ni Kansuru Kaiso Choshuroku" (Records of Recollections about Counter-Intelligence) (NIDSMA).

61   "Security of British and Allied Communications," HW 40/8, PRO.

62   Sanbo Honbu, "Tokushu Joho-bu Rinji Hensei Shiryo" (Records of the Extraordinary Establishment of the Special Intelligence Department) (NIDSMA).

63   Ibid. and Ariga, op. cit., p.156.

64   According to ex-Lieutenant Colonel Takeo Hagino, officer in the HQ of the Kwantung Army (Intelligence), the number of people employed in IJA intelligence was about 3,000 at the end of the war. Takeo Hagino, "Tokujo ni Kansuru Senkun" (Maxims on Signals Intelligence) (NIDSMA).

65   Yokoyama, op. cit.

66   Ibid.

67 Eizo Hori, *Daihon'ei Sanbo no Joho Senki* (Intelligence War of an Army Staff Officer in the Imperial HQ) (Bunshun Bunko, 1996), pp.257–58.

68 "Security of British and Allied Communications," HW 40/8, PRO.

69 Okubo, op. cit.

70 Ariga, op. cit., p.149.

71 Osawa, op. cit., p.41.

72 Fumimaro Konoe, *Heiwa eno Doryoku* (Effort for Peace) (Nihon Denpou Tushin-sha, 1946) p.5; Nakamuta, op. cit., p.89.

73 Kumao Harada, *Saionji-ko to Seikyoku* (Duke Saionji and Political Affairs), Vol. 7 (Iwanami Shoten, 1952) p.364.

74 Yokoyama, op. cit.

75 Ibid.

76 "Security of British and Allied Communications," HW 40/8, PRO.

77 Barbara Tuchman, *Stillwell and the American Experience in China, 1911–45* (Macmillan, 1970) p. 386.

78 "Leakage of Information through Cipher Messages of Chinese Service Attaché," HW 40/207, PRO.

79 Ibid.

80 Richard Aldrich, *Intelligence and the War against Japan: Britain, America and the Politics of Secret Service* (Cambridge UP, 2000) p.249.

81 Yokoyama, op. cit.

82 Kita-shina Homen-gun Shirei-bu, *Kita-shina Homen-gun Joho Shuninsha Kaido Kankei Shiryo* (Records about the Senior Intelligence Officer Meeting of the North China Area Army) (NIDSMA).

83 Hagino, op. cit.

84 Yokoyama, op. cit.

85 Etsuo Koutani, *Manshu ni Okeru Joho Kinmu* (Intelligence Work in Manchuria) (NIDSMA).

86 Koyukai, op. cit., p.193.

87 Ibid, p.747.

88 Gunzo Ota, "Hokubu-gun Karahuto Tushinsho Gyomu Kiroku" (Service Records of the Northern Army Sakhalin Communication Site) (NIDSMA).

89 Saburo Hayashi, "Wareware wa Donoyoni Taiso Joho Kinmu wo Yattaka" (How Did We Conduct Intelligence Operations Against the Soviet Union?) (NIDSMA).

90 Hirose, op. cit., p.60.

91 Osawa, op. cit., p.182.

Notes

92   NIDS, *Senshi Sosho, Daitoa Senso Kaisen Keii (4)* (The Process of the Outbreak of the Pacific War Vol. 4, War History Series) (Asagumo Shinbunsha, 1974) pp.307–08.

93   Koutani, op. cit.

94   HW 40/236, PRO.

95   Hayashi, op. cit.

96   "Security of British and Allied Communications," HW 40/8, PRO.

97   HW 40/236, PRO.

98   "Security of British and Allied Communications," HW 40/8, PRO. "About the Decrypted Records of the Soviet Code," see "Japanese R/I on Soviet Communications," NND9G301, US National Archives and Records Administration (NARA).

99   Hayashi, op, cit.

100   Hagino, op. cit.

101   Kazuo Kamaga, "Daitoa Senso ni Okeru Ango-sen to Gendai Ango" (Covert Operations in the Pacific War and Modern Code), in Dodai Kurabu Keizai Konwakai, op. cit., Vol. 2, p.199.

102   Yokoyama, op. cit.

103   Okura-sho Showa Zaisei-shi Henshu-shitsu, *Showa Zaisei-shi* (Financial History of the Showa Period, Vol. 4) (Toyo Keizai Shinposha, 1955) p.266.

104   Nakano Koyukai, op. cit., p.889. The name *Tokumu Kikan* derived from the Russian term for a military board. Originally, the IJA applied *Tokumu* to named agencies that did not belong officially to any forces.

105   Rikugun-sho, *Tokumu Kikan ni Kansuru Soukatsu-teki Hokoku* (Summary Report on the Special Duty Agencies) (NIDSMA).

106   Masatane Kanda, "Joho Kinmu ni Taisuru Kaiso" (Memories of Intelligence Service) (NIDSMA).

107   For more on the Harbin Agency, see Yukio Nishihara, op. cit.

108   *Kanto-gun Shozoku no Tokushu Butai (2)* (Special Divisions of the Kwantung Army, Vol. 2) (NIDSMA).

109   Nishihara, op. cit., pp.46–58.

110   Ibid, p.45.

111   James Harris, "Encircled by Enemies: Stalin's Perception of the Capitalist World", *The Journal of Strategic Studies*, Vol. 30, No. 3 (June 2007) p.525.

112   Kanto-gun Sanbo-bu, *Showa 11 Nen 9 Gatsu Tai-so Choho Kikan Kyoka Keikaku* (The Plan for Reinforcing the Intelligence Apparatuses against the Soviet Union, September 1936) (NIDSMA).

113 John Stephan, *The Russian Fascists: Tragedy and Farce in Exile 1925–1945* (Harper & Row 1978) p.202.

114 *Showa 14 Nen Riku Shi Ju Dai-Nikki Dai 32 Go* (Chinese Army Highly Confidential Daily Report, 1939, Vol. 32) (NIDSMA).

115 Nakano Koyukai, op. cit., p.23. The majority of the Army General Staff were indifferent to the foundation of the Nakano School, so the school was placed in the annex building of the *Aikoku Fujinkai* (Patriotic Ladies' Association) in Kudan, Tokyo.

116 Rikugun Nakano Gakko Koyukai, *Himitsu-sen Gairon* (Introduction to Covert War) (NIDSMA).

117 *Showa 14 Nen Mitudai Nikki Dai 5 Satsu* (Highly Confidential Daily Report, 1939, Vol. 5) (NIDSMA).

118 Hayashi, op. cit.

119 Ibid.

120 Ibid.

121 Paul W. Doerr, "The Changkufeng/Lake Khasan incident of 1938: British Intelligence on Soviet and Japanese Military Performance," *Intelligence and National Security* (July 1990) p.187.

122 Albin Coox (trans. by Yasuo Kobayashi), "Ryushikofu Hoan Iin no Bomei" (Exile of Directorate Ryushkov), *Gunji Shigaku* (The Journal of Military History), Vol. 92 (Mar 1998) p.77.

123 Koutani, op. cit.

124 Hayashi, op. cit.

125 Koutani, op. cit.

126 Ibid.

127 Ibid.

128 Yutaka Kudo, *Cho-ho Kenpei* (Espionage by the Military Police) (Tosho Shuppansha, 1984) p.90; Zenkoku Kenyukai Rengokai, *Nippon Kenpei Gaishi* (Unofficial History of the Military Police) (Kenbun Shoin, 1983) p.694.

129 Ibid, p.693.

130 Koutani, op. cit.

131 Nishihara, op. cit., pp.144–47.

132 "Report on Interrogation of Col Nishihara Yukio by Maj. Ralli at the War Ministry on 2 Apr. 1946," HW 40/208, PRO.

133 "Security of British and Allied Communications," HW 40/8, PRO.

134 Koutani, op. cit.

135 *So-gun Kokkyo Chikujo Joho Kiroku* (The Record of Information about the Soviet Construction of Tochkas along the Border) (NIDSMA).

136 Tatsumi Kusaba, "Shaso yori Rokoku wo Mite" (Watching Russia from Train Windows) (NIDSMA).

137 Koyukai, op. cit., p.70.

138 "Arisue Seizo Bunsho" (Private Collections of Seizo Arisue), Kokuritsu Kokkai Toshokan (National Diet Library, Japan).

139 Hayashi, op. cit.

140 Koyukai, op. cit., p.144.

141 Gunji-shi gakkai (eds.), *Kimitsu Senso Nisshi* (Secret War Record) Vol. 2 (Kinshosha 1998), p.703.

142 Nishihara, op. cit., p.152.

143 Koutani, op. cit.

144 Mantetsu Chosa-bu, *So-ren Chosa Siryo Geppo* (Monthly Soviet Research Report) (NIDSMA).

145 Hayashi, op. cit.

146 Yuriko Onodera, *Baruto-kai no Hotori nite* (On the Edge of the Baltic Sea) (Kyodo Tsushinsha, 1985) p.37.

147 "Copy of Statement Handed in by Kraemer," 14, 9, 45, KV 2/243, PRO.

148 Hayashi, op. cit.

149 Ibid.

150 Koutani, op. cit.

151 NIDS, *Senshi Sosho Hokushi no Chian Sen (1)* (Counter-Insurgency in North China, Vol. 1) (Asagumo, 1968) p.215.

152 Tobe, op. cit., p.221.

153 For details, see Imai, op. cit.; Rechard Deacon, *Kempei Tai: A History of the Japanese Secret Service* (Berkley Publishing Group, 1985); Tobe, op. cit.

154 Tobe, op. cit., pp.221–23.

155 NIDS, *Senshi Sosho Hokushi no Chian Sen (1)*, p.218.

156 *Shina Chuton Kenpei-tai Shirei-bu Shiryo* (Documents of the Military Police HQ in China) (NIDSMA).

157 Zenkoku Kenyukai Rengokai, *Nihon Kenpei Seishi* (Orthodox History of the Japanese Military Police) (Kenbun Shoin, 1975) p.834.

158 Ibid., pp.833–35.

159 *Shina Chuton Kenpei-tai Shirei-bu Shiryo*.

160 NIDS, *Senshi Sosho Hokushi no Chian Sen (1)*, p.220.

161 *Hokushina Homen Gun Sakusen Kiroku* (North China Army Operational Record) (NIDSMA).

162 Yokoyama, op. cit.

163 Japanese Military Espionage Agencies, RG 38 ONI Records, NARA. Taketoshi Yamamoto (ed.), *Daini-ji Sekai Taisen-ki: Nippon no Choho Kikan Bunseki, Dai 4 kan Chugoku-hen 1* (WWII: Analysis of the Japanese Intelligence Agencies, Vol. 4, China Series 1) (Kashiwa Shobo, 2000) p.6.

164 Nakano Koyukai, op. cit., p.18.

165 Imai, op. cit., pp.186–92.

166 Nakano Koyukai, op. cit., p.12.

167 Chu-shi Haken Tokumu Kikan Honbu, *Chu-shi Haken Tokumu Kikan Honbu (Dai 13 gun) Enkaku* (History of the HQ of Special Agencies sent to Central China (the Thirteenth Army)) (NIDSMA).

168 Nakano Koyukai, op. cit., p.312.

169 Ibid, p.313.

170 Aldrich, op. cit., p.29.

171 Nakano Koyukai, op. cit., p.313.

172 Zenkoku Kenyukai Rengokai, *Nihon Kenpei Gaishi* (Another History of the Military Police) (Kenbun Shoin, 1983) p.782.

173 Yoshitane Haruke, *Boryaku no Shanhai* (Conspiracies in Shanghai) (Ato Shobo, 1951) pp.122–23.

174 Ibid, p.38.

175 Ibid, pp.82–83.

176 Zenkoku Kenyukai Rengokai, *Nihon Kenpei Gaishi*, p.780.

177 Yoshimasa Okada, "Hong Kong Kosaku no Kaiso" (Recollections of Espionage and Plot Activities in Hong Kong) (NIDSMA).

178 J. W. M. Chapman (ed.), *The Price of Admiralty* (Salitre Press, 1984), Vol. 2 and 3, pp.262–67.

179 COS (40) 592, CAB 66/10, PRO. See also Peter Elphick, *Far Eastern File: The Intelligence War in the Far East, 1930–1945* (Hodder and Stoughton, 1997) pp.255–67; James Rusbridger, "The Sinking of the *Automedon* and the Capture of the *Nankin*," *Encounter*, Vol. 64, No. 5 (May 1985) pp.8–14.

180 Rikugun-sho, *Showa 17 Nen Riku-gun-sho Riku A Mitsu Dai-nikki, dai 07 go* (Asian Army Highly Confidential Daily Report, 1942, War Ministry) (NIDSMA).

181 Rikugun-sho, *Showa 14 Nen Riku Kimitsu Dai-nikki, dai 2 satsu* (Army Highly Confidential Daily Report 1939) (NIDSMA).

182 Sugita, op. cit., p.20.

183 Doudai Keizai Konwakai, Vol. 2, pp.274–75.

184 Ibid., p.274.

185 Ibid., Vol. 2, p.267.

186 Nakano Koyukai, op. cit., p.892.

187 Hiroshi Tamura, "Taikoku Kankei Tamura Bukan Memo" (Military Attaché Tamura's Memo on Thailand) (NIDSMA).

188 Sugita, op. cit., p.146.

189 Sanbo Honbu, *Showa 16 Nen, Eiryo Malai Joho Kiroku* (Intelligence Record on British Malaya, 1941) (NIDSMA).

190 Iwaichi Fujiwara, *F Kikan* (F Agency) (Hara Shobo, 1966), p.36.

191 Ibid., pp.75–8.

192 Ibid., pp.118–20.

193 Peter Fay, *The Forgotten Army: India's Armed Struggle for Independence, 1942–1945,* (University of Michigan Press, 1993) p.83.

194 Nakano Koyukai, op. cit., p.427.

195 Rikichiro Sawamoto, "Minami Kikan Gai-shi" (Unofficial History of Minami Agency) (NIDSMA).

196 Nakano Koyukai, op. cit., p.355.

197 Ariga, op. cit., p.116.

198 Kimitada Miwa, "Tai-bei Kessen eno Imeji" (View on the War against the United States)," in Hidetoshi Kato and Shunsuke Kamei (eds.), *Nihon to Amerika* (Japan and the United States) (Nihon Gakujutsu Shinkokai, 1976) p.262.

199 Hayashi, op. cit. p.256.

200 Ariga, op. cit. pp.119–21.

201 Keijiro Otani, *Showa Kenpei Shi* (History of the Military Police in the Showa Era) (Misuzu Shobo, 1966) p.578.

202 "Bocho no Sanko" (Textbook for Counter-Intelligence) (NIDSMA).

203 Otani, op. cit., p.615.

204 Minoo Hidaka, *Gunki Hogo-ho* (Military Secret Act) (Haneda Shoten, 1937) pp.24–98; Takeshichiro Otake, *Kokubo Hoan-ho* (National Security Act) (Haneda Shoten, 1941) pp.18–60.

205 Zenkoku Kenyukai Rengokai, *Nihon Kenpei Seishi*, p.296.

206 Kita-shina Haken Kenpeitai Kyoshutai, *Sokyo Jitsumu Kyoan: Kita-shina Haken Kenpeitai Kyoshutai* (Textbook for Anti-Communist Activities: North China Expeditionary Military Police Training Troop) (NIDSMA).

207 Ibid.

208 Zenkoku Kenyukai Rengokai, *Nihon Kenpei Seishi*, p.337.

209 Kudo, op. cit., p.110.

210 Rikugun-sho, *Riku Man Mitsu Dai Nikki, Showa 16 Nen Dai 10* (Manchurian Army Highly Confidential Daily Report, No. 10) (1940) (NIDSMA).

211 Zenkoku Kenyukai Rengokai, *Nihon Kenpei Gaishi*, pp.240–48.

212 "Showa 2 Nen Oshu Shitaru Himitsu Bunsho Dai 6 Go, Sanbo Honbu (Confiscated Document No. 6 of 1927, Army General Staff) (NIDSMA).

213 Antony Best, *British Intelligence and the Japanese Challenge in Asia, 1914–1941* (Palgrave 2002) p.57.

214 Zenkoku Kenyukai Rengokai, *Nihon Kenpei Gaishi*, p.779.

215 Ibid., pp. 851–52.

216 Ibid.

217 Zenkoku Kenyukai Rengokai, *Nihon Kenpei Seishi* (Orthodox History of the Japanese Military Police) (Kenbun Shoin, 1975) p.672.

218 Hidaka, op. cit., pp.223–28.

219 Kubo, op. cit.

220 Elphick, op. cit., pp.249–50.

221 F4313, September 20, 1940, FO371/24740, PRO.

222 Antony Best, *Britain, Japan and Pearl Harbor: Avoiding War in East Asia, 1936–41* (Routledge, 1995) p.124.

223 Kubo, op. cit.

224 Ibid.

225 Mitsukuni Saito, *Showa-shi Hakkutsu: Maboroshi no Tokumu Kikan "Yama"* (Examination of the History of the Showa Period: "Yama," the Illusory Special Agency) (Shincho Shinsho, 2003).

226 Gordon Prange, *Target Tokyo: The Story of the Sorge Spy Ring* (McGraw-Hill, 1984) p.407.

3. Japanese Navy Intelligence

227 Yuzuru Sanematsu, *Nihon Kaigun no Taigai Joho Kiko* (Intelligence Apparatus of the IJA) (NIDSMA).

228 Denpa Kankei Bukkosha Kensho Ireikai, *Kaigun Denpa Tsuioku-shu Dai 1 go* (The Naval Signal Traffic Records, Vol. 1) (not for sale, 1955) p.247.

229 Toshiyuki Yokoi, *Nihon no Kimitsushitsu* (Japanese Black Chamber) (Rokumeisha, 1951) p.6.

230 Denpa Kankei Bukkosha Kensho Ireikai, op. cit., p.248.

231 *Showa 7 Nen Kobun Biko T – Jiken Fuzoku* (Notes for Official Documents of 1932 T – Attached to incidents) (NIDSMA). On the IJN's SIGINT records, there remain reasonable numbers of records in *Takagi Sokichi Nikki*, *Saionji-ko to Seikyoku* and *Showa Shakai Keizai Shiryo Shusei* etc.

232 Yokoi, op. cit., p.14.

233 Gunrei-bu, *Showa 6, 7 Nen Jihen Kaigun Senshi* (Naval History of incidents in 1931 and 1932) (Suikosha, 1934, not for sale) p.246.

234 Denpa Kankei Bukkosha Kensho Ireikai, op. cit., p.249.

235 "Wachi Tsunezo," HW 40/211, PRO.

236 Yokoi, op. cit., pp.32–34.

237 Denpa Kankei Bukkosha Kensho Ireikai, op. cit., p.250.

238 Samejima, op. cit., pp.209–10.

239 Ibid., p.251.

240 Motonao Samejima, op. cit., p.173.

241 Ibid, p.209.

242 Kazuo Kamaga, "Daitoa Senso ni Okeru Ango-sen to Gendai Ango" (Covert Operations in the Pacific War and Modern Code), in Dodai Kurabu Keizai Konwakai, *Showa Gunji Hiwa (Jo)* (Secret Military Stories of the Showa Era, Vol. 1) (Doudai Keizai Konwakai 1989) p.186.

243 Denpa Kankei Bukkosha Kensho Ireikai, op. cit., p.253.

244 HW 40/211, PRO.

245 Samejima, op. cit., pp.180–81.

246 Ibid., p.189.

247 Ibid., p.182.

248 Denpa Kankei Bukkosha Kensho Ireikai, op. cit., p.257.

249 Samejima, op. cit., p.182.

250 Security of British and Allied Communications, HW 40/8, PRO.

251 *Jokyo Handan Shiryo* (Situation Estimate Document), (NIDSMA).

252 Kahn, op. cit., pp. 582–83.

253 Samejima, op. cit., p.211–2.

254 Samejima, op. cit., p.213.

255 "Security of British and Allied Communications," HW 40/8, PRO.

256 Denpa Kankei Bukkosha Kensho Ireikai, op. cit., p.259.

257 "Ougi Kazuto Bunsho" (Private Collections of Kazuto Ougi), Kokuritsu Kokkai Toshokan (National Diet Library) Kensei Siryo-shitsu.

258 Okura-sho Showa Zaisei-shi Henshu-shitsu, *Showa Zaisei-shi* (Financial History of the Showa Period) Vol. 4 (Toyo Keizai Shinposhan, 1955) p.266.

259 Taketoshi Yamamoto (ed.), *Daini-ji Sekai Taisen-ki: Nippon no Choho Kikan Bunseki, Dai 1 kan* (WWII: Analysis of the Japanese Intelligence Agencies, Vol. 1) (Kashiwa Shobo, 2000) p.28.

260 Ibid, Vol. 1, p.53.

261 "Decypher Telegram, Gov of India, Defence Dep to Secretary of State for India" (February 3, 1941) L/WS/1/290, WS 3039, India Office Library, British Library.

262 Koshiba Naosada, "Shina Kinmu no Kaisoroku" (Memories of Service in China) (NIDSMA).

263 Chu-shi Haken Tokumu Kikan Honbu, op. cit.

264 Rigun-sho, *Riku Shi Mitsu Dai Nikki, Showa 13 Nen Sono 12* (China Army Highly Confidential Daily Report, 1938, Vol. 12) (NIDSMA).

265 Koshiba Naosada, *Kaisen Zengo no Sento Oyobi Taikoku ni Okeru Kaigun no Kakyo Kosaku (Sono 1)* (The Navy's Operations against Overseas Chinese in Swatow and Thailand before and after the Outbreak of the War, Vol. 1) (NIDSMA).

266 Ibid.

267 "Correspondence between Sempill and Toyoda," KV 2/871, PRO.

268 "The Case of Lt. Commander Collin Mayers," KV 2/689, PRO.

269 *Daily Express* (March 18, 1927).

270 The Security Service's files on Rutland were opened in 2000 as "Japanese Intelligence Agents and Suspected Agents" (KV2 series) at the National Archives, Kew. There are several articles on the topic: Antony Best, "Intelligence, Diplomacy and the Japanese Threat to British Interests, 1914–41", *Intelligence and National Security*, Vol. 17, No. 1 (Spring 2002); Ken Kotani, "Nihon Kaigun to Rutland Ei Kaigun Shosa" (The IJN and Squadron Leader Rutland), *Gunji Shigaku* (The Journal of Military History), Vol. 38, No. 2 (September 2002); Max Everest-Phillips, "Reassessing Pre-War Japanese Espionage: The Rutland Naval Spy Case and the Japanese Intelligence Threat before Pearl Harbor," *Intelligence and National Security*, (Vol. 21, No. 2 (April 2006).

271 "Notes on the Case of Squadron Leader Rutland, RAF," KV 2/328, PRO.

272 "Frederick Joseph Rutland," KV 2/333, PRO.

273 "Philby (SIS) to Young (MI5)" (April 22, 1946) KV 2/337, PRO.

274 "London to Tokyo" (June 1933) KV 2/338, PRO.

275 "F. J. Rutland" (September 13, 1941) KV 2/331, PRO.

276 "F. J. Rutland," KV 2/332, PRO.

277 "MI5 Report" (September 30, 1941) KV 2/332, PRO.

278 "Note on Interview with Squadron Leader Rutland" (November 3, 1941) KV 2/332, PRO.

279 "Note on Personal Activities in the US" KV 2/333, PRO.

280 "MI5 Report" (December 31, 1941) KV 2/333, PRO.

281 "Stott Memorandum" (June 14, 1943) KV 2/336, PRO.

282 "Japanese Naval Attaché London to Director Naval Intelligence Tokyo" (March 13, 1935) KV 2/338, PRO.

283 "Director Naval Intelligence Tokyo to Japanese Naval Attaché London" (May 28, 1935) KV 2/338, PRO.

284 "Herbert Greene," KV 2/635, PRO.

285 "Employment of Midorikawa," KV 2/636, PRO.

286 "Daily Worker" (December 22, 1937) KV 2/635, PRO.

287 "F. J. Rutland," KV 2/333, PRO.

288 "Japanese Naval Attaché London to Director Naval Intelligence, Tokyo" (May 8, 1935) KV 2/338, PRO.

289 "Japanese Naval Attaché London to the Director of Naval Intelligence, Tokyo" (May 1, 1935) KV 2/338, PRO.

290 "Shinkawa-Report, from Japanese Naval Attaché, London to Director of Naval Intelligence, Tokyo" (March 20, 1935) KV 2/338, PRO.

291 "Memorandum, American Embassy in London" (July 2, 1943) KV 2/336, PRO.

292 If "Ito" was the real name of the staff officer, he was probably Commander Risaburo Ito, the specialist in naval codes.

293 "F. J. Rutland," KV 2/336, PRO.

294 Zacharias was a Japanese intelligence expert on the US forces, and was an old acquaintance of Admiral Kichisaburo Nomura, who would later be Japanese ambassador to the US.

295 "Fukuti to Rutland" (June 1941) KV 2/335, PRO.

296 "BJ 093616: Japanese Intelligence Network in Central and South America" (July 24, 1941) HW 12/266, PRO.

297 "Butler to Russell" (September 15, 1960) HO 45/25105, PRO.

298 "Rutland's Statement" (December 19, 1941) HW 12/266, PRO.

299 The GC&CS decoded and reported communications between Tokyo and Japanese representatives in the Navy Disarmament Conference held in London from 1935 to 1936. HW12/248, PRO.

300 "H. A. R. Philby (SIS) to Young (MI5)" (April 22, 1946) KV 2/337, PRO.

301 On the IJA's control of the secrets, see Kosaku Urata, *Dare mo Kakanakatta Nihon Rikugun* (The Unwritten IJA) (PHP Kenkyusho, 2003).

302 "Rondon Kaigun Kaigi Ikken/Ango ni Kansuru Kaigun-sho Iken" (Matters Regarding the London Navy Conference/A Suggestion of the Ministry of Navy on the Codes), Gaimu-sho Gaiko Shiryokan (Diplomatic Library of the Ministry of Foreign Affairs). Ito warned in the paper that however strong a code was, the content could be leaked out if it was sent to the other departments by another weaker code.

303 Samejima, op. cit., pp.142–43.

304 As more coded communications are used, more materials to break the code are supplied to the opponent. Therefore, the rapid increase of the use of coded communications raised the possibility that the code would be broken. Indeed, the chief of the Communications Section of the Navy Ministry gave his view to the chief of the Operations Section of the Navy General Staff, "There are too many telegrams on supply, maintenance, and repair dispatched while we are preparing for the operation. Won't these cause the exposure of the plan?" Samejima, op. cit., p.147.

305 About this point, see Junko Nagata, *Ango* (Cryptology), (Daiyamondosha, 1971) pp.291–341; Kanya Miyauchi, *Niitaka-yama Nobore 1208* (Climb up Mt. Niitaka 1208) (Rokko Shuppan, 1975), pp. 446–57.

306 Ryunosuke Kusaka, "Middowe Kaisen ni Okeru Seikakunaru Nihon-gawa Kantai Hensei to Honkaisen Sanka-sha no Kojin-teki Iken" (Accurate Formation of the Japanese Fleet in the Sea Battle of Midway and the Private View of a Participant in the Battle) (NIDSMA).

307 Gunrei-bu, *Gunrei-bu Sakusen Nisshi (2)* (Operations Journal of the Naval General Staff, Vol. 2) (NIDSMA).

308 Matome Ugaki, "Sensoroku Sono 3" (War Diary) (NIDSMA).

309 Hiroyuki Agawa, *Shinpan Yamamoto Isoroku* (Isoroku Yamamoto, New Edition) (Shinchosha, 1969) p.377.

310 Samejima, op. cit., p.153.

311 Kaigun-sho Gunmu Dai 1 Ka, *Kaigun Otsu Jiken Kankei Shorui Tsuzuri* (Document File on the Navy Otsu incident) (NIDSMA).

312 On the Navy *Otsu* incident, see Akira Yoshimura, *Kaigun Otsu Jiken* (Navy Otsu incident) (Bunshun Bunko, 1982), pp.111–15; *Senshi Sosho; Nansei Homen Kaigun Sakusen: Dai Ni Dan Sakusen Iko* (War History Series; Navy Operation in the Southwest: after the Second Stage of the Operation) (Choun Shinbunsha, 1972), p.380.

313 "Ougi Kazuto Bunsho" (Private Collections of Kazuto Ougi).

4. The Analysis and Evaluation of Intelligence

314 Alvin Coox, "Japanese Net Assessment in the Era before Pearl Harbor," in Alland Millett and Williamson Murray (eds.), *Calculations* (Free Press, 1992) p.298.

315 Saburo Hayashi, "Wareware wa Donoyoni Taiso Joho Kinmu wo Yattaka" (NIDSMA).

316 Imai, op. cit.

317 Ibid.

Notes

318 Yuzuru Sanematsu, "Nihon Kaigun no Taigai Joho Kiko" (Intelligence Apparatus of the IJA) (NIDSMA).

319 Ibid., pp. 249–309.

320 Richard Betts, *Enemies of Intelligence: Knowledge and Power in American National Security* (Columbia UP, 2007), p.23.

321 Tsutao Ariga, *Nihon Riku Kai Gun no Joho Kiko to Sono Katsudo* (The Organizations and Activities of the IJA and IJN) (Kindai Bungeisha, 1994) p.56; Sanematsu, op. cit.

322 "Ougi Kazuto Bunsho".

323 Roberta Wohlstetter, *Pearl Harbor: Warning and Decision* (Stanford UP, 1962) p. 280.

324 Hayashi, op. cit.

325 Sugita, op. cit., p.85.

326 Dodai Kurabu Keizai Konwakai, *Showa Gunji Hiwa (Jo)* (Secret Military Stories of the Showa Era, Vol. 1) (Doudai Keizai Konwakai, 1989) p.44.

327 Regarding this point, the German Army General Staff was in a similar situation. German intelligence also specialized in the intelligence for operations. Michael Handel, "Intelligence and Military Operations," in Michael Handel (ed.), *Intelligence and Military Operations* (Frank Cass, 1990) p.23.

328 Shiro Inoue, *Shogen Senji Bundan-shi: Joho-kyoku Bungeika-cho no Tsubuyaki* (Witness to a Literary World: a Memoir of the Chief of the Literature Section of the Intelligence Bureau) (Ningen no Kagakusha, 1984) p.8. On the Cabinet Intelligence Department, see Takumi Sato, *Genron Tosei* (Regulation of Speech) (Chuko Shinsho, 2004).

329 Kumao Harada, *Saionji-ko to Seikyoku* (Duke Saionji and Political Affairs), Vol. 7 (Iwanami Shoten, 1952) p.311.

330 Ariga, op. cit., p.48. On the British Army's intelligence, see Peter Gudgin, *Military Intelligence* (Sutton Publishing, 1999).

331 Ariga, op. cit., p.49.

332 Hisashi Takahashi, "Nihon Rikugun to Taichu Joho" (The IJA and its Intelligence in China), in Gunji-shi Gakkai (ed.) *Dai Ni ji Sekai Taisen (2)* (World War II Vol. 2) (Kinshosha, 1990) p.241.

333 Philip Davies, *MI6 and the Machinery of Spying* (Frank Cass, 2004) pp.336–46.

334 Etsuo Koutani, "Manshu ni Okeru Joho Kinmu" (Intelligence Work in Manchuria) (NIDSMA).

335 Yuichi Tsuchihashi, "Dai Ni Bucho Jidai no Omoide" (Memories of the 2nd Department's Chief) (NIDSMA).

336 Susumu Nishiura, "Hokubu Futsuin Shinchu no Senshi-teki Kansatsu" (The Military History of the Japanese advance into North Indo-China) (NIDSMA).

337 Sugita, op. cit., p.127.

338 NIDS, *Senshi Sosho, Daitoa Senso Kaisen Keii (4)* (The Process of the Outbreak of the Pacific War, Vol. 4) (Asagumo Shinbunsha, 1974) p.146.

339 Akio Doi, *Gekokujo* (Supplanting One's Superior) (Nihon Kogyo Shinbunsha, 1982) p.85.

340 Sugita, op. cit., p.127.

341 Masatane Kanda, "Kyugun ni Kansuru Kaiso" (Memories of the Imperial Forces).

342 Ibid.

343 Doi, op. cit., p.88.

344 NIDS, *Senshi Sosho Mare Shinko Sakusen* (Operation of Malaya Invasion, War History Series) (Asagumo Shinbunsha, 1966), p.52.

345 Sugita, op. cit., p.146.

346 Koutani, op. cit.

347 Stephen Mercado, *The Shadow Warriors of Nakano: A History of the Imperial Japanese Army's Elite Intelligence School* (Brassey's, 2002) p.23.

348 Kiichiro Higuchi, "Hoppo Joho Gyomu ni Kansuru Kiroku" (Record on the Intelligence Service in the Northern Area) (NIDSMA).

349 Yukio Nishihara, op. cit., p.40.

350 Sanematsu, op. cit., p.236.

351 *Jokyo Handan Shiryo* (Situation Estimate Document) (NIDSMA).

352 NIDS, *Senshi Sosho Kaigun Sho Go Sakusen (1)* (The Navy *Sho Go* Operation, Vol.1, War History Series) (Asagumo Shinbunsha, 1966) pp.713–29.

353 Sanematsu, op. cit., p.232.

354 Atsushi Oi, *Kaijo Goei-sen* (Defensive Battle on the Sea) (Koyosha, 1953) p.229.

355 Imai, op. cit.

356 Sanematsu, op. cit., p.228.

357 Ibid., p.229.

358 Marder, op. cit., p.335.

359 Sanematsu, op. cit., p.312.

360 Imai, op. cit.

361 Kamaga, op. cit., p.186.

362 Koutani, op. cit.

363 "Jokyo Handan Shiryo."

364 Wohlstetter, op. cit., p.314., Richard Aldrich, *Intelligence and the War against Japan: Britain, America and the Politics of Secret Service* (Cambridge UP, 2000) p.243.

5. Pre-War and Early-War Intelligence on Enemy Forces

365 John Ferris, " 'Worthy of Some Better Enemy?: The British Estimate of the Imperial Japanese Army 1914–1941, and the Fall of Singapore," *Canadian Journal of History* (August 1993); W. Wark, "In Search of a Suitable Japan: British Intelligence in the Pacific before the Second World War", *Intelligence and National Security*, Vol. 1, No. 2 (May 1986); Antony Best, "This Probably Over-Valued Military Power: British Intelligence and Whitehall's Perception of Japan, 1939–1941," *Intelligence and National Security* (July 1997); Douglas Ford, *Britain's Secret War against Japan, 1937–45* (Routledge 2006).

366 "Malaya and Singapore, Report Drawn up by Major H. P. Thomas, O.B.E., I.A." (May 30, 1942) WO 208/1529, PRO.

367 "Value of the Japanese Army for War" (May 18, 1940) WO 208/1445, PRO.

368 "Craigie to Foreign Office" (November 1, 1937) FO 371/21038, PRO.

369 "Vivian Memo" (February 18, 1935) ADM 116/3862, PRO.

370 Marder, op. cit., p. 352.

371 "Dispatch of a Fleet to the Far East, CID" (April 5, 1939) CAB 16/183A, PRO.

372 Thomas Mahnken, *Uncovering Ways of War: US Intelligence and Foreign Military Innovation, 1918–1941* (Cornell UP, 2002) p. 71.

373 "Estimated Strength of First Line Aircraft" (February 1939) ADM 116/4393, PRO.

374 "Japanese Aircraft Performance" (February 19, 1941) AIR 22/74, PRO.

375 Denis Richards and Hilary Saunders, *Royal Air Force 1939–1945*, Vol. 2 (HMSO, 1954) p. 11.

376 Mahnken, op. cit., p. 79.

377 "Craigie to Foreign Office" (May 2, 1941) FO 371/1296, PRO.

378 John Dower, *War Without Mercy: Race and Power in the Pacific War* (Faber & Faber 1986) p. 99.

379 Ryohei Osawa (ed.), *Sakae Butai-shi* (The History of the 'Sakae' Troop) (not for sale, 1995) p14.

380 Dodai Kurabu Keizai Konwakai, *Showa Gunji Hiwa, Chu* (Secret Military Stories of the Showa Era, Vol. 2) (Doudai Keizai Konwa Kai, 1988) pp. 274–75.

381 Teikoku Zaigou Gunjinkai Honbu, *So-gun Joshiki* (Basic Knowledge of the Soviet Army) (NIDSMA).

382 Niimi Seiichi, *Showa 16 Nen 7 Gatsu, So-gun Heiki Oyobi Soren Kogyo ni Kansuru Shisatsu* (Situation Report on Soviet Military and Industry in July 1941) (NIDSMA).

383 Rikugun Sanbo Honbu (Army General HQ) (ed.), *Eiryo Malaya Joho Kiroku* (The Intelligence Record of British Malaya) (NIDSMA).

384 Ibid.

385 *Koredake Yomeba Ikusa wa Kateru* (Surefire Method of Winning the War) (NIDSMA).

386 Akira Fujiwara, "Nihon Rikugun to Tai Bei Senryaku" (The Japanese Army and their Strategy against the United States)," in Chihiro Hosoya, *Nichi Bei Kankeishi (The History of US–Japanese Relations)* (Tokyo UP, 1971), p.13.

387 Sanbo Honbu, *Hito Sakusen Kiroku* (Record of the Philippines Operation) (NIDSMA).

388 Sugita, op. cit., p.288

389 NIDS (ed.), *Senshi Sosho Daihonei Rikugunbu (3)* (Army Department, Imperial HQ, Vol. 3, Military History Series) (Asagumo Shinbunsha, 1970) p.366.

390 Taro Tanimitsu, *Taiheiyo Senshi ni Miru Soshiki to Joho Senryaku* (The History of Japanese Intelligence Strategy in the Pacific War) (Piason Education, 1999) p.208.

391 Takayama, p.355.

392 *Showa 16 Nen Kaisen Madeno Kouryaku Senryaku Sono 5* (Strategy in the Pacific War, 1941, Vol. 5) (NIDSMA).

393 Nihon Kokusai Seiji Gakkai (The Japan Association of International Relations) (eds.), *Taiheiyo Senso eno Michi, 7* (The Road to the Pacific War, Vol. 7) (Asahi Shinbunsha, 1987) p.324.

394 Teiji Yabe, *Konoe Fumimaro* (Jijitsushin, 1986) p.162.

395 Tasuku Nakazawa, "Nakazawa Tasuku Kaisoroku" (Memoir of Nakazawa Tasuku) (NIDSMA).

396 *Jokyo Handan Shiryo* (Situation Estimate Document) (NIDSMA).

397 Satoshi Iwama, *Sekiyu de Yomitoku Kanpai no Taiheiyo Senso* (Japanese Oil Crisis in the Pacific War) (Asahi Sensho, 2007).

398 There were several reasons for the delay in delivering the declaration. The primary reason was an ongoing estrangement between the Navy and the Japanese Ministry of Foreign Affairs. The Ministry of Foreign Affairs was not informed of a detailed plan of operation until just a day before it was launched, and that led to the late delivery of the final draft.

399 *Showa 15 Nen Ei Tai-nichi Sakusen Yoso Heiryoku* (Estimation of British Forces in the Far East, 1940) (NIDSMA).

400 Marder, op. cit., p.340.

401 Marder, op. cit., p.339.

6. Tactical and Strategic Intelligence
in Japanese War Planning

402 Barnhart, op. cit., p.424.

403 Hajime Kitaoka, *Interijensu Hisutori* (Intelligence History) (Keio UP, 2006) p.202.

404 Alvin Coox, *The Anatomy of a Small War: the Soviet-Japanese Struggle for Changkufeng–Khasan, 1938* (Greenwood Press, 1977).

405 Saburo Hayashi, *Kantogun to Kyokuto Sorengun* (The Kwantung Army and the Soviet Far Eastern Army) (Fuyo Shobo, 1974) pp.113–34.

406 Etsuo Koutani, "Manshu ni Okeru Joho Kinmu" (Intelligence Work in Manchuria) (NIDSMA).

407 NIDS, *Senshi Sosho, Hokushi no Chian Sen (1)* (Battles in North China, Vol.1, War History Series) (Asagumo, 1970) p.472.

408 Yokoyama, op. cit.

409 Hokushina Homengun Shireibu (Japanese Expeditionary Army, North China Command) (ed.), *Sougun Joho Kaigi Teishutsu Syorui* (Report to Intelligence Meeting, Army General HQ) (NIDSMA).

410 This point is discussed by Edward Dreyer, *China at War 1902–1949* (Longman, 1995) pp.239–45.

411 Nicholas Tarling, *Britain, Southeast Asia and the Onset of the Pacific War* (Cambridge UP, 1996).

412 Negotiations between Japan and French Indo-China are described in Eric Jennings, *Vichy in the Tropics* (Stanford UP, 2000); John Dreifort, *Myopic Grandeur* (Kent State UP, 1991); Martin Thomas, *The French Empire at War* (Manchester UP, 1998).

413 COS (39) 941 (July 11, 1940) CAB 53/52, PRO.

414 COS (40) 592 (July 31, 1940) CAB 66/10, PRO.

415 *Toku-jo*, Bei (US) 1719, 11th Section, the Navy General Staff (7552) (July 3, 1940) Futsuin (NIDSMA).

416 Sanbo Honbu (Army General Staff) (ed.), *Sugiyama Memo* (Hara Shobo, 1969) pp.10–15.

417 Paul Baudouin, *The Private Diaries of Paul Baudouin* (Eyre and Spottiswoode, 1948) p.199.

418 BJ 082514 (August 5, 1940) HW 12/255, PRO.

419 WM (40) 221 (August 7 1940) CAB 66/10, PRO.

420 Nicholas Tarling, "The British and the First Japanese Move into Indo-China," *Journal of Southeast Asian Studies*, Vol. 21, No. 1 (1990) p.45.

421 BJ082724 (August 15 1940) HW 12/255, PRO.

422 *The Times* (August 17, 1940).

423 Tarling, "The British and the First Japanese Move into Indo-China", p.51.

424 WM (241)40, CAB 65/9 (September 4, 1940) PRO.

425 *Toku-jo*, Bei (US) 2488, 11th Section, the Navy General Staff (13879) (September 7, 1940) Futsuin Shinchu Mondai (French Indo-China Operational Problems) (NIDSMA).

426 *Toku-jo*, Ei (UK) 1874, 11th Section, the Navy General Staff (8984) (September 9, 1940), Futsuin Shinchu Mondai (NIDSMA); see also "Henderson to Halifax" (September 6, 1940), F4163/3429/61, FO 371/24719, PRO.

427 *Toku-jo*, Ei 1884, 11th Section, the Navy General Staff (9009) (September 9, 1940), Futsuin Shinchu Mondai (NIDSMA); see also "Telegram" (September 8, 1940) F4204/3429/61, FO 371/24719, PRO.

428 NIDS, *Senshi Sosho, Daitoa Senso Kaisen Keii (2)* (The Process of the Outbreak of the Pacific War, Vol. 2, War History Series) (Asagumo Shinbunsha, 1974) p.68.

429 Ibid., p.70.

430 *Toku-jo*, Shi (China) 8640, 11th Section, the Navy General Staff (6284) (September 9, 1940), Futsuin Shinchu Mondai (NIDSMA); see also "Minute by Butler" (September 5, 1940) F4219/3429/61, FO 371/24719, PRO.

431 *Toku-jo*, Ei 1882, 11th Section, the Navy General Staff (9006) (September 10, 1940), Futsuin Shinchu Mondai (NIDSMA); see also "Halifax to Kerr" (September 7, 1940) F4163/3429/61, FO 371/24719, PRO.

432 "Nishihara to Tokyo" (September 11, 1940) Futsuin Shinchu Mondai (NIDSMA).

433 "Matsuoka to Suzuki" (September 11, 1940) Futsuin Shinchu Mondai (NIDSMA).

434 Futsuin Shinchu Mondai, Vol. 2 (NIDSMA).

435 *Toku-jo*, Ei 1428, 11th Section, Navy General Staff (14211) (September 17, 1940) Futsuin Shinchu Mondai (NIDSMA); see also "Halifax to Lothian" (September 14, 1940) F4229/3429/61 (September 15, 1940) F4163/3429/61, FO 371/24719, PRO.

436 *Toku-jo*, Shi 2775, 11th Section, Navy General Staff (14211) (September 18, 1940) Ei 1406, 11th Section, Navy General Staff (9188), Futsuin Shinchu Mondai (NIDSMA); see also "Telegram from Clark Kerr" (September 13, 1940) F4204/3429/61, FO 371/24719, PRO.

437 "Matsuoka to Suzuki" (September 19, 1940) Futsuin Shinchu Mondai (NIDSMA).

438 BJ 083584 (September 20, 1940) HW 12/256, PRO.

Notes

439 "Eden to Amery" (September 21, 1940) F 4248/G, FO 371/24719, PRO.

440 "Tokyo to Foreign Office" (September 16, 1941) F 4126/3429/61, FO 371/24719, PRO.

441 NIDS, *Senshi Sosho, Daitoa Senso Kaisen Keii (2)*, p.93.

442 Cordell Hull, *The Memoirs of Cordell Hull*, Vol. 1 (Macmillan, 1948) p.906.

443 *Toku-jo*, Ei 1452, 11th Section, the Navy General Staff (9887) (September 21, 1940) Futsuin Shinchu Mondai (NIDSMA); see also "Telegram" (Septembe 16, 1940) F4204/3429/61, FO 371/24719, PRO.

444 Hull, op. cit., p.905; "Shinajihen Futsuryo Indo China Shinchu Mondai" (NIDSMA).

445 *Toku-jo*, Bei 2657, 11th Section, the Navy General Staff (15780) (September 20, 1940) Futsuin Shinchu Mondai (NIDSMA).

446 Hull, op. cit., p.907.

447 *Toku-jo*, Ei 1489, 11th Section, the Navy General Staff (9455) (September 26, 1940) Futsuin Shinchu Mondai (NIDSMA).

448 *Toku-jo*, Bei 2673 and 2685, 11th Section, the Navy General Staff (15813), (16125) (September 22, 1940) Futsuin Shinchu Mondai (NIDSMA).

449 Gordon Prange, *At Dawn We Slept* (Penguin Books, 1981) pp.75–76.

450 Toshihide Maejima and Hide Suzuki, "Hawai Homen Teisatsu Hokoku" (The Reconnaissance Report on Hawaii) (NIDSMA).

451 Laurance Safford, "A Brief History of Communications Intelligence in the United States," SRH-149, declassified per sec, 3 E. 0. 12065 by Director NSA/Chief. CSS (March 6, 1982).

452 Dai San Sentai Senji Nisshi (War Diary of the 3rd Battleship Division), *Gordon Prange Papers, Special Collections*, University of Maryland Libraries.

453 Nakano Koyukai, op. cit., p.491.

454 Yuichi Tsuchihashi, "Tsuchihashi Yuichi Kaiso Roku, 5" (Memoir of Yuichi Tsuchihashi, Vol. 5) (NIDSMA).

455 *Kokusai Josei Geppo* (Monthly Report on International Affairs), Vol. 17 (NIDSMA).

456 *Kaiko* (February 1982) p.22.

457 Oi, op. cit., p.117.

458 Marder, op. cit., p.335.

459 Nishiura, op. cit.

460 Shinobu Takayama, *Sanbo Honbu Sakusen-ka* (The Operations Section, Army General Staff) (Fuyo Shobo, 1985) pp.315–16.

461 Masaki Miyake, *Nichidokui Sangoku Domei no Kenkyu* (Study of the Tripartite Pact) (Nansosha, 1975) p.255.

462 Ibid., p.332.

463 Ryouei Saito, *Azamukareta Rekishi* (History Deceived) (Yomiuri Shinbun, 1955) p.109.

464 NIDS, *Senshi Sosho, Daitoa Senso Kaisen Keii*, Vol. 2., pp.141–42.

465 Also see, Chapman, op. cit.; James Rusbridger, op. cit.; Elphick, op. cit.

466 COS(40)592, Cab 66/10, PRO.

467 Chihiro Hosoya, "Sangoku Domei to Nisso Churitsu Joyaku" (The Russo-Japanese Neutrality Pact and the Tripartite Pact), in *Taiheiyo Senso eno Michi, 5* (Japan's Road to Pearl Harbor, Vol. 5) (Asahi Shinbunsha, 1963) p.284.

468 Martin Gilbert, *The Churchill War Papers,* Vol. 3 (William Heinemann, 2000) pp.439–40; "Prime Minister's Message to Mr. Matsuoka" (April 1, 1941) PREM 3/252/, PRO.

469 "Matsuoka to Churchill" (April 22, 1941) FO 371/27891, PRO.

470 Sugita, op. cit., p.308.

471 Barnhart, op. cit., p.424.

472 NIDS, *Daihonei Rikugunbu (2)* (The IJA, Vol. 2) (Asagumo, 1968) pp.120–22.

473 "Rikugun Chujo Muto Akira Shuki" (Memoir of Lieutenant General Akira Muto) (NIDSMA).

474 Shiro Hara, *Daisenryaku Naki Kaisen (*War without Grand Strategy) (Hara Shobo, 1987) p.218.

475 NIDS, *Senshi Sosho, Daitoa Senso Kaisen Keii (4)*, p. 92; F. H. Hinsley (ed.), *British Intelligence in the Second World War*, Vol. 1 (HMSO, 1979) p.478.

476 BJ 090789 (June 15, 1941) HW 12/264, PRO.

477 JIC (41) 252, CAB 81/103, PRO.

478 Gilbert, op. cit., pp.806–07.

479 David Dilks, *The Diaries of Sir Alexander Cadogan* (Putnam, 1972) p.338.

480 Yuriko Onodera, *Baruto-kai no Hotori nite* (On the Edge of the Baltic Sea) (Kyodo Tsushinsha, 1985) p.105.

481 Gunji-shi gakkai (eds.) *Kimitsu Senso Nisshi* (Secret War Record), Vol. 2 (Kinshosha, 1998) pp.111–12.

482 NIDS, *Senshi Sosho, Daitoa Senso Kaisen Keii (4)*, p.143.

483 Koichi Kido, *Kido Koichi Nikki (Ge),* (Diary of Kido Koichi, Vol. 2) (Tokyo UP, 1966) p.879.

484 Sin'ichi Kamata, "Taibei Kaisen Keii to Ishikettei Moderu" (Decision-Making Model in the War Planning Process of the Pacific War), *Gunji Shigaku* (The Journal of Military History), Vol. 100 (1990) p.89.

485 Ryoichi Tobe, "Doku-So Sen no Hassei to Nihon Rikugun" (The IJA and the

Outbreak of the Soviet-German War), *Gunji Shigaku* (The Journal of Military History), Vol. 100 (1990) p.277.

486 Isamu Asai, "Soren no Tainichi Sakusen (Soviet Operations against Japan) (NIDSMA).

487 Ibid.

488 Ibid.

489 NIDS, *Daihonei Rikugunbu*, Vol. 2, pp.294–303.

490 Ibid.

491 Kanehara, op. cit., p.331.

492 "Ishii Akiho Nikki Sono 2" (Diary of Akiho Ishii, Vol. 2) (NIDSMA).

493 Asai, op. cit.

494 "Showa 16 Nen Tanaka Shin'ichi Chujo Gyomu Nissi Sono 7" (Business Diary of General Shinichi Tanaka in 1941, Vol. 7) (NIDSMA).

495 Atsushi Moriyama, *Nichibei Kaisen no Seiji Katei* (The Policy-Making Process in the Pacific War) (Yoshikawa Kobunkan, 1998) p.6.

496 Hara, op. cit., p.214.

497 Naoki Inose, *Showa 16 Nen Natsu no Haisen* (The Defeat in Summer 1941) (Bunshun Bunko, 1986) p.193.

498 Kimitada Miwa, "Tai-bei Kessen eno Imeji" (View on the War against the United States), in Hidetoshi Kato, Shunsuke Kamei (eds.), *Nihon to Amerika* (Japan and the United States) (Nihon Gakujutsu Shinkokai, 1976) p.244.

499 Sadao Asada, "Nihon Kaigun to Taibei Seisaku Oyobi Senryaku" (The IJN and its Strategy and Policy toward the United States), in Kato and Kamei, op. cit.

500 Antony Best, "Straws in the Wind: Britain and the February 1941 War-Scare in East Asia," *Diplomacy & Statecraft*, Vol. 5, No. 3 (November 1994).

501 JIC (41) 55 (February 5, 1941) CAB 81/100, PRO.

502 *The Times* (January 30, 1941).

503 "The Director, American Visit" (February 1, 1941) HW 14/45, PRO; Prescott Currier, "My Purple Trip to England in 1941," *Cryptologoa*, Vol. 20, No. 3 (July 1996) pp.194–98. According to the GC&CS document, it can be assumed that the GC&CS broke the Purple Code on February 15, 1941; BJ 087754 (February 15, 1941) HW 12/261, PRO.

504 (February 16, 1941) PREM3 252/6A, PRO.

505 BJ 092418 (June 21, 1941) HW 12/265, PRO.

506 BJ 092889 (July 4, 1941) HW 12/266, PRO.

507 F 5883/523/G (July 4, 1941) FO 371/27892, PRO.

508 F 5883/523/G (July 4, 1941) FO 371/27892; "Eden to Craigie" (July 4, 1941) FO 371/27892, PRO.

509 Chuichi Ohashi, *Taiheiyo Senso Yurai-ki* (The Origins of the Pacific War) (Yumani, 2002) p.165.

510 Kido Nikki Kenkyukai, *Kido Koichi Nikki (Ge)* (Diary of Kouichi Kido, Vol. 2) (Tokyo UP, 1966) p.888.

511 F 7459/1299/23, FO 371/27975, PRO.

512 Dilks, op. cit.

513 "Washington to London" (July 21, 1941) FO 371/27972, PRO.

514 *Kimitsu Senso Nisshi*, p.136.

515 "Ishii Akiho Nikki" (NIDSMA).

516 Muto, op. cit.; Tasuku Nakazawa, "Nakazawa Tasuku Kaisoroku" (Memoir of Nakazawa Tasuku) (NIDSMA).

517 Shigenori Togo, *Jidai no Ichi Sokumen* (A Dimension of Time) (Hara Shobo, 1989) pp.241–46.

518 Kanehara, op. cit., p.364.

519 Ibid., p.366.

520 Waldo Heinrichs, *Threshold of War, Franklin D. Roosevelt and American Entry into World War*, (Oxford UP, 1988) p.210.

521 *Nichi Bei Gaiko Kankei Zassan dai 6 kan* (Record of US–Japan Diplomatic Relations, Vol. 6).

522 Heinrichs, op. cit., p.210.

523 "From Washington to Foreign Office" (November 29, 1941) CAB 121/114, PRO.

524 Kanehara, op. cit., p.369.

525 Togo, op. cit., p.262.

Conclusion

526 Sugita, op. cit. p.283.

527 Percy Cradock, *Know Your Enemy: How the Joint Intelligence Committee Saw the World*, (John Murray, 2002), p.296.

528 Ferris, op. cit., p.233.

529 Kamaga, op. cit.; Dodai Kurabu, op. cit., p.186.

530 Mark Lowenthal, *Intelligence from Secrets to Policy, (Third Edition)* (CQ Press, 2006) p.174.

531 Drea, "Reading Each Other's Mail", pp.185–205.

BIBLIOGRAPHY

PRIMARY SOURCES

Japan
The National Institute for Defense Studies Military Archives (NIDSMA)

Official documents

Chu-shi Haken Tokumu Kikan Honbu (Dai 13 gun) Enkaku (History of the HQ of Special Agencies sent to Central China (the Thirteenth Army))

Eiryo Malaya Joho Kiroku (The Intelligence Record of British Malaya)

Futsuin Shinchu Mondai (French Indo-China Operational Problems)

Gunrei-bu Sakusen Nisshi (2) (Operations Journal of the Naval General Staff, Vol. 2)

Himitsu-sen Gairon (Introduction to Covert War)

Hito Sakusen Kiroku (Record of the Philippines Operation)

Hokushina Homen Gun Sakusen Kiroku (North China Army Operational Record)

Joho Kinmu no Sanko (Textbook for the Intelligence Service)

Jokyo Handan Shiryo (Situation Estimate Document)

Kaigun Otsu Jiken Kankei Shorui Tsuzuri (Document file on the Navy Otsu incident)

Kanto-gun Shozoku no Tokushu Butai (Special Divisions of the Kwantung Army)

Kita-shina Homen-gun Joho Shuninsha Kaido Kankei Shiryo (Records about the Senior Intelligence Officer Meetings of the North China Area Army)

Kokusai Josei Geppo (Monthly Report on International Affairs)

Koredake Yomeba Ikusa wa Kateru (Surefire Method of Winning the War)

Matome Ugaki, Sensoroku, Vol. 3 (War Diary)

Nai Gai Josei no Gaiyo Hyo (Summary of Domestic and Foreign Affairs)

Riku Man Mitsu Dai Nikki, Showa 16 Nen (Manchurian Army Highly Confidential Daily Report, 1940)

Riku Shi Mitsu Dai Nikki, Showa 13 Nen (China Army Highly Confidential Daily Report, 1938)

Shina Chuton Kenpei-tai Shirei-bu Shiryo (Documents of the Military Police HQ in China)

Showa 2 Nen Oshu Shitaru Himitsu Bunsho, Sanbo Honbu (Confiscated Document of 1927, Army General Staff)

Showa 7 Nen Kobun Biko T (Notes for Official Documents, 1932 T)

Showa 11 Nen 9 Gatsu Tai-so Choho Kikan Kyoka Keikaku (The Plan for Reinforcing the Intelligence Apparatuses against the Soviet Union, September 1936)

Showa 14 Nen Mitudai Nikki Dai 5 Satsu (Highly Confidential Daily Report, 1939)

Showa 14 Nen Riku Kimitsu Dai-nikki, dai 2 satsu (Army Highly Confidential Daily Report, 1939)

Showa 14 Nen Riku Shi Ju Dai-Nikki Dai 32 Go (Chinese Army Highly Confidential Daily Report, 1939, Vol. 32)

Showa 15 Nen Ei Tai-nichi Sakusen Yoso Heiryoku (Estimation of British Forces in the Far East, 1940)

Showa 16 Nen, Eiryo Malai Joho Kiroku (Intelligence Record on British Malaya, 1941)

Showa 16 Nen Kaisen Madeno Kouryaku Senryaku (Strategy in the Pacific War, 1941)

Showa 16 Nendo Tai-shi Boryaku Keikaku no Yoko (Summary of the Plan for Espionage against China, 1941)

Showa 17 Nen Riku-gun-sho Riku A Mitsu Dai-nikki, dai 07 go (Asian Army Highly Confidential Daily Report, 1942, War Ministry)

So-gun Joshiki (Basic Knowledge of the Soviet Army)

So-gun Kokkyo Chikujo Joho Kiroku (The Record of Information about the Soviet Construction of Tochkas along the Border)

Sokyo Jitsumu Kyoan: Kita-shina Haken Kenpeitai Kyoshutai (Textbook for Anti-Communist Activities: North China Expeditionary Military Police Training Troop)

So-ren Chosa Siryo Geppo (Monthly Soviet Research Report)

Sougun Joho Kaigi Teishutsu Syorui (Report to Intelligence Meeting, Army General HQ)

Tekisei Joho Shusen Zenya (Information on Enemies at the Last Stage of the War)

Tokumu Kikan ni Kansuru Soukatsu-teki Hokoku (Summary Report on the Special Duty Agencies)

Tokushu Joho-bu Rinji Hensei Shiryo (Records of the Extraordinary Establishment of the Special Intelligence Department)

Private papers

Hagino, Takeo, "Tokujo ni Kansuru Senkun" (Maxims on Signals Intelligence)

Hayashi, Saburo, "Wareware wa Donoyoni Taiso Joho Kinmu wo Yattaka" (How Did We Conduct Intelligence Operations Against the Soviet Union?)

Higuchi, Kiichiro, "Hoppo Joho Gyomu ni Kansuru Kiroku" (Record on the Intelligence Service in the Northern Area)

Imai, Nobuhiko, "Gunrei-bu Tai-bei Joho Buin Imai Nobuhiko Shuki" (Memoir of Nobuhiko Imai, Staff Officer of US Intelligence Section, the Navy General Staff)

Ishii, Akiho, "Ishii Akiho Nikki" (Diary of Akiho Ishii)Kanda, Masatane, "Joho Kinmu ni Taisuru Kaiso" (Memories of Intelligence Service)

Koutani, Etsuo, "Manshu ni Okeru Joho Kinmu" (Intelligence Work in Manchuria)

Koshiba, Naosada, "Kaisen Zengo no Sento Oyobi Taikoku ni Okeru Kaigun no Kakyo Kosaku (Sono 1)" (The Navy's Operations against Overseas Chinese in Swatow and Thailand before and after the Outbreak of the War, Vol. 1) (NIDSMA).

Koshiba, Naosada, "Shina Kinmu no Kaisoroku" (Memories of Service in China)"

Kubo, Muneharu, "Bocho ni Kansuru Kaiso Choshuroku" (Records of Recollections about Counter-Intelligence)

Kusaba, Tatsumi, "Shaso yori Rokoku wo Mite" (Watching Russia from Train Windows)

Kusaka, Ryunosuke, "Middowe Kaisen ni Okeru Seikakunaru Nihon-gawa Kantai Hensei to Honkaisen Sanka-sha no Kojin-teki Iken" (Accurate Formation of the Japanese Fleet in the Sea Battle of Midway and the Private View of a Participant in the Battle)

Muto, Akira, "Rikugun Chujo Muto Akira Shuki" (Memoir of Lieutenant General Akira Muto)

Nakazawa, Tasuku, "Nakazawa Tasuku Kaisoroku" (Memoir of Nakazawa Tasuku)

Niimi, Seiichi, "Showa 16 Nen 7 Gatsu, So-gun Heiki Oyobi Soren Kogyo ni Kansuru Shisatsu" (Situation Report on the Soviet Military and Industry in July 1941)

Nishiura Susumu, "Hokubu Futsuin Shinchu no Senshi-teki Kansatsu" (The Military History of the Japanese Advance into Northern Indo-China)

Okada, Yoshimasa, "Hong Kong Kosaku no Kaiso" (Recollections of Espionage and Plot Activities in Hong Kong)

Okubo, Toshijiro, "Tai-ro Ango Kaidoku ni Kansuru Soushi Narabi ni Senkun-to ni Kansuru Shiryo" (Materials on the Origins of Codebreaking against the Soviet Union and on the Guidelines for the War etc.)

Ota, Gunzo, "Hokubu-gun Karahuto Tushinsho Gyomu Kiroku" (Service Records of the Northern Army Sakhalin Communication Site)

Sanematsu, Yuzuru, "Joho Sakusen ni Tsuite" (On Intelligence in Operations)

Sanematsu, Yuzuru, "Nihon Kaigun no Taigai Joho Kiko" (Intelligence Apparatus of the IJA)

Sawamoto, Rikichiro, "Minami Kikan Gai-shi" (Unofficial History of the Minami Agency)

"Showa 16 Nen Tanaka Shin'ichi Chujo Gyomu Nissi" (Business Diary of General Shinichi Tanaka in 1941)

Tamura, Hiroshi, "Taikoku Kankei Tamura Bukan Memo" (Military Attaché Tamura's memo on Thailand)

Tsuchihashi, Yuichi, "Dai Ni Bucho Jidai no Omoide" (Memories of the 2nd Department's Chief)

Tsuchihashi, Yuichi, "Tsuchihashi Yuichi Kaiso Roku" (Memoir of Yuichi Tsuchihashi)

Yokoyama, Yukio, "Tokushu Joho Kaiso-ki" (Memories of Special Intelligence)

Kokuritsu Kokkai Toshokan (National Diet Library)
Kensei Siryo-shitsu

Arisue Seizo Bunsho (Private collections of Seizo Arisue)

Ougi Kazuto Bunsho (Private collections of Kazuto Ougi)

Gaimu-sho Gaiko Shiryokan
(Diplomatic Library of the Ministry of Foreign Affairs)

Nichi Bei Gaiko Kankei Zassan dai 6 kan (Record of US–Japan Diplomatic Relations, Vol. 6)

"Rondon Kaigun Kaigi Ikken/Ango ni Kansuru Kaigun-sho Iken" (Matters Regarding the London Navy Conference/A Suggestion of the Ministry of Navy on the Codes)

United Kingdom
The National Archives, Kew (UKNA)

ADM 116: Admiralty and Secretariat Papers

AIR 22: Air Ministry

CAB 16: Committee of Imperial Defence

CAB 53: Chiefs of Staff Committee Minutes and Memoranda

CAB 65: War Cabinet Minutes

CAB 66: War Cabinet Memoranda

CAB 121: Cabinet Office: Special Secret Information Centre

FO 371: Foreign Office

HW 12: GC&CS, Decrypts of Intercepted Diplomatic Communications

HW 40: GC&CS, Security of Allied Cyphers Section

KV 2–3: Security Service

PREM 3: Operational Papers of the Prime Minister's Office

WO 208: Directorate of Military Intelligence Papers

India Office Library, British Library

L/WS/1/290: Military Department, War Staff Files

United States

National Archives II, Maryland

RG 38: ONI Records, Records of the Oriental Desk, 1936–46 Box 18
RG 457: SRH-149 Laurance Safford, "A Brief History of Communications
Intelligence in the United States"

Gordon Prange Papers, Special Collections,
University of Maryland Libraries

Dai San Sentai Senji Nisshi (War Diary of the 3rd Battleship Division, IJN)

SECONDARY SOURCES
Books

Agawa, H., *Shinpan Yamamoto Isoroku* (Isoroku Yamamoto, New Edition) (Shinchosha, 1969)

Aldrich, R., *Intelligence and the War against Japan: Britain, America and the Politics of Secret Service* (Cambridge UP, 2000)

Ariga, T., *Nihon Riku Kai Gun no Joho Kiko to Sono Katsudo* (The Organizations and Activities of the IJA and IJN) (Kindai Bungeisha, 1994)

Barrett, D. and Shyu, L., *Chinese Collaboration with Japan 1932–1945; The Limits of Accommodation* (Stanford UP, 2001)

Baudouin, P., *The Private Diaries of Paul Baudouin* (Eyre and Spottiswoode, 1948)

Bennett, J.W., Hobart, W.A., and Spitzer, J.B., *Intelligence and Cryptanalytic Activities of the Japanese during World War II* (Aegean Park Press, 1986)

Best, A., *Britain, Japan and Pearl Harbor: Avoiding War in East Asia, 1936–41* (Routledge, 1995)

Best, A., *British Intelligence and the Japanese Challenge in Asia, 1914–1941* (Palgrave, 2002)

Betts, R., *Enemies of Intelligence: Knowledge and Power in American National Security* (Columbia UP, 2007)

Boei-cho Boei Kenkyu-jo (The National Institute for Defense Studies), *Senshi Sosho, Daitoa Senso Kaisen Keii* (The Process of the Outbreak of the Pacific War, War History Series) (Asagumo Shinbunsha, 1974)

Boei-cho Boei Kenkyu-jo (The National Institute for Defense Studies), *Senshi Sosho Hokushi no Chian Sen* (Battles in North China, War History Series) (Asagumo Shinbunsha, 1970)

Boei-cho Boei Kenkyu-jo (The National Institute for Defense Studies), *Senshi Sosho Kaigun Sho Go Sakusen (1)* (The Navy *Sho Go* Operation, Vol. 1, War History Series) (Asagumo Shinbunsha ,1966)

Boei-cho Boei Kenkyu-jo (The National Institute for Defense Studies), *Senshi Sosho, Mare Shinko Sakusen* (Operations of the Malaya Invasion, War History Series) (Asagumo, Shinbunsha 1966)

Boei-cho Boei Kenkyu-jo (The National Institute for Defense Studies), *Senshi Sosho, Nansei Homen Kaigun Sakusen: Dai Ni Dan Sakusen Iko* (Navy Operations in the Southwest: After the Second Stage of the Operation, War History Series) (Asagumo Shinbunsha, 1972)

Brook, T., *Collaboration: Japanese Agents and Local Elites in Wartime China* (Harvard UP, 2007)

Chapman, J. W. M. (ed.), *The Price of Admiralty* (Salitre Press, 1984)

Coox, A., *The Anatomy of a Small War: the Soviet–Japanese Struggle for Changkufeng–Khasan, 1938* (Greenwood Press, 1977)

Cradock, P., *Know Your Enemy: How the Joint Intelligence Committee Saw the World* (John Murray, 2002)

Davies, P., *MI6 and the Machinery of Spying* (Frank Cass, 2004)

Deacon, R., *Kempei Tai: A History of the Japanese Secret Service* (Berkley Publishing Group, 1985)

Deakin, F. W. and Storry, G. R., *The Case of Richard Sorge* (Chatto & Windus, 1966)

Denpa Kankei Bukkosha Kensho Ireikai, *Kaigun Denpa Tsuioku-shu Dai 1 go* (The Naval Signal Traffic Records, Vol. 1) (not for sale, 1955)

Dilks, D., *The Diaries of Sir Alexander Cadogan* (Putnam, 1972)

Dodai Kurabu Keizai Konwakai, *Showa Gunji Hiwa (Secret Military Stories of the Showa Era)* (Dodai Keizai Konwakai, 1989)

Doi, A., *Gekokujo* (Supplanting One's Superior) (Nihon Kogyo Shinbunsha, 1982)

Dower, J., *War without Mercy: Race and Power in the Pacific War* (Faber & Faber, 1986)

Dreifort, J., *Myopic Grandeur* (Kent State UP, 1991)

Dreyer, E., *China at War 1902–1949* (Longman, 1995)

Elphick, P., *Far Eastern File: The Intelligence War in the Far East, 1930–1945* (Hodder & Stoughton, 1997)

Fay, P., *The Forgotten Army: India's Armed Struggle for Independence, 1942–1945* (University of Michigan Press, 1993)

Ford, D., *Britain's Secret War against Japan, 1937–45* (Routledge, 2006)

Bibliography

Fujiwara, I., *F Kikan* (F Agency) (Hara Shobo, 1966)

Gilbert, M., *The Churchill War Papers, Vol. 3* (William Heinemann, 2000)

Gudgin, P., *Military Intelligence* (Sutton Publishing, 1999)

Gunji-shi gakkai (eds.), *Kimitsu Senso Nisshi* (Secret War Record) (Kinshosha, 1998)

Gunrei-bu, *Showa 6, 7 Nen Jihen Kaigun Senshi* (Naval History of incidents in 1931 and 1932) (Suikosha, 1934)

Hara, S., *Daisenryaku Naki Kaisen* (War without Grand Strategy) (Hara Shobo, 1987)

Harada, K., *Saionji-ko to Seikyoku* (Duke Saionji and Political Affairs) Vol. 7 (Iwanami Shoten, 1952)

Haruke, Y., *Boryaku no Shanhai* (Conspiracies in Shanghai) (Ato Shobo, 1951)

Hayashi, S., *Kantogun to Kyokuto Sorengun* (The Kwantung Army and the Soviet Far Eastern Army) (Fuyo Shobo, 1974)

Heinrichs, W., *Threshold of War: Franklin D. Roosevelt and American Entry into World War* (Oxford UP, 1988)

Herman, M., *Intelligence Power in Peace and War* (Cambridge UP, 1996)

Hidaka, M., *Gunki Hogo-ho* (Military Secret Act) (Haneda Shoten, 1937)

Hinsley, F. H. (ed.), *British Intelligence in the Second World War, Vol. 1* (HMSO, 1979)

Hori, E., *Daihon'ei Sanbo no Joho Senki* (Intelligence War of an Army Staff Officer in the Imperial HQ) (Bunshun Bunko, 1996)

Hori, E., *Nichibei Joho Senki* (Record of the US–Japanese Intelligence War) (Bungei Shunju, 1994)

Hull, C., *The Memoirs of Cordell Hull, Vol. 1* (Macmillan, 1948)

Imai, T., *Showa no Boryaku* (Conspiracies in the Showa Era) (Hara Shobo, 1967)

Inose, N., *Showa 16 Nen Natsu no Haisen* (The Defeat in Summer 1941) (Bunshun Bunko, 1986)

Inoue, S., *Shogen Senji Bundan-shi: Joho-kyoku Bungeika-cho no Tsubuyaki* (Witness to a Literary World: a Memoir of the Chief of the Literature Section of the Intelligence Bureau) (Ningen no Kagakusha, 1984)

Iwama, S., *Sekiyu de Yomitoku Kanpai no Taiheiyo Senso* (Japanese Oil Crisis in the Pacific War) (Asahi Sensho, 2007)

Jennings, E., *Vichy in the Tropics* (Stanford UP, 2000)

Kahn, D., *The Codebreakers: The Story of Secret Writing* (Macmillan, 1967)

Kanehara, S., *Daitoa Senso Rikugun Eiseishi* (The Army Medical History of the Pacific War) (not for sale, 1971)

Kenpei-tai (Military Police) HQ, *Nihon Kenpei Showa Shi* (History of the Japanese Military Police in the Showa Era) (original text was reprinted by Kyokuto Shuppan Kenkyukai in 1969)

Kido, K., *Kido Koichi Nikki (Ge)* (Diary of Kido Koichi, Vol.2) (Tokyo UP, 1966)

Kitaoka, H., *Interijensu Hisutori* (Intelligence History) (Keio UP, 2006)

Konoe, F., *Heiwa eno Doryoku* (Effort for Peace) (Nihon Denpo Tsushinsha, 1946)

Kudo, Y., *Cho-ho Kenpei* (Espionage by the Military Police) (Tosho Shuppansha, 1984)

Lebra, J., *Japanese Trained Armies in South-East Asia* (Columbia UP, 1971)

Lowenthal, M., *Intelligence from Secrets to Policy* (Third Edition) (CQ Press, 2006)

Mahnken, T., *Uncovering Ways of War: US Intelligence and Foreign Military Innovation, 1918–1941* (Cornell UP, 2002)

Marder, A., *Old Friends, New Enemies: The Royal Navy and the Imperial Japanese Navy* (Oxford UP, 1981)

Matthews, T., *Shadow Dancing: Japanese Espionage against the West, 1939–1945* (St. Martin's Press, 1993)

Mercado, S., *The Shadow Warriors of Nakano: A History of the Imperial Japanese Army's Elite Intelligence School* (Brassey's, 2002)

Miyake, M., *Nichidokui Sangoku Domei no Kenkyu* (Study of the Tripartite Pact) (Nansosha, 1975)

Miyauchi, K., *Niitaka-yama Nobore 1208* (Climb up Mt. Niitaka 1208) (Rokko Shuppan, 1975)

Moriyama, A., *Nichibei Kaisen no Seiji Katei* (The Policy-Making Process in the Pacific War) (Yoshikawa Kobunkan, 1998)

Nagata, J., *Ango* (Cryptology) (Daiyamondosha, 1971)

Nakamuta, K., *Joho Shikan no Kaiso* (Memoir of an Intelligence Officer) (Daiyamondosha, 1974)

Nakano Koyukai, *Rikugun Nakano Gakko* (Army Nakano School) (Hara Shobo, 1978)

Nihon Kokusai Seiji Gakkai (The Japan Association of International Relations) (eds.), *Taiheiyo Senso eno Michi, 7* (The Road to the Pacific War, Vol. 7) (Asahi Shinbunsha, 1987)

Nishihara, Y., *Zen Kiroku Harbin Tokumu Kikan* (Complete Record of the Harbin Special Agency) (Mainichi Shinbunsha, 1980)

Ohashi, C., *Taiheiyo Senso Yurai-ki* (The Origins of the Pacific War) (Yumani, 2002)

Oi, A., *Kaijo Goei-sen* (Defensive Battle on the Sea) (Koyosha, 1953)

Okura-sho Showa Zaisei-shi Henshu-shitsu, *Showa Zaisei-shi* (Financial History of the Showa Period) (Toyo Keizai Shinposha, 1955)

Onodera, Y., *Baruto-kai no Hotori nite* (On the Edge of the Baltic Sea) (Kyodo Tsushinsha, 1985)

Osawa, R. (ed.), *Sakae Butai-shi* (The History of the "Sakae" Troop) (not for sale, 1995)

Bibliography

Otake, T., *Kokubo Hoan-ho* (National Security Act) (Haneda Shoten, 1941)

Otani, K., *Showa Kenpei shi* (History of the Military Police in the Showa Era) (Misuzu Shobo, 1966)

Prados, J., *Combined Fleet Decoded: The Secret History of American Intelligence and the Japanese Navy in World War II* (Annapolis, 1995)

Prange, G., *At Dawn We Slept* (Penguin Books, 1981)

Prange, G., *Target Tokyo: The Story of the Sorge Spy Ring* (McGraw-Hill, 1984)

Richards, D. and Saunders, H., *Royal Air Force 1939–1945* (HMSO, 1954)

Saito, M., *Showa-shi Hakkutsu: Maboroshi no Tokumu Kikan "Yama"* (Examination of the History of the Showa Period: "Yama," the Illusory Special Agency) (Shincho Shinsho, 2003)

Saito, R., *Azamukareta Rekishi* (History Deceived) (Yomiuri Shinbun, 1955)

Samejima, M., *Moto Gunreibu Tsushin Kacho no Kaiso* (Memoir of an Ex-Chief of Communications, Navy General Staff) (not for sale, 1981)

Sanbo Honbu (Army General Staff) (ed.), *Sugiyama Memo* (Hara Shobo, 1969)

Sanematsu, Y., *Joho Senso* (Intelligence War) (Tosho Shuppansha, 1972)

Sato, K., *Sonshi no Shisoteki Kenkyu* (Studies of Sun Tzu's Thought) (Hara Shobo, 1980)

Sato T., *Genron Tosei* (Regulation of Speech) (Chuko Shinsho, 2004)

Shimanuki, S., *Senryaku Nichiro Senso, Jo* (Strategy in the Russo-Japanese War, Vol. 1) (Hara Shobo, 1980)

Slim, W. J., *Defeat into Victory* (David McKay, 1961)

Stephan, J., *The Russian Fascists: Tragedy and Farce in Exile 1925–1945* (Harper & Row, 1978)

Sugita, I., *Joho Naki Senso Shido* (Conducting War Without Intelligence) (Hara Shobo, 1987)

Takayama, S., *Sanbo Honbu Sakusen-ka* (The Operations Section, Army General Staff) (Fuyo Shobo, 1985)

Tanimitsu, T., *Taiheiyo Senshi ni Miru Soshiki to Joho Senryaku* (The History of Japanese Intelligence Strategy in the Pacific War) (Piason Education, 1999)

Tarling, N., *Britain, Southeast Asia and the Onset of the Pacific War* (Cambridge UP, 1996)

Thomas, M., *The French Empire at War* (Manchester UP, 1998)

Tobe, R., *Nihon Riku-gun to Chugoku: "Shina-tsu" ni Miru Yume to Satetsu* (The Japanese Imperial Army and China: Dream and Failure of China-hands) (Kodansha Sensho Metier, 1999)

Togo, S., *Jidai no Ichi Sokumen* (A Dimension of Time) (Hara Shobo, 1989)

Tuchman, B., *Stillwell and the American Experience in China, 1911–45* (Macmillan, 1970)

Urata, K., *Dare mo Kakanakatta Nihon Rikugun* (The Unwritten IJA) (PHP Kenkyusho, 2003)

Utsunomiya, N., *Koga,Yosuko, Shuko: Chugoku Kinmu no Omoide* (The Yellow River, the Yangtze River, and the Chu River: Memories of Service in China) (not for sale, 1980)

Wohlstetter, R., *Pearl Harbor:Warning and Decision* (Stanford UP, 1962)

Yabe, T., *Konoe Fumimaro* (Jijitsushin, 1986)

Yamaga, S., *Sonshi Kogi* (Lecture of Sun Tzu) (1911)

Yamamoto, I., *Nihon Bocho shi* (History of Japanese Counter-Intelligence) (Jinbunkaku, 1942)

Yamamoto, T. (ed.), *Daini-ji Sekai Taisen-ki: Nippon no Choho Kikan Bunseki* (WWII: Analysis of the Japanese Intelligence Agencies) (Kashiwa Shobo, 2000)

Yokoi, T., *Nihon no Kimitsu shitsu* (Japanese Black Chamber) (Rokumeisha, 1951)

Yoshimura, A., *Kaigun Otsu Jiken* (Navy Otsu incident) (Bunshun Bunko, 1982)

Zenkoku Kenyukai Rengokai, *Nihon Kenpei Seishi* (Orthodox History of the Japanese Military Police) (Kenbun Shoin, 1975)

Zenkoku Kenyukai Rengokai, *Nihon Kenpei Gaishi* (Unofficial History of the Military Police) (Kenbun Shoin, 1983)

Articles and essays

Asada, S., "Nihon Kaigun to Taibei Seisaku Oyobi Senryaku" (The IJN and its Strategy and Policy toward the United States), in H. Kato and S. Kamei (eds.), *Nihon to Amerika* (Japan and the United States) (Nihon Gakujutsu Shinkokai, 1976)

Barnhart, M., "Japanese Intelligence before the Second World War: 'Best Case' Analysis," in E. May, *Knowing One's Enemy* (Princeton UP, 1986)

Best, A., "Intelligence, Diplomacy and the Japanese Threat to British Interests, 1914–41," *Intelligence and National Security*, Vol. 17, No. 1 (Spring 2002)

Best, A., "Straws in the Wind: Britain and the February 1941 War-Scare in East Asia," *Diplomacy & Statecraft*, Vol. 5, No. 3 (November 1994)

Best, A., "This Probably Over-Valued Military Power: British Intelligence and Whitehall's Perception of Japan, 1939–1941," *Intelligence and National Security* (July 1997)

Chapman, J. W. M., "Japanese Intelligence 1918–1945: A Suitable Case for Treatment."

Bibliography

in C. Andrew and J. Noakes (eds.), *Intelligence and International Relations 1900–1945* (Exeter UP, 1987)

Coox, A., "Japanese Net Assessment in the Era before Pearl Harbor," in A. Millett and W. Murray (eds.), *Calculations* (Free Press, 1992)

Coox, A. (trans. by Y. Kobayashi), "Ryushikofu Hoan Iin no Bomei" (Exile of Directorate Ryushkov), *Gunji Shigaku* (The Journal of Military History) Vol. 92 (March 1998)

Currier, P., "My Purple Trip to England in 1941," *Cryptologoa*, Vol. 20, No. 3 (July 1996)

Doerr, P.W., "The Changkufeng/Lake Khasan incident of 1938: British Intelligence on Soviet and Japanese Military Performance," *Intelligence and National Security* (July 1990)

Drea, E., "New Evidence on Breaking the Japanese Army Codes," *Intelligence and National Security,* Vol. 14, No. 1 (Spring 1999)

Drea, E., "Reading Each Other's Mail: Japanese Communications Intelligence, 1920–1941," *Journal of Military History,* Vol. 55, No. 2 (April 1991)

Everest-Phillips, M., "Reassessing Pre-War Japanese Espionage: The Rutland Naval Spy Case and the Japanese Intelligence Threat before Pearl Harbor," *Intelligence and National Security*, Vol. 21, No. 2 (April 2006)

Ferris, J., " 'Worthy of Some Better Enemy?': The British Estimate of the Imperial Japanese Army 1914-1941, and the Fall of Singapore," *Canadian Journal of History* (August 1993)

Fujiwara, A., "Nihon Rikugun to Tai Bei Senryaku" (The Japanese Army and their Strategy against the United States)," in C. Hosoya (ed.), *Nichi Bei Kankeishi* (The History of US–Japanese Relations) (Tokyo UP, 1971)

Handel, M., "Intelligence and Military Operations," in M. Handel (ed.), *Intelligence and Military Operations* (Frank Cass, 1990)

Harris, J., "Encircled by Enemies: Stalin's Perception of the Capitalist World," *The Journal of Strategic Studies*, Vol. 30, No. 3 (June 2007)

Hirose, E., "Finrando ni Okeru Tsushin Choho" (Signals Intelligence in Finland), in Dodai Kurabu Keizai Konwakai, *Showa Gunji Hiwa (Jo)* (Secret Military Stories of the Showa Era, Vol. 1) (Doudai Keizai Konwakai, 1989)

Hosoya, C., "Sangoku Domei to Nisso Churitsu Joyaku" (The Russo-Japanese Neutrality Pact and the Tripartite Pact), in Nihon Kokusai Seiji Gakkai (The Japan Association of International Relations) (eds.), *Taiheiyo Senso eno Michi*, 5 (Japan's Road to Pearl Harbor, Vol. 5) (Asahi Shinbunsha, 1963)

Igarashi, K., "Nisshin Senso Kaisen Zengo no Teikoku Riku Kai Gun no Josei Handan to Joho Katsudo" (IJA and IJN Intelligence Activities and their Estimations before the Sino-Japanese War), in Boei-cho Boei Kenkyu-jo (The National Institute for Defense Studies) *Senshi Kenkyu Nenpo* (Military History Studies Annual), Vol. 4 (2001)

Igarashi, K., "Teikoku Riku Kaigun no Joho to Josei Handan: Hokushinjihen kara Nichiro Senso e" (Intelligence and Analysis of the IJA and IJN: From the Boxer Rebellion to the Russo-Japanese War), *NIDS Security Report*, Vol. 5, No. 2 (March 2003)

Kamaga, K., "Daitoa Senso ni Okeru Ango-sen to Gendai Ango" (Covert Operations in the Pacific War and Modern Code), in Dodai Kurabu Keizai Konwakai, *Showa Gunji Hiwa Chu* (Secret Military Stories of the Showa Era, Vol. 2) (Dodai Keizai Konwakai, 1989)

Kamata, S., "Taibei Kaisen Keii to Ishikettei Moderu" (Decision-Making Model in the War Planning Process of the Pacific War), *Gunji Shigaku* (The Journal of Military History) Vol. 100 (1990)

Kondo, T., "Ango-sen 3: Bei Kokumu-sho Gure Kodo no Kaidoku" (Codebreaking War, Vol. 3: Decrypt of the Gray Code of the US Department of State), *Kaiko* (March 2000)

Kotani, K., "Could Japan Read Allied Signal Traffic?: Japanese Codebreaking and the Advance into French Indo-China, September 1940," *Intelligence and National Security*, Vol. 20, No. 2 (June 2005)

Kotani, K., "Nihon Kaigun to Rutland Ei Kaigun Shosa" (The IJN and Squadron Leader Rutland), *Gunji Shigaku* (The Journal of Military History), Vol. 38, No. 2 (September 2002)

Miwa, K., "Tai-bei Kessen eno Imeji" (View on the War against the United States), in H. Kato and S. Kamei (eds.), *Nihon to Amerika* (Japan and the United States) (Nihon Gakujutsu Shinkokai, 1976)

Miyasugi, H., "Senzen Nihon no Ango Kaidoku Joho no Dentatsu Ruto" (Communication Routes of Japanese Signal Intelligence before the Pacific War), *Nihon Rekishi* (December 2006)

Moriyama, A., "Senkanki ni okeru Nihon no Ango Nouryoku ni Kansuru Kiso Kenkyu" (Basic Research on Japanese Codebreaking Capability in the Inter-War Period), *Kokusai Kankei Hikaku Bunka Kenkyu*, Vol. 3, No. 1 (September 2004)

Nish, I., "Japanese Intelligence, 1894–1922" in C. Andrew and J. Noakes (eds.), *Intelligence and International Relations 1900–1945* (Exeter UP, 1987)

Nish, I., "Japanese Intelligence and the Approach of the Russo-Japanese War," in C. Andrew and D. Dilks (eds.), *The Missing Dimension* (University of Illinois Press, 1984)

Potter, E., "The Crypt of Cryptanalysts," *US Naval Institute Proceedings*, Vol. 109, No. 8 (August 1983)

Rusbridger, J., "The Sinking of the *Automedon* and the Capture of the *Nankin*," *Encounter*, Vol. 64, No. 5, May 1985)

Sato, M., "Joho Senso to shite no Nichiro Senso (3)" (Russo-Japanese War as an Intelligence War, Vol. 3), *Hokudai Hogaku Ronshu* (Hokkaido University Collection of Scholarly and Academic Papers, Graduate School of Law) Vol. 51, No. 2 (2000)

Takahashi, H., "Nihon Rikugun to Taichu Joho" (The IJA and its Intelligence in China), in *Gunji Shigaku* (The Journal of Military History) WWII (2) (1996)

Tarling, N., "The British and the First Japanese Move into Indo-China," *Journal of Southeast Asian Studies*, Vol. 21, No.1 (1990)

Tobe, R., "Doku-So Sen no Hassei to Nihon Rikugun" (The IJA and the Outbreak of the Soviet–German War), *Gunji Shigaku* (The Journal of Military History), Vol.100 (1990)

Wark, W., "In Search of a Suitable Japan: British Intelligence in the Pacific before the Second World War," *Intelligence and National Security*, Vol. 1, No. 2 (May 1986)

INDEX

Estonia, intelligence
cooperation with IJA 40

F
Fairbanks, Alaska 24
Far Eastern Combined
Bureau (FECB),
Singapore 15, 71, 113,
132, 135
Federal Bureau of
Investigation (US)
Rutland surveillance 82,
83, 84, 86
Tachibana arrest 85
Feng Yu-hsiang 63
Ferris, John 161
Finland 24
codebreaking teams 125,
169
intelligence cooperation
with IJA 40
SIGINT operations 25
'Flying Tigers',
American Volunteer
Group114
Formosa 128
Four-Powers Pact/Treaty
142, 162
French Indo-China 48, 78,
92, 100, 104, 107, 122,
126–35, 142, 145, 153,
158, 163
Fujiwara, Major Iwaichi
53–4
Fukai, Major Eiichi 22
Fukudome, Vice Admiral
Shigeru 89, 105
Fukumoto, Major Kameji
30, 67
Fukushima, General
Yasumasa 6, 7

G
Genda, Commander
Minoru 136, 137

*Genjo Sekai ni Oite Teikoku
Kaigun no Torubeki Taido*
(IJN report) 119
Genro (veteran advisers to
the Emperor) 138–9
German Abwehr 41
German Air Force 143
German Army 120
German-Japanese Traffic
and Information
Exchange Agreement
11, 15, 24–5
Germany (Nazi) 127, 129,
138, 139
intelligence cooperation
with IJA 11, 40
Nazi Party 82
planned invasion of
Britain 139
and the Tripartite Pact
132
Gray Code (AF2) US DoS
13–14, 15, 70
Great Asian Co-Prosperity
Sphere 138, 155
'Great Terror', Soviet
Russia (1936) 34
Great War (World War I) 99
Greene, Graham 82
Greene, Herbert
codename 'Green River'
82–3
Greene, William 82
Grew, Joseph, US
Ambassador 128, 134
Guadalcanal, battle of 16,
57, 144, 160

H
Hagino, ex-Lieutenant
Colonel Takeo 169
Halifax, Lord 128, 130,
132, 134, 154, 158
Hamda, Colonel Taira 42
Hanoi, US Consul 130,
132
Hara, Ex-Lieutenant

Intelligence) 76–86, 90, 109, 137
intelligence-gathering against the US/Pacific Fleet 69, 81, 85, 86
intelligence/operation dysfunction 98–107, 108, 122, 159
interception stations 74
Kikan, Minami (Special Agency) 55
and "Nii Taka Yama Nobore 1208" 158
operation code JN-25b 137
Pearl Harbour operation 161
Pearl Harbour/Hawaii intelligence gathering 84, 86
personnel numbers in department 95
RDF (Radio Direction Finders) 75–6, 137
role of department 107–10
shortage of staff 97
SDS (Special Duty Section) 73–4, 76–7, 78
SIGINT (Signals Intelligence) 9, 10, 69–76, 90, 109
anti-British 74
anti-Chinese 70, 74
anti-Soviet 74
anti-US 74
technology 73
SIS (Special Intelligence Section) 77, 105, 162
Soviet codes 74
SRS (Special Research Section) 72
status and standing (of intelligence department) 94–8
Tachibana interception

station 70
Takao (*Kaoshun*) Communication Unit, Taiwan 74
tactical intelligence 160
techniques of analysis/evaluation 91–4
techniques of analysis/evaluation compared with US 92–3
Toku-jo units 108
US Navy Task Binder (captured document) 10
US Planning of Amphibious Operations in Okinawa (captured document) 10
Imai, Lieutenant Colonel Nobuhiko 10, 92
Imaizumi, Lieutenant 71
Imperial University, Tokyo 97
'Imperial Wartime Communication Plan of Showa 16' (1941) 74
Imphal operation (1944) 101
India 138
Indian Army, British 54
Indian Independence League (IIL) 53–4
Indian National Army (INA) 54
Inoue, Captain Yoshihisa 13
Inoue, Vice Admiral Shigeyoshi 139
Institute for Sino-Japanese Trade 6
'intelligence cycle' 6, 122, 162
Ishii, Lieutenant Colonel Akiho 148, 155
Ishikawa, Captain Shingo 119